SALES FORECASTING MANAGEMENT

To Brenda, Ashley, Erin, and Steven

SALES FORECASTING MANAGEMENT

John T. Mentzer & Carol C. Bienstock

SAGE Publications
International Educational and Professional Publisher
Thousand Oaks   London   New Delhi

For information:

SAGE Publications, Inc.
2455 Teller Road
Thousand Oaks, California 91320
E-mail: order@sagepub.com

SAGE Publications Ltd.
6 Bonhill Street
London EC2A 4PU
United Kingdom

SAGE Publications India Pvt. Ltd.
M-32 Market
Greater Kailash I
New Delhi 110 048 India

Printed in the United States of America

Library of Congress Cataloging-in-Publication Data

Mentzer, John T.
    Sales forecasting management / by John T. Mentzer and
  Carol C. Bienstock.
      p. cm.
    Includes bibliographical references and index.
    ISBN 0-7619-0823-4 (cloth : acid-free paper).—ISBN 0-7619-0822-6
  (pbk. : acid-free paper)
    1. Sales forecasting—Management.   2. Marketing research—Management.
  I. Bienstock, Carol C.   II. Title.   III. Title: Sales forecasting management.
  HF5415.2.M393 1997
  658.8'18—dc21   97-33746

01 02 03 10 9 8 7 6 5 4

Acquiring Editor:	Harry Briggs
Editorial Assistant:	Anna Howland
Production Editor:	Michele Lingre
Production Assistant:	Denise Santoyo
Typesetter/Designer:	Marion Warren
Indexer:	Julie Grayson
Cover Designer:	Ravi Balasuriya
Print Buyer:	Anna Chin

Contents

Preface

If this book is a labor of love, then the delivery process has taken 25 years. Our research with companies in the area of sales forecasting management began back in the early 1970s with Whirlpool, Johnson & Johnson, and Union Carbide. From that point on, we have worked with more than 400 companies in the areas of sales forecasting technique development and application, sales forecasting systems, and sales forecasting management processes.

The early work led to the first of what has become four phases of sales forecasting benchmarking research. Phase 1 was a survey in the early 1980s of sales forecasting technique usage and satisfaction, and accuracy achieved, in 157 companies. Phase 2 broadened this survey 10 years later to include sales forecasting techniques, systems, and management practices in 208 companies. Phase 3 was an in-depth analysis of the sales forecasting management practices of 20 top-performing companies. Phase 4, which still is ongoing today, applies what we learned in the first three phases to improve the sales forecasting performances of specific companies. We call this last phase *sales forecasting audits* and collectively refer to all four phases as the *benchmarking studies*.

In addition to the benchmarking studies and our applied work with specific companies, we have worked with many companies to develop sales forecasting software systems. This stream of work has culminated in a sales forecasting system, called *MULTICASTER*, which is used by many companies to develop their quantitative sales forecasts. A demonstration version of this powerful software is included with this book.

We have tried to bring the results of all this research and experience into this book and the software that accompanies it. As such, this book is designed to give sales forecasting analysts more of an understanding of the role their function plays in the organization *and* to give managers of the sales forecasting function more of an understanding of the technical aspects of developing and analyzing sales forecasts.

In addition, the book is designed to give users of the sales forecast (marketing, finance/accounting, sales, production/purchasing, and logistics managers) a better understanding of how forecasts are developed and the sales forecasting needs of all the business functions. Thus, readers of this book should include new and experienced forecast analysts as well as new and experienced managers of the sales forecasting function or of functions using the sales forecasts.

In addition, this book is designed to serve as a text for the stand-alone sales forecasting course or as a required reading for the sales forecasting section of other business undergraduate or graduate courses. Thus, readers of this book should also include undergraduate and graduate students in business schools.

Therefore, the book is intended to be a tool for both students and practitioners of sales forecasting management. The software is intended as an environment in which students can apply what they have learned from the book. The demand histories of actual products from real companies are included with the software to provide the basis for realistic sales forecasting projects and assignments. Instructors in courses using this book are encouraged not only to assign the products that accompany the software as class projects but also to have the students gather their own data from local companies to make projects more interesting.

For practitioners, the software is intended to provide a readily available environment in which to test what you have just learned in reading the book in your company. The products already loaded in the software can be used, or we encourage practitioners to load their own demand histories and apply the forecasting concepts learned in the book to see the immediate impact on their sales forecasting.

The combined key objectives of the book and the software are as follows:

- To prepare sales forecasting analysts to understand the uses of their sales forecasts in their companies
- To provide sales forecasting managers with a technical foundation in the techniques, approaches, and systems used to develop sales forecasts
- To provide managers of functions that use sales forecasts with an understanding of how the forecasts are developed and the limitations of these forecasts
- To provide undergraduate and graduate business students with an appreciation of all three previous points

- To expose all these groups to the "state of the art" in sales forecasting today, based on experience gathered by the authors with more than 400 companies
- To give all these groups a chance to apply what they have learned to their own data with a state-of-the-art sales forecasting system (a demonstration copy of which is included with the book) designed to provide relevant sales forecasts to all the user functions in a variety of company sizes and types.

In terms of the relevancy of the book to these two target readers—students and practitioners—we are especially pleased with the feedback the book has received. For the classroom environment, we are pleased and flattered that the executive committee of the Academy of Marketing Science has endorsed the book. For the practitioners, we are very pleased with the positive reviews received from our panel of practitioner-reviewers of the book. Some of these comments included the following:

> Excellent book. I commend you for putting this together in such a readable form. (John A. Hewson, manager of forecasting, Eastman Chemical)

> Great book. I really enjoyed reading [the book]. It contains a lot of new ideas which would be very useful in practical applications of sales forecasting. I like the way you balanced theory . . . for practicality of use. (James W. Martin, automotive aftermarket, AlliedSignal, Inc.)

> A genuinely wonderful text . . . a monumental work in the area. I congratulate you on what I believe will be the new benchmark which others will be judged against for many years to come. (Jon B. Schroeter, director of upstream supply chain management, General Cable Corporation)

Again, it is gratifying to receive such positive feedback from the very people for whom the book was written.

As with any effort of this sort, it is not the work of just the authors; it also includes the input, guidance, efforts, and understanding of a legion of colleagues. We thank all of those who have provided this support to us in writing this book. In general, we thank the many undergraduate and graduate students we have had in our sales forecasting classes over the years for challenging us to think more thoroughly about the topics and issues involved in sales forecasting.

We also thank the many people with whom we have interacted on the topic of sales forecasting. In particular, we thank the many individuals who provided us with their insights while we were working with the following companies:

AT&T

Advance Auto

AlliedSignal

Anheuser-Busch

Becton-Dickinson

Brake Parts, Inc.

Canadian Tire Company

Carter-Wallace

CBIS Federal

Coca Cola

Colgate Palmolive

Computer Data Systems, Inc.

Courtlauds Performance Films

DG Products

DJR Products

DuPont Corporation

Eastman Chemical

Essex Chemical

Federal Express

Federal 2DMogul

Gallo Wineries

General Mills

General Motors

Gordon's Furniture

W. R. Grace

Greyhound

Heritage Healthcare

Hershey Corporation

The IJ Company

International Brake Industries

James River Limestone

Johnson & Johnson

Kelsan Company

Kimberly Clark

Litton Industries

The Longaberger Company

Lucent Technologies

Lykes Pasco

MAC Group

Magnetek

Martin Brower Corporation

Martin Processing

Mary Kay Cosmetics

Metro and Company Realtors

Michelin

Midlab Corporation

Motorola

Nabisco

O'Connor Products

Owens Corning Fiberglas

J. C. Penney

Pfizer

Pillsbury

Planters LifeSavers Company

ProSource

Reckitt Colman

Red Lobster

Resource Optimization Corporation

Sandoz

Schering Plough

SeaLand

Sysco

Tropicana

Union Pacific Railroad

United Telecom

U.S. Defense Logistics Agency

U.S. Internal Revenue Service

Warner Lambert

Westwood Squibb

Weyerhauser

Whirlpool Corporation.

Our special thanks go to the following individuals for taking a considerable amount of time out of their already busy schedules to review this book:

Nancy Haslip, global logistics manager, Digital Equipment Corporation

R. A. (Rhe) Desjardins, demand manager, Agricultural Products, DuPont Canada, Inc.

James W. Martin, automotive aftermarket, AlliedSignal, Inc.

John A. Hewson, manager of forecasting, Eastman Chemical

Jon B. Schroeter, director of upstream supply chain management, General Cable Corporation

Dwight E. Thomas, Jr., manager of forecast planning, Lucent Technologies, Inc., Bell Labs Innovations

The insight and dedication of these individuals helped us greatly in revising the book to meet their exacting standards—efforts that we believe have greatly strengthened the result. Again, we thank you.

Speaking of insight, dedication, and guidance, we certainly would be remiss if we did not thank the following academic colleagues for their input on the book:

Kenneth B. Kahn, assistant professor of marketing, Georgia Tech

John L. Kent, assistant professor of marketing, Southwest Missouri State University

Mark A. Moon, assistant professor of marketing, University of Tennessee

Michael Garver, research associate, University of Tennessee

Carlo D. Smith, research associate, University of Tennessee

Special appreciation goes to Carlo Smith for reading *every single page* of the manuscript and providing us with incredibly detailed feedback.

Finally, this book would not have been possible without the understanding, love, and support of our families. For the many hours in the evenings and on weekends that we had to work on the manuscript, and received understanding in return, we most sincerely thank Brenda, Ashley, and Erin Mentzer and Steven Bienstock.

CHAPTER 1

Managing the
Sales Forecasting Process

*S everal years ago, a manufacturer of snack foods
decided to develop a new approach to forecasting its
products. When it started, much talk went into which
techniques to use for which products, and the word
statistics got thrown around at most meetings. It did not
take long, however, to realize several facts. First, the
product managers (who were responsible for sales
forecasting) considered forecasting a tedious,
unrewarding, and unimportant part of their job. Second,
there was no common database of historical information;
each product manager kept his or her own records. Third,
there was no direct communication of sales forecasts to
the other planning functions (i.e., sales, distribution,
production, and finance). Fourth, even when the forecasts
were communicated to this group, they were not believed.
So, we backed off from our initial talks about
statistics and spent considerable time talking about issues
such as how to give the product managers the
information they needed to forecast well; how to motivate
the product managers to forecast well; and how to bring
production, finance, sales, and distribution "into the
fold" so that they were a part of—and not critics of—the
forecasts.*

1

Part of the result was the forerunner to the sales forecasting system discussed later in this book, but the result was much more than just a forecasting system. Sure, the forecasting system analyzed sales history to select the best forecasting techniques, but the system also put at the product managers' fingertips more information on sales, promotions, pricing, and economic changes than they had ever dreamed possible before. In fact, part of the project was to begin gathering actual demand data rather than just factory shipments so that the product managers could see how much demand was missed by low forecasts. This same information also was available on a local area network—the first time any of us had heard that term, by the way—to finance, production, sales, and distribution so that they could give their input to the forecasts. In short, we created a corporate-wide system of information relevant to developing sales forecasts.

Perhaps more important were the managerial changes. The roles of each functional area in developing the sales forecasts were clearly defined in a monthly schedule that described what had to be done to develop the sales forecast on each day and who was responsible for its completion. A "forecasting champion" was named with the sole responsibility of seeing that each daily step was completed. Finally, the vice president of marketing changed the reward structure for the product managers such that 25% of their performance appraisals became based on improving forecasting accuracy over the previous forecasting period. Whereas product managers previously had spent an average of $\frac{1}{2}$ day each month developing their forecasts, with this change the average grew to 4 days.

Of course, selecting the proper forecasting technique for each product had a profound impact on accuracy; however, the largest improvements in forecasting performance came not from techniques but rather from improvements in the systems and management of the sales forecasting function.

Much like the example just given, this book is about much more than just techniques. It is about the management of the sales forecasting function within an organization. It is about recognizing that, although the function typically is called sales forecasting, we really are trying to forecast *demand*; that is, we want to know what our customers demand so that we can plan on achieving sales at or near that level.

Sales forecasting involves the proper use of various techniques, use and interaction with corporate information systems, meeting the myriad needs of the different users of the sales forecasts, and managing all these aspects. To manage these multidimensional aspects, we have to understand each in turn and the management structures in which sales forecasting must operate. These are the topics of this book. Before going any further, however, we should understand exactly what we mean by sales forecasting and the area with which it often is confused: planning.

Forecasting Versus Planning

For the purposes of this book, we define sales forecasting as *a projection into the future of expected demand given a stated set of environmental conditions.* This should be distinguished from the sales plan, which we define as *a set of specified managerial actions to be undertaken to meet or exceed the sales forecast.*

Notice that our definition of a sales forecast does not specify the technique (quantitative or qualitative), does not specify who develops the forecast within the company, and does not include managerial plans. The reason for this is that *many companies confuse the functions of the sales forecast and the sales plan.* Managerial plans for the level of sales to be achieved should be based on the forecast of demand, but the two management functions should be kept separate. For this reason, our definition of the sales plan (or of any other managerial plans, for that matter) does not include the activities of making projections of demand levels.

Notice that these definitions imply different performance measures for sales forecasts than for sales plans. Because the goal of the sales forecast is to make the projections within a defined environment, one of the key measures of performance is accuracy of the forecast, and one of the key methods to explain variances in accuracy is how the environment varied from the one defined. This explanation is not intended to excuse forecast inaccuracy;

rather, it is to help us understand the business environment and forecast more accurately in the future.

By contrast, the goal of the sales plan is not accuracy but rather to meet, and in some cases to exceed, the plan. The purpose of the sales plan is not to accurately project future demand levels; rather, it is to provide sales goals for marketing and sales based on this projected future demand and the motivation to meet or exceed these goals.

Why Is a Sales Forecast Needed?

If we can simply set a sales goal and expect marketing and sales to exceed it, then why do we even need a sales forecast in the first place? This is a question many managers ask and often answer incorrectly (i.e., we do not need a forecast), to their eventual sorrow.

The correct answer is that every time we develop a plan of any type, we first make a forecast. This is true of individuals, profit and nonprofit companies, and government organizations; in fact, it is true of any entity that makes a plan. It can be as simple as planning what we will wear tomorrow. When we decide to lay out wool slacks and a sweater for the next day, we are forecasting that the weather will be cool. When we add an umbrella to our ensemble, we are forecasting rain. The plan was predicated on the forecast, whether we consciously thought about it or not.

This is not much different from a company making financial plans based on expected sales and the costs of meeting those sales. The trick is to not get caught in the trap of making *inadvertent sales forecasts.* Inadvertent sales forecasts are made when we are so intent on developing the plan that we simply assume what sales will be rather than giving any concentrated thought and analysis to the market conditions that will be necessary to create this level of sales.

One great example of such an inadvertent forecast came from a manufacturer in the grocery products industry. The owner of the company explained to us that the sales plan called for an increase in sales of 5% for the next year. However, we also had been told that this industry in this country was not growing and that any attempt to grab market share from the competition was only met by countermoves that caused greater promotional expenditures but no shift in market share. "Wait a minute," we said to the owner. "How can industry size not change, market share not change, but sales grow? It does not take a math major to figure out that this is not going to work." The answer was that management would simply have to motivate everyone to work harder to achieve the (mathematically impossible) plan. Of course, it is obvious what happened; no amount of motivation is going to overcome an impossible situation, and the sales plan was not achieved. It was not achieved because it was based on an inadvertent and uninformed forecast.

Let us look at one more example. A large regional distributor of food products to restaurants develops an elaborate annual profit plan. Hundreds of person-days go into the development of this plan, but it always starts with comments such as "We need profits to increase next year by 6%. Let's figure out how much sales have to be to achieve that goal." Notice that the term "goal" sneaked into that quote. Where these executives should have started was to ask about market and environmental conditions facing the company during the planning horizon and what levels of sales could be expected based on these conditions. The plan then becomes one of determining what marketing and sales efforts will be necessary to meet and exceed these projections to a level necessary to achieve the profit plan. The plan cannot drive the forecast; it has to be the other way around.

Thus, one of our goals in this book it to help managers see the importance of the sales forecast as *input* to their plans and to understand how these forecasts can and should be developed. To do this, as a first step, we should talk about the sales forecast needs of the primary managerial functions within an organization. In other words, what do marketing, sales, finance/accounting, production/purchasing, and logistics need from the sales forecast as input to their plans? To answer this question, we first define the related concepts of sales forecasting level, time horizon, and time interval, mainly because different management functions require different levels, horizons, and intervals of sales forecasts.

The *sales forecasting level* is the focal point in the corporate hierarchy where the forecast is needed. A corporate forecast, for instance, is a forecast of overall sales for the corporation. The *sales forecasting time horizon* generally coincides with the time frame of the plan for which it was developed. If, for instance, we continue the example just given, a corporate plan may be for the next 2 years, and, thus, we need a sales forecast for that 2-year time horizon. The *sales forecasting time interval* generally coincides with how often the plan is updated. If our 2-year corporate sales plan must be updated every 3 months (not an unusual scenario), then we can say that the level is corporate, the horizon is 2 years, and the interval is quarterly.

Sales Forecasting Needs of Marketing

Marketing typically is concerned with the success of individual products and product lines the company offers to its customers. This concern usually manifests itself in annual plans (updated monthly or quarterly) of marketing efforts for new and existing products. The marketing plans, in turn, usually involve projected product changes, promotional efforts, channel placement, and pricing. To develop these plans, marketing needs sales forecasts that take these various efforts into account and project sales at the product and product line levels for an annual time horizon and with monthly or quarterly intervals.

Sales Forecasting Needs of Sales

Sales, as a management function, typically is concerned with setting goals for the individual members of the sales force and motivating those salespeople to exceed these goals. The territories of salespeople can be defined in numerous ways (e.g., geographically, by industry, by customer, by product), and it is this definition that helps define the sales forecasting level for a particular sales function. The common factor in the sales forecasting level for the sales function is the product, for this is what a salesperson is rewarded for selling. Thus, the territorial aspect of the sales forecasting level may vary by company, but all sales functions need sales forecasts at the product level.

The horizon and interval are largely defined by the time frame of the compensation plan. If, for instance, members of a certain sales force receive their commissions based on quarterly sales and the sales manager must plan for the next 4 quarters, then the horizon will be 1 year and the interval will be quarterly. At the very least, most companies' sales management functions need sales forecasts at the product level, with typical horizons of 1 or 2 years and monthly or quarterly intervals.

Sales Forecasting Needs of Finance/Accounting

Among other responsibilities, finance (with input from the accounting function) is charged with the job of projecting cost and profit levels and capital needs based on a given sales forecast. These *profit plans* typically are annual intervals and can extend anywhere from 1 to 5 years. Although individual product sales are an input to this planning process (because costs of different products may vary), the concern with the profit plan typically is at the corporate or divisional level. Thus, the sales forecasting needs of finance typically are at the corporate, to divisional, to product line level; the horizon typically is 1 to 5 years; and the interval is quarterly or monthly (depending on how often the plan is updated).

Sales Forecasting Needs
of Production/Purchasing

Production must concern itself with two very different forecasts, one long term and one very short term. The long-term forecast is used for planning the development of plant and equipment, which can take several years. Because this long-term plan of plant and equipment is dependent on the mixture of sales of products to be made in the plant, it must be at the individual product level (in forecasting terminology, often referred to as stock keeping units [SKUs]). The horizon is dependent on the time it takes to bring new plant and equipment on line and, thus, can range from 1 to 3 years. The interval for updating these forecasts typically is quarterly.

The short-term production forecast is based on the needs of the production planning schedule, which can range from 1 to 6 months (depending on the raw materials purchasing order cycle) and needs a specific detail of which products to produce. Thus, this short-term production/purchasing sales forecast is at the SKU level, has a horizon seldom greater than 6 months, and has intervals ranging from weekly to monthly.

Sales Forecasting Needs of Logistics

Because it is the responsibility of logistics to move the products (SKUs) production creates to the specific locations where they will be demanded, logistics needs sales forecasts at the stock keeping unit by location (SKUL) forecast level. The horizons for these forecasts also are twofold: one for the long-term plan and one for the short-term plan. The long-term plan is needed to develop the storage facilities in various locations and the transportation equipment to move the products between these facilities. Again, the horizon is determined by the time it takes to bring these facilities on line. A large chemical company, for instance, needs an 18-month planning horizon to contract the construction of new rail cars to move its various products. Thus, the long-term logistics plan has as input a forecast with an 18-month horizon.

Across companies, these long-term horizons can range from monthly for rented facilities or contract carriage to several years for customized facilities or transportation equipment built specifically for the companies. Because both often are used, the interval typically is monthly. Because the plans are influenced by specifically what is moved and where it is moved, the level is product by location (SKUL).

Short-term logistics plans are concerned with specific decisions of what products to move to what locations and when to move them. Thus, the sales forecast has a horizon defined by the order cycle time from the plant to the facility and, thus, can be extremely short term (often monthly, weekly, or, in some extreme cases, daily forecasts). The intervals for updating these forecasts also typically are at the monthly or weekly (and sometimes even daily) level.

Summary: Organizational Sales Forecasting Needs

As Table 1.1 illustrates, not only are sales forecasts needed as input to all the plans of the organization, but different functions within the organization have very different needs from the sales forecast as input to their plans. It is the purpose of this book to help the reader understand these different needs and how advanced companies solve these disparate needs through the sales forecasting management tools of techniques, systems, management approaches, and performance measurement.

Tools of Sales Forecasting Management

Just as any modern management function must make use of the state of the art in techniques to get the job done, the information systems available to it, the latest in managerial approaches to managing the function, and some method of measuring and rewarding performance, so too must sales forecasting management. We provide a brief overview of each of these areas here, but we will devote considerably greater attention to each in later chapters.

Sales Forecasting Techniques

Myriad forecasting techniques exist and are available to the sales forecasting manager. In fact, it often seems that too many techniques are available and so the choice decision can border on information overload (at last count, there were more than 60 different time-series techniques alone). Such a scenario often causes decision makers to give up any hope of understanding the full field of techniques and to consistently use only one or two with which they are familiar, whether those techniques are appropriate for the forecasting situation or not.

Fortunately, this scenario can be simplified considerably. To understand the sales forecasting technique selection process, the sales forecasting manager needs to understand the characteristics of a relatively small set of groups of techniques and to realize in what situations each group of techniques works

TABLE 1.1 Forecasting Requirements of Various Managerial Functions

	Marketing	Sales	Finance/ Accounting	Production: Long Term	Production/ Purchasing: Short Term	Logistics: Long Term	Logistics: Short Term
Needs	Annual plans (updated monthly or quarterly) for new and existing products or product changes, promotional efforts, channel placement, and pricing	Setting goals for the sales force and motivating salespeople to exceed those goals	Projecting cost and profit levels and capital needs	Planning the development of plant and equipment	Planning specific production runs	Planning the development of storage facilities and transportation equipment	Specific decisions of what products to move to what locations and when to move them
Level	Product or product line	Product by territory	Corporate, division, product line	Product (SKU)	Product (SKU)	Product by location (SKUL)	Product by location (SKUL)
Horizon	Annual	1-2 years	1-5 years	1-3 years	1-6 months	Monthly to several years	Daily, weekly, or monthly
Interval	Monthly or quarterly	Monthly or quarterly	Monthly or quarterly	Quarterly	Weekly or monthly	Monthly	Daily, weekly, or monthly

NOTE: SKU = stock-keeping unit; SKUL = SKU by location.

best. Once the technique group has been chosen, selection of the specific technique to use is a much more straightforward decision—a decision that can be influenced by a great deal of research that has looked at which techniques are used most often and when they work best (Armstrong, 1983, 1986; Carbone, Anderson, Corriveau, & Corson, 1983; Chambers, Mullick, & Smith, 1971; Dalrymple, 1975; Fildes & Lusk, 1984; Gardner, 1985; Makridakis & Wheelwright, 1977; Mentzer, 1988; Mentzer & Cox, 1984a, 1984b; Mentzer & Kahn, 1995).

The common categories for sales forecasting techniques are based on whether the techniques use subjective or statistical analysis, whether endogenous data (a forecasting term that means using only the history of sales, not any other factors that may explain changes in sales) or exogenous data (a forecasting term that means using other data such as price or promotional changes, competitive actions, or economic measures to explain the changes in sales) are analyzed, and whether these data are actually analyzed by the forecaster or simply input to a technique for calculation of the forecast. These characteristics of forecasting techniques lead to three broad categories of sales forecasting techniques: time-series (both fixed-model and open-model technique categories), regression (also called correlation techniques and incorrectly called causal techniques), and judgmental (also called qualitative or subjective techniques). We briefly discuss each here, but much more detail on each category and the specific techniques within each category will be discussed in later chapters.

Open-Model Times-Series Techniques

Open model time-series (OMTS) techniques (e.g., Box Jenkins) build a forecast model after analyzing sales history data to identify its existing patterns (because only sales history is examined, OMTS techniques are considered endogenous). OMTS techniques are based on the interrelationship of four data patterns: level, trend, seasonality, and noise. *Level* is a horizontal sales history, or what sales patterns would be if there was no trend, seasonality, or noise. *Trend* is a continuing pattern of a sales increase or decrease, and that pattern can be a straight line or a curve. *Seasonality* is a repeating pattern of sales increases and decreases such as high sales every summer for air conditioners, high sales of agricultural chemicals in the spring, or high sales of toys in the fall; the point is that the pattern of high sales in certain periods of the year and low sales in other periods repeats itself every year. *Noise* is random fluctuation, that part of the sales history that a time series technique cannot explain. This does not mean the fluctuation could not be explained by regression analysis or judgment; it means that the pattern has not happened consistently in the past, so the time-series technique cannot pick it up and forecast it.

OMTS techniques analyze the data to determine which patterns exist and then build an appropriate forecast equation. This is in contrast to fixed-model time-series (FMTS) techniques, which have fixed equations that are based on a priori assumptions that certain patterns do or do not exist in the data. Although much academic research has been conducted with OMTS techniques, these techniques have been of little use in business because of their complexity and limited incremental accuracy over FMTS or subjective techniques (Mentzer & Cox, 1984a).

Most OMTS forecasting techniques require extensive training and considerable analysis time. Throughout the analysis, numerous subjective decisions must serve as input to the model. Thus, the accuracy of the forecast is largely influenced by the abilities of the user. Many periods of sales history (often more than 48 data periods) are required to obtain usable results. Because of these factors, OMTS techniques are used when substantial sales history data but little exogenous data are available, personnel are well trained in the use of the technique, and when only a limited number of forecasts are to be made. For these reasons, OMTS techniques have seen little applicability in sales forecasting, and so we will spend only a little time discussing them later in Chapter 3.

Fixed-Model Time-Series Techniques

In short-range (horizons of less than 6 months) product forecasting, rapid changes in sales and the large number of forecasts needed often dictate the use of a simple yet adaptable technique. FMTS forecasting techniques can be effectively used in such instances. FMTS techniques use the same four patterns (level, trend, seasonality, and noise) as do OMTS techniques. However, FMTS techniques arrive at a forecast by assuming that at least one of these patterns exists in a previous sales history and projecting this pattern (or these patterns) into the future. Exponential smoothing is a common FMTS technique.

FMTS techniques often are simple and inexpensive to use and require little data storage. Many of the techniques also adjust very quickly to changes in sales conditions and, thus, are appropriate for short-term forecasting. FMTS techniques, however, probably will be less accurate than correlation analysis if the forecaster uses an FMTS technique that assumes data patterns do not exist when in fact such patterns are in the sales history. Simple exponential smoothing assumes, for example, that the sales history consists of only level and noise. If trend and seasonality exist in the sales history, then simple exponential smoothing will consistently err in its forecast.

As mentioned earlier, there are more than 60 different FMTS techniques in existence. However, a discussion of less than 10 of these techniques will give the manager the necessary grasp of how these techniques work and which to use in any given situation. It is these representative techniques on which we will concentrate in the chapter on time-series techniques (Chapter 3).

Regression (Correlation) Analysis

Correlation analysis is a statistical approach to forecasting that seeks to establish a relationship between sales and exogenous variables that affect sales such as advertising, product quality, price, logistics service quality, and/or the economy. Past data on exogenous variables and sales data are analyzed to determine the strength of their relationship; for instance, the fact that every time the price goes up, sales of the product go down is a strong negative relationship. If a strong relationship is found, then the exogenous variables can be used to forecast future sales. Corporate, competitive, and economic variables can be used together in a correlation analysis forecast, thus giving it a broad environmental perspective. Correlation analysis also can provide a statistical value estimate of each variable. Thus, variables contributing little to the forecast can be dropped.

Correlation analysis is potentially one of the most accurate forecasting techniques available, but it requires a large amount of data. These large data demands also make correlation analysis slow to respond to changing conditions. Understanding the advantages and disadvantages of correlation analysis helps clarify when it is more useful, as in longer range (greater than 6-month time horizon) corporate level forecasts for which a large amount of data on exogenous variables is readily available.

Qualitative (Subjective) Techniques

Subjective techniques are procedures that turn the opinions of experienced personnel (e.g., marketing planners, salespeople, corporate executives, outside experts) into formal forecasts. An advantage of subjective techniques is that they take into account the full wealth of key personnel experience and require little formal data. They also are valuable when little or no historical data are available such as in new product introductions.

Subjective forecasting, however, takes a considerable amount of key personnel time. Because of this drawback, subjective techniques typically are used as a part of long range, corporate level forecasting or for adjustment purposes in short range product forecasting. For example, the forecast committee of one auto parts manufacturer with which we have worked meets once a quarter to subjectively generate a 3 year forecast and once a month to subjectively adjust the product forecasts by product line (e.g., all product forecasts in a particular product line may be raised by 3%). Individual product forecasts by inventory location, however, are left to an appropriate FMTS technique determined by the forecast managers. Individual product forecasts by the forecast committee would be a waste of valuable executive time.

Sales Forecasting Systems

This dimension of sales forecasting management encompasses the computer and electronic communications hardware and software used to develop, analyze, and distribute sales forecasts. It includes the storage, retrieval, and transfer of all information related to sales forecasting.

Systems sophistication can range from individual analyses of isolated databases, often called *islands of analysis,* to fully electronically interconnected analysis and communication of the information that is part and parcel of developing a sales forecast. At the lower end of this scale, companies have a number of separate information systems that are not interconnected. As a result, information that is transferred from one functional area to another is transferred via printed reports and often is not in a format nor sufficiently complete for what is needed by the receiving area. This information must be input manually to the receiving function's computer system and augmented by additional information from numerous sources. Because the systems are disjointed and complex, few people outside the management information systems function understand the functionality of the systems.

At the more sophisticated end of this scale are companies with system-user interfaces that allow greater access to a common information base and understanding of the functionality of the systems by users in the various functional areas developing and using the sales forecasts. Some companies at this end of the scale have open systems that allow electronic data interchange linkages with key customers for point-of-sale customer demand input to the forecasting process.

Sales Forecasting Managerial Approaches

The management of sales forecasting is concerned with how we organize and how we efficiently and effectively conduct the business of developing and using sales forecasts. Organization of the sales forecasting function typically follows one of four forms: independent, concentrated, negotiated, or consensus.

In the *independent* form of sales forecasting organization, each functional department develops its own forecasts independently of all other departments for its own internal uses. This is a naive approach to forecasting that ignores the synergistic advantages of input from various perspectives. Furthermore, it lacks any form of coordination of plans based on the sales forecasts.

In the *concentrated* form of sales forecasting organization, one department is assigned the responsibility for developing the sales forecast and all other departments must use it. Although it solves some of the coordination problems of the independent approach, the concentrated approach gives the sales forecast a decided bias of the department developing it. For example, if residing in logistics, the forecast will be SKUL oriented. If residing in marketing, the forecast will be product line oriented. If residing in sales, the forecast will be sales territory oriented. If residing in production, the forecast will be SKU oriented. If residing in finance, the forecast will be dollars oriented. Of course, each of these functional areas has a different time horizon orientation that will affect the orientation of the forecast.

Within the *negotiated* form of organization, each functional area makes its own independent forecast for each product grouping, but representatives from each functional area must come together each forecasting interval to reach a negotiated final forecast. This overcomes some of the bias problems of the concentrated approach and some of the coordination problems of the independent approach. However, the fact that each function brings its own orientation does create an environment of politics that can bias the results.

Finally, under the *consensus* organizational form, a committee is formed for each product grouping with representatives from various functional areas and one person in charge of the forecast. This committee develops one forecast that has the input of all functional areas. This approach overcomes some of the coordination problems of the independent approach, some of the bias problems of the concentrated approach, and some of the political problems of the negotiated approach. Although superior sales forecasts can result from this management approach, it often requires more personnel resources and more interfunctional integration than are possible within many companies.

This discussion of approaches to sales forecasting management leads to a concern over how we efficiently and effectively conduct the business of developing and using sales forecasts—a concern for functional integration. Functional integration of the sales forecasting function embodies the concept of Forecasting C[3]—communication, coordination, and collaboration. *Communication* encompasses all forms of written, verbal, and electronic communication among these functional areas. *Coordination* is the formal structure and required meetings among these functional areas. *Collaboration* is an orientation between the sales forecasting function and the other functional areas of the company that use the forecast toward common goal setting and working together. More will be said about each of these in the chapter on managing the sales forecasting function (Chapter 10), so suffice it to say here that the proper matching of Forecasting C^3 to the needs of the organization can significantly lower the costs of forecasting and increase performance on the relevant performance measurements.

Sales Forecasting Performance Measurement

Just what are the relevant performance measurements for the sales forecasting function? The obvious answer is accuracy, and the advantages and disadvantages of various forms of measuring forecasting accuracy will be discussed in the chapter on sales forecasting performance measurement (Chapter 2). However, this chapter also will address the concept of multidimensional metrics of sales forecasting performance measurement. There is more to sales forecasting performance than just accuracy. For example, what about the inexpensive product that holds a monopoly position in its market (i.e., customers cannot get it anywhere else)? The cost of overstocking this product is low, and the potential to lose customers due to temporary unavailability also is low. Why should we spend much money on accurately forecasting this product when the penalties for inaccuracy are nonexistent? Although this example is rather extreme to make the point, the fact remains that desired accuracy in sales forecasting should be weighed against the dimensions of the supply chain costs, the revenue-generating potential, and the customer satisfaction implications of inaccuracy. In the next chapter, we will explore this topic further to provide clearcut measures of all the dimensions of sales forecasting performance.

Overview of This Book

This book has been designed to give sales forecasting analysts more of an understanding of the role their function plays in the organization *and* to give managers of the sales forecasting function more of an understanding of the technical aspects of developing and analyzing sales forecasts and of managing this process. In addition, users of the sales forecast (i.e., marketing, finance/accounting, sales, production/purchasing, and logistics managers) will receive a better understanding of how sales forecasts are developed and of the sales forecasting needs of all the business functions.

Furthermore, numerous schools teach a course in sales forecasting and/or require sales forecasting as part of certain undergraduate and M.B.A. courses. This book is designed to serve as a text for the stand-alone forecasting course and as a required reading for the forecasting section of other marketing courses.

The book is the result of more than 25 person-years of experience with the sales forecasting management practices of more than 400 companies. This experience includes the personal experience of the authors in advising companies on how to improve their sales forecasting management practices and a program of research that includes two major surveys of companies' sales forecasting practices (one conducted in 1982 and the other in 1992), an in-depth study during 1994-1996 of the sales forecasting management practices of 20 major companies, and an ongoing study of how to apply the findings from the 1994-1996 study in conducting sales forecasting audits of additional companies. These studies in total are referred to as the *benchmarking studies,* with the 1982 study referred to as Phase 1, the 1992 study as Phase 2, the in-depth study as Phase 3, and the sales forecasting audits as Phase 4. Although the first three phases of the benchmarking studies will be discussed in detail in Chapters 7 and 8, where relevant, the findings from these studies, Phase 4, and our experience are laced throughout the book.

Following Chapter 1 are thorough, yet easy to understand, chapters on performance measurement (Chapter 2) and the technique categories of time-series (Chapter 3), regression (Chapter 4), and qualitative techniques (Chapter 5). These chapters will provide the reader with a fundamental understanding of how each technique works, its advantages and disadvantages, and under what circumstances each works best.

Because the communication and computer systems used by, and interacting with, the sales forecasting function can profoundly affect sales forecasting effectiveness, Chapter 6 examines our *seven principles of sales forecasting systems* and presents an example system that embodies all of these principles. From this base of understanding, we will move on to chapters describing what a benchmark of companies are doing in managing sales forecasting. This discussion is based on the two surveys of more than 360 companies (Chapter 7) and how they manage their sales forecasting function *and* the in-depth Phase 3 of the benchmarking studies (Chapter 8) of how the best 20 companies in these surveys manage the sales forecasting function and its use in management planning.

Next, we will turn in Chapter 9 to a discussion of a demonstration version of the sales forecasting software system presented in Chapter 6, a system that has been used successfully by numerous companies to provide accurate forecasts to all the functions affected by future sales forecasts. The purpose of this chapter, and the demonstration copy of the software that is included with this book, is to allow the reader to load some of his or her own demand data and to apply what has been learned in the book to his or her own organization.

The book concludes with Chapter 10 pulling together the managerial implications of what we know about sales forecasting techniques, systems, and management.

References

Armstrong, J. S. (1983). Relative accuracy of judgmental and extrapolative methods in forecasting annual earnings. *Journal of Forecasting, 2,* 437-447.

Armstrong, J. S. (1986). Research on forecasting: A quarter century review. *Interfaces, 16,* 89-109.

Carbone, R., Anderson, A., Corriveau, Y., & Corson, P. (1983). Comparing for different time series methods: The value of technical expertise, individualized analysis, and judgmental adjustment. *Management Science, 29,* 559-566.

Chambers, J. C., Mullick, S. K., & Smith, D. D. (1971, July-August). How to choose the right forecasting technique. *Harvard Business Review, 49,* 45-74.

Dalrymple, D. J. (1975, December). Sales forecasting methods and accuracy. *Business Horizons,* pp. 69-73.

Fildes, R., & Lusk, E. J. (1984). The choice of a forecasting model. *Omega, 12,* 427-435.

Gardner, E. S., Jr. (1985). Exponential smoothing: The state of the art. *Journal of Forecasting, 4*(1), 1-28.

Makridakis, S., & Wheelwright, S. (1977, October). Forecasting: Issues and challenges. *Journal of Marketing, 24,* 24-38.

Mentzer, J. T. (1988). Forecasting with adaptive extended exponential smoothing. *Journal of the Academy of Marketing Science, 16*(4), 62-70.

Mentzer, J. T., & Cox, J. E., Jr. (1984a). Familiarity, application, and performance of sales forecasting techniques. *Journal of Forecasting, 3*(1), 27-36.

Mentzer, J. T., & Cox, J. E., Jr. (1984b). A model of the determinants of achieved forecast accuracy. *Journal of Business Logistics, 5*(2), 143-155.

Mentzer, J. T., & Kahn, K. B. (1995). Forecasting technique familiarity, satisfaction, usage, and application. *Journal of Forecasting, 14,* 465-476.

CHAPTER 2

Sales Forecasting Performance Measurement

*W*hen we first visited a company we work with in the grocery products industry, we spent several days interviewing everyone involved in the sales forecasting process—those involved in either developing or using the forecasts. One of the surprising results of these interviews was the response to questions about how well the present forecasting process worked.

Everyone interviewed was unanimous that the first need for the company was some allowance in the process for measuring and rewarding forecasting performance. However, no one could define what the basis for that performance measurement should be. Everyone felt accuracy of the forecast should be part of it but that there must be something more.

In fact, the estimates of accuracy alone ranged from 30% error to 60% error, with nobody able to explain where they got their estimates or to actually define how they calculated them.

Clearly, this company had a management problem; here they had an important management function (sales forecasting) and no conception of how well they were

> *doing in that function or on what basis to reward those performing the function.*
>   *Unfortunately, this is not an unusual situation in companies today.*

The example just described is not unusual because we, as managers, often forget a basic management principle when applied to the function of sales forecasting:

What gets measured gets rewarded
and
What gets rewarded gets done.

It is not just business practitioners of sales forecasting management who are guilty of forgetting this simple concept. A quick review of the indexes from forecasting textbooks over the past 20 years reveals that very few actually even mention the word *accuracy* and that none mention the concept of *performance measurement*.

So, our job in managing the sales forecasting function is to determine what it is we want to get done, then how we will measure it so that we can reward those who do it. In other words, what is it we want to accomplish when we set out to forecast sales? The answer, often and immediately, is *accuracy,* but accurate sales forecasts are only a means to a management end. What we really want to accomplish with the sales forecast is to obtain a level of accuracy that helps us plan better. *Better* in this case means lowering the marketing and operations costs to market and deliver the product in a way that creates customer satisfaction.

Thus, we have three dimensions to sales forecasting performance:

- Accuracy
- Costs
- Customer satisfaction

If we can develop measures that tap all three of these dimensions, then we will have what we term *multidimensional metrics* of sales forecasting performance: metrics that will help us define for those responsible for sales forecasting what needs to be improved. It is the purpose of this chapter to do just this: develop multidimensional metrics of sales forecasting performance measurement. We accomplish this by taking each of these three dimensions in turn and then conclude by bringing the three together into one set of metrics.

Sales Forecasting Accuracy

Accuracy in sales forecasting seems like a fairly straightforward concept, but it gets a bit more complicated when we try to implement it. The straightforward part is that we just want to know how much we missed the actual demand in a given time period with our forecast of sales for that period. The complicated part is interpreting exactly what the accuracy numbers mean after we get them.

For example, suppose that we found our forecast for one product was off by 2% each month for the last year. That is a straightforward statement, but what does it mean? Did we forecast high or low? What was the actual unit amount the forecast was off? Is that a good or bad forecast?

If we sold 100 units per month of a fairly low-value product that did not upset our customers when it was not available and we were off by only ±2 units each month, then it probably is acceptable accuracy; that is, the cost of marketing it, the cost of carrying it in inventory, and the likelihood of losing the customer all were negligible. However, suppose that it was an expensive product that was vital to our customers' satisfaction with our company and that we sold 1 million units per month? A 2% error means that our forecast was off each month by ±20,000 units! Clearly, there is something wrong with this rather simple performance measure because it does not distinguish between these two situations.

Sales forecasting accuracy is further complicated by the fact that myriad accuracy statistics may be provided by any given forecasting system. What do all these numbers mean? To answer both questions (How do we find an accuracy metric that works with different forecasting problems? What do all these different accuracy measures mean?), we review the range of forecasting accuracy statistics available, discuss the advantages and disadvantages of each, and suggest a practical solution to the sales forecasting accuracy measurement problem.

Actually, myriad forecasting accuracy measures fall into three categories:

- Actual measures
- Measures relative to a perfect forecast

- Measures relative to a perfect forecasting technique

We discuss each of these categories in turn to understand what each provides as a metric for measuring sales forecasting accuracy performance.

Before we can do this, however, we have to forecast something. Table 2.1 presents a record of monthly demand for a product manufactured by a company in the business of providing replacement parts to the aerospace industry. We forecast this demand with a technique called *Mentzer's adaptive extended exponential smoothing* (more on this technique in Chapter 3). For simplicity, we tried to forecast only next month's demand during each month, although later in this chapter we have to deal with the problem of measuring forecasting performance when we are forecasting further into the future.

Actual Measures of Forecasting Accuracy

Several measures of forecasting accuracy exist that, in some way, describe the difference between what the actual sales were for a product in a given period and what was forecast to be the sales for that period at some previous date. All are based on the simple calculation of

$$\text{Error}_t = E_t = \text{Forecast}_t - \text{Sales}_t , \tag{2.1}$$

where t = time period in which the sales occurred.

Notice that although we could have calculated error as either forecast minus sales or sales minus forecast, the former gives us a more meaningful number. When calculated as forecast minus sales, a positive sign always tells us that we forecast high for that period and a negative sign always tells us that we forecast low for that period. It is a minor point, but one that has strong intuitive value to managers.

Mean error. The first actual measure of forecasting accuracy is called the mean error (*ME*) and is simply a running average of how much the forecast has been off in the past. It is calculated as

$$ME = \Sigma \, E \, / \, N, \tag{2.2}$$

where N = number of periods for which we have been tracking the error.

For example, the *ME* for May 1995 in Table 2.1 is

TABLE 2.1 Aerospace Aftermarket Product Demand and Forecast: Actual
              Measures

Month	Sales (S)	Forecast (F)	Error (F–S)	Mean Error	Mean Absolute Error	Sum of Squared Errors	Mean Squared Error
January 1995	100	103	3	3	3	9	9
February 1995	119	120	1	2	2	10	5
March 1995	478	441	–37	–11	3.66667	13.79	459.6667
April 1995	98	118	20	–3.250000	15.25000	1,779	444.7500
May 1995	110	104	–6	–3.800000	13.40000	1,815	363
June 1995	93	103	10	–1.500000	12.83333	1,915	319.1667
July 1995	104	105	1	–1.142860	11.14286	1,916	273.7143
August 1995	96	101	5	–0.37500	10.37500	1,941	242.6250
September 1995	96	98	2	–0.111111	9.44444	1,945	216.1111
October 1995	103	109	6	0.500000	9.10000	1,981	198.1000
November 1995	94	99	5	0.909091	8.72727	2,006	182.3636
December 1995	102	105	3	1.083333	8.25000	2,015	167.9167
January 1996	98	101	3	1.230769	7.84615	2,024	155.6923
February 1996	120	119	–1	1.071429	7.35714	2,025	144.6429
March 1996	469	453	–16	–0.066667	7.93333	2,281	152.0667
April 1996	99	115	16	0.937500	8.43750	2,537	158.5625
May 1996	99	106	7	1.294118	8.35294	2,586	152.1176
June 1996		101					

$$ME_{May95} = (Jan_{95} + Feb_{95} + Mar_{95} + Apr_{95} + May_{95}) / 5$$
$$= (3 + 1 - 37 + 20 - 6) / 5 = -3.8,$$

which apparently tells us that we have forecast, on average, 3.8 units low
(notice the negative sign) in each of the first 5 months. However, an important
problem with this measure is that the positive and negative errors in each

period are canceling each other out. If you look more closely at Table 2.1, you can see that our forecasts actually have been off by far more than 3.8 units, but the large –37 in March 1995 is mostly canceled in this calculation by the large +20 in the following month. So, we need a similar calculation in which the positive errors and the negative errors do not cancel each other out and cause us to draw misleading conclusions about forecasting accuracy.

Mean absolute error. The mean absolute error (*MAE*) overcomes the problem of cancellation of positive and negative signs by simply looking at the absolute value of each error. For example, the error in March 1995 of –37 would be treated in the calculation as 37 (the negative sign is dropped). This is represented in the calculation as

$$MAE = \Sigma \ |E| \ / \ N, \qquad (2.3)$$

where $|E|$ = absolute value of the error (i.e., drop all the negative signs).
For example, the *MAE* for May 1995 in Table 2.1 is

$$MAE_{May95} = (3 + 1 + 37 + 20 + 6) \ / \ 5 = 13.4,$$

which now tells us that, on average, our forecast has been off by 13.4 units in each of the first 5 months. This is a truer representation of how much the forecast has been off each month than is the *ME*.

However, the *MAE* does not tell us much else. Is an error of 13.4 units a good forecast or a bad forecast? For a base of around 100 units, it probably is not bad, but if we did not have this base number in a report, then we would not know how much the error is relative to overall volume. An additional problem with this measure is that now we do not know (by simply looking at the number) whether the forecasts were high or low. We need to look at the history of sales and forecasts to determine that.

A final problem for some companies is that the months in which the forecasts were off a little count as heavily in the calculation of *MAE* as do the months in which forecasts were off a lot. If very large errors have a greater impact on company operations, then we probably want a measure of forecasting accuracy that puts more weight on larger errors.

Sum of squared errors. The simplest way to magnify larger errors and still keep the positive and negative signs from canceling each other out is to square the error in each period. This calculation causes all the resultant numbers to be positive and magnifies the larger errors. For example, a ratio of an actual error of 5 in one month and an actual error of 10 in another month is $\frac{1}{2}$ (or 5/10), but a ratio of the same two errors *squared* is $\frac{1}{4}$ (or 25/100). Thus, the larger errors are magnified.

By adding these squared errors together, we obtain an overall measure of how much the forecast has been off. The calculation for sum of squared errors (*SSE*) is

$$SSE = \Sigma\, E^2. \tag{2.4}$$

For example, the *SSE* for May 1995 in Table 2.1 is

$$SSE_{May95} = (3^2 + 1^2 + (-37)^2 + 20^2 + (-6)^2) = 1{,}815,$$

which now tells us that the sum total of our squared forecast error up to this point has been 1,815. Unfortunately, this calculation does not tell us much else. To make matters worse, this calculation has lost all intuitive information for the manager. Is 1,815 good or bad? In fact, just what does 1,815 squared units mean? It is impossible to tell anything other than the closer the *SSE* gets to zero, the better the forecast. For this reason, we need a more intuitive measure of absolute error than *SSE*.

Mean squared error. A small improvement in the preceding measure is the mean squared error (*MSE*), a number that often is displayed in forecasting software reports. The *MSE* still magnifies larger errors and still keeps the positive and negative signs from canceling each other out by squaring the error in each period. By taking an average of these squared errors, we obtain an overall measure of how much the forecast has been off that is a little more intuitive than the *SSE*. The calculation of *MSE* is as follows:

$$MSE = \Sigma\, E^2\,/\,N. \tag{2.5}$$

For example, the *MSE* for May 1995 in Table 2.1 is

$$MSE_{May95} = (3^2 + 1^2 + (-37)^2 + 20^2 + (-6)^2)\,/\,5 = 363,$$

which now tells us that, on average, our squared forecast error has been 363 for each period. Unfortunately, this still is not a very intuitive number but (as we will see later) can be useful when used with another, more intuitive measure of relative performance, particularly if management considers the ability to magnify larger actual errors to be important.

Accuracy Measures Relative to a Perfect Forecast

Obviously, what we would like from a sales forecast is perfection—to be able to forecast in advance *exactly* what sales will be. If we could do this, then the forecasting error in each period would be zero. To overcome some of the disadvantages of the actual measures of accuracy just discussed, three measures of accuracy relative to such a perfect forecast have been developed.

Percent error. Because a perfect forecast would have a zero error in any given period, it is of some value to calculate the percent by which the forecasting technique we are using is off in each period. This is accomplished by the following calculation:

$$\text{Percent Error}_t = PE_t = [(\text{Forecast}_t - \text{Sales}_t) / \text{Sales}_t] * 100, \qquad (2.6)$$

where t = time period in which the sales occurred.

For example, the *PE* for May 1995 in Table 2.2 is

$$PE_{\text{May95}} = [(104 - 110) / 110] * 100 = 5.45455\%,$$

which tells us that in May 1995 our forecast was low (remember the negative sign) by a little more than 5.45%.

Notice that this calculation divides the actual error ($\text{Forecast}_t - \text{Sales}_t$) in each Period t by the *actual sales* that occurred in Period t, not by the *forecast*. This is an important point. Sometimes this is calculated incorrectly as actual error divided by forecast, but this calculation gives a misleading metric. The reason it is misleading takes us back to our discussion at the beginning of this chapter that focused on what are we trying to accomplish with sales forecasting performance measurement; we want metrics that allow us to measure how well we are doing in anticipating *actual sales*. Expressing *PE* as a percent of forecast tells us the percentage the *forecast* was off from *sales,* not the other way around. Take May 1995 again; the correct way in which to interpret this number is that our forecast was 5.45% below what actually occurred. If we calculate it with the forecast in the denominator, then it becomes

$$\text{Incorrect } PE_{\text{May95}} = [(104 - 110) / 104] * 100 = -5.76923\%,$$

which is a different answer and must be interpreted as the percent that *sales* was off from the *forecast.* This may seem like a minor point, but the difference in the answers can be significant. (Try a forecast of 200 and actual sales of

TABLE 2.2 Aerospace Aftermarket Product Demand and Forecast:
Relative Measures

Month	Sales (S)	Forecast (F)	Error (F–S)	Percent Error [(F–S)/S]	Mean Absolute Percent Error	Year-to-Date Mean Absolute Percent Error	Sales Forecasting Technique Accuracy Benchmark
January 1995	100	103	3	3	3.00		
February 1995	119	120	1	0.84034	1.92		.2405
March 1995	478	441	–37	–7.74059	3.86		.1272
April 1995	98	118	20	20.40816	8.00		.0668
May 1995	110	104	–6	–5.45455	7.49		.0765
June 1995	93	103	10	10.75269	8.03		.0948
July 1995	104	105	1	0.96154	7.02		.0948
August 1995	96	101	5	5.20833	6.80		.1032
September 1995	96	98	2	2.08333	6.27		.1071
October 1995	103	109	6	5.82524	6.22		.1165
November 1995	94	99	5	5.31915	6.14		.1243
December 1995	102	105	3	2.94118	5.88	5.88	.1280
January 1996	98	101	3	3.06122	5.66	5.88	.1325
February 1996	120	119	–1	–0.83333	5.32	5.88	.1299
March 1996	469	453	–16	–3.41151	5.19	5.52	.1201
April 1996	99	115	16	16.16162	5.88	5.16	.0921
May 1996	99	106	7	7.07071	5.95	5.30	.0990
June 1996		101					

100 to demonstrate this difference; using *PE* the correct way comes out to
100% error, whereas using it the incorrect way comes out to only 50% error.)
In performance measurement, we always are trying to compare our performance (in forecasting, this means our forecast) to what actually happened (in
forecasting, this means actual sales).

One of the values of the *PE* calculation is its ability to graphically give
us insights into what we are doing wrong in our forecasts. Figure 2.1 illustrates
such a simple graphical analysis of the *PE* for the technique we are using in
Tables 2.1 and 2.2. Regardless of whether we are satisfied with the *PE*'s we
are receiving, an examination of Figure 2.1 indicates that most of our forecasts

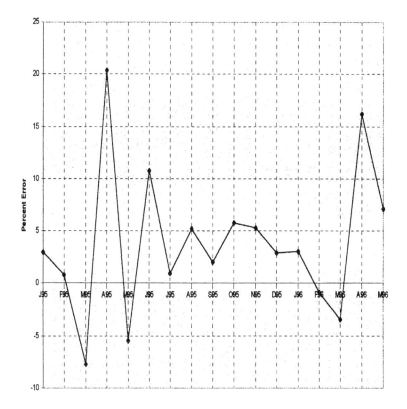

Figure 2.1. Percent Error Plot

are high (all but 4 periods have positive *PE*'s). This could indicate that the technique we are using is overforecasting a positive trend (we are forecasting sales going up at a faster rate than they actually are) or is underforecasting a negative trend (we are forecasting sales going down at a slower rate than they actually are), either of which would cause more overforecasting than under-forecasting. It may merely indicate that we need to subjectively lower the technique forecast. Which of these is correct is not important now. What is important is to realize the value of a *PE* plot in measuring the performance of any sales forecasting technique.

Let us look at another example. The *PE* plot in Figure 2.2 (which is derived from a different set of data and a different technique from those used in Tables 2.1 and 2.2) indicates that we overforecast during certain periods of the year and underforecast during other periods. This is a rather classic *PE* plot that results when we use a forecasting technique that does not consider seasonality to forecast sales that are seasonal. In the periods when we are experiencing positive *PE*'s, the technique assumes that there is no seasonal effect when, in fact, this is the season of low sales; that is, we overforecast. The opposite logic works when we are underforecasting. Such a plot would indicate we need to switch our forecasting technique to one that considers seasonality. Thus, the *PE* plot can help us make subjective adjustments to technique forecasts and/or to select more appropriate techniques to use.

Finally, the *PE* in any given month has strong intuitive appeal; it tells us by what percent the forecast was off in any given month. Although the *PE* plot is valuable, the *PE* itself does not tell us how we are performing over a number of periods. For this information, we need to turn to two other relative accuracy measures.

Mean absolute percent error. To measure how well we are doing over time in terms of *PE,* we need only to take an average of the *PE* calculation in Equation 2.6. However, to avoid the problems of positive and negative signs canceling each other out (as we had with the *ME*), we take an average of the *absolute value* of the *PE* as follows:

$$\text{Mean Absolute Percent Error} = MAPE = \Sigma |PE| / N, \qquad (2.7)$$

where N = number of periods for which we have been tracking the *PE* and $|PE|$ = absolute value of the *PE* (i.e., drop the negative sign).

For example, the *MAPE* for May 1995 in Table 2.2 is

$$MAPE_{\text{May95}} = (3 + 0.840336 + |-7.740586| + 20.40816 + \\ |-5.454545|) / 5 = 7.49\%,$$

which tells us that by May 1995 our forecast had been off, on average, by 7.49%. Again, this calculation has strong intuitive appeal; it tells us, at any point in time, what average percent the forecast has been off. When managers say the forecast error in the past has been 7%, they typically are referring to the *MAPE* whether they realize it or not.

One problem with this measure is that it continues to consider all *PE*'s as far back as we have been forecasting, regardless of how old those numbers may be. This may be undesirable if the errors back when we first started forecasting were very high (due to lack of data) and no longer are representative of forecasting accuracy. In other words, the *MAPE* does not give a good measure of how well we have been forecasting *in the recent past.*

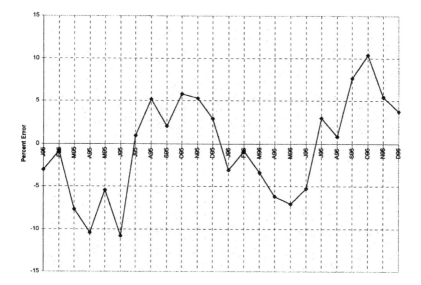

Figure 2.2. Percent Error Plot: Seasonal Sales With a Nonseasonal Technique

Year-to-date mean absolute percent error. What a manager may need is a type of *MAPE* measure that measures recent performance. This is precisely what year-to-date (*YTD*) *MAPE* is designed to do. It is a rolling 12-month (or 52-week, or 4-quarter, etc., depending on the forecasting time intervals used) calculation of *MAPE* that gives recent performance. For monthly forecasting, it is calculated as follows:

$$YTD\ MAPE = \sum_{t}^{t-11} |PE|/12. \tag{2.8}$$

For example, the *YTD MAPE* for May 1996 in Table 2.2 is

$$
\begin{aligned}
YTD\ MAPE_{May96} = {}& (10.75269 + 0.96154 + 5.20833 + 2.08333 + \\
& 5.82524 + 5.31915 + 2.94118 + |-0.83333| + \\
& |-3.41151| + 16.16162 + 7.07071) / 12 = 5.30\%,
\end{aligned}
$$

which tells us that over the 12 months ending May 1996 our forecast had been off, on average, 5.30%. This calculation still has strong intuitive appeal with the added benefit of telling us, at any point in time, what percent the forecast has been off for the preceding year.

Although the measures of forecast accuracy relative to a perfect forecast give the manager much more intuitively appealing numbers, what neither they nor the absolute measures give is any indication of whether the forecast is "good" or "bad." By the way, this was part of the motivation for the benchmarking studies discussed in Chapters 7 and 8: to establish benchmarks of what levels of *MAPE* companies were achieving in different sales forecasting situations so that companies could determine whether their *MAPE* numbers were good or bad compared to the benchmarks. However, we also can provide a metric that addresses this question without always resorting to a comparison to other companies' performances.

Accuracy Measures Relative to a Perfect Forecasting Technique

The original attempt to overcome this lack of a standard against which to gauge whether we have a good forecast was developed by Theil (1966). The logic of Theil's *U* statistic was that a perfect forecasting technique is one that forecasts well and is easy to use. What could be easier, Theil reasoned, than to simply take sales from last month as our forecast for next month (this is called a naive forecast)? If any other technique we try cannot come up with a more accurate forecast than this relatively easy one, then why bother using it?

Theil's *U* statistic simply calculates a ratio of the accuracy of the technique we are using to the naive forecast's accuracy. If the *U* statistic is greater than 1.0, then our technique is worse than the naive forecast and should be discarded. If the *U* statistic is less than 1.0, then our technique is better than the naive technique and should be kept until we find another technique that gives an even lower *U* statistic. (A technique that provides perfect forecasts will yield a *U* statistic of zero.)

Unfortunately, the calculation of Theil's *U* statistic is sufficiently complicated that it is seldom used in practice. However, we can accomplish the same thing by developing a simple ratio of the *MAPE* our forecast divided by the *MAPE* of the naive forecast. We can call this ratio the sales forecasting technique accuracy benchmark (*SFTAB*), and the calculation for this benchmark is

$$SFTAB = MAPE_E \,/\, MAPE_N, \tag{2.9}$$

where $MAPE_E$ = *MAPE* for the technique we are evaluating and $MAPE_N$ = *MAPE* for the naive technique.

For example, the *SFTAB* for May 1996 is the *MAPE* for our technique of 5.95 divided by the *MAPE* for the naive technique during the same month of 60.10, or

$$SFTAB_{May95} = 0.0990,$$

indicating that our technique is much better than the naive standard. If, however, we can find another technique that provides an even lower *SFTAB* (i.e., one closer to zero), then it would be better than the one we are presently using.

Of course, a similar measure could be developed that compares the naive technique to the one we are evaluating, based on *YTD MAPE* instead of *MAPE*.

Multidimensional Measures of Accuracy

Given that none of these measures of forecasting accuracy seems to be perfect, perhaps what we need is a combination of several to provide the best performance measurement of forecasting accuracy, one that provides the pattern of a relative monthly measure of a *PE* plot, the relative overall measure of *MAPE* and/or *YTD MAPE,* an actual measure of error, and some comparison to a standard forecast.

This is precisely what is provided in Figure 2.3. The *PE* plot of Figure 2.1 is maintained but is augmented by several cumulative statistics. Specifically, we provide *MAPE, YTD MAPE, MAE,* and *SFTAB.* By using this combination (and also providing plots over time of *MAPE, YTD MAPE, MAE,* and *SFTAB*), the manager can look at the patterns of error (the *PE* plot), an overall measure of relative accuracy (*MAPE*), a current measure of relative accuracy (*YTD MAPE*), an overall measure of magnitude of error (*MAE*), and a comparison standard (*SFTAB*). *MSE* could be substituted for *MAE* if management feels that larger forecasting errors should be emphasized, but we prefer *MAE* because it still offers some intuitive appeal, whereas *MSE* has no real intuitive meaning.

Examining Figure 2.3 tells us that we have fairly good overall accuracy performance with this technique. On average, we have been off about 8 units in our forecast, representing a 5.95% error (5.30% in the preceding year), and we are forecasting much more accurately than the standard (naive) forecasting technique. There is room for improvement, however, because our forecasts typically are high. Such an analysis is just the type of conclusions for performance improvement that should be provided by our accuracy metric.

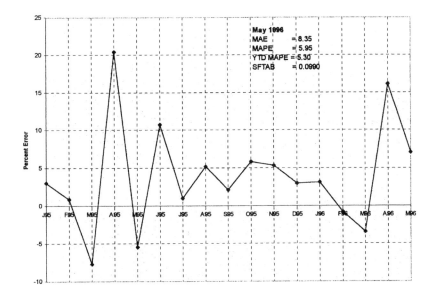

Figure 2.3. Multidimensional Metrics of Sales Forecasting Accuracy

Measuring Accuracy Across Multiple Products

All of the measures presented so far have been intended to evaluate forecasting performance with respect to one product. Suppose, however, that we have several thousand products to forecast and want a metric of how well we are doing. How do we evaluate the forecasting accuracy for a large number of products? The answer lies in a weighted *MAPE* or a weighted *YTD MAPE*.

If we simply took the *MAPE*'s for all products and averaged them, we would get considerable distortion in the result. For instance, a product for which demand was only 2 units that we forecast to be 1 unit would have a *MAPE* of 50%, whereas a product for which demand was 1,000 units that we forecast to be 1,100 units would have a *MAPE* of 10%. When we average them together, the average *MAPE* is 30%. The low unit demand product had the same weight in the metric as did the high unit demand product, which makes our forecasting performance look much worse than it actually is.

If we weight this calculation by unit volume, then we get distortions from products with different prices. In the preceding example, if the first product had a unit price of $5,000 and the second had a unit price of $0.01, then the unit volume *MAPE* would put too much weight on the second (high unit volume) product and would not represent the contribution of each to overall dollar revenue.

The solution is to take the *MAPE* or *YTD MAPE* (whichever is preferred) for each product and to multiply it by the ratio of that product's dollar demand volume divided by the total dollar demand for the company. If these calculations are added together for all products, then a realistic and representative metric for aggregate forecasting accuracy is the result. This calculation for *MAPE* is as follows:

$$\text{Aggregate } MAPE = \sum_{p=1}^{P} MAPE_p * (D_p/D_t), \qquad (2.10)$$

where $MAPE_p = MAPE$ for Product p, D_p = dollar demand for Product p, and D_T = total dollar demand for all P products.

In our original example, dollar demand for the first product is \$10,000 (2 * \$5,000) and dollar demand for the second product is \$10 (\$0.01 * 1,000), so the aggregate *MAPE* is

$$\text{Aggregate } MAPE = [0.50 * (10,000 / 10,010)] +$$
$$[0.10 * (10 / 10,010)] = 0.4996,$$

which tells us that, on a revenue basis, we are not doing a very good job of forecasting, in spite of the fact that the forecast accuracy for most *units* is quite good.

Of course, this aggregate *MAPE* does not provide us with any insight into which products are forecast well and which are not (we need to look at individual product *MAPE*'s for that insight), but it does give us an overall metric of how well we are forecasting on a corporate or product line level.

Sales Forecasting Time Horizon

With this multidimensional metric of sales forecasting accuracy defined, we need to briefly turn our attention to the issue of sales forecasting time horizon. As we discussed in Chapter 1, the time horizon is determined by the planning purpose to which the sales forecast will be applied. If, as in the example used in this chapter, the sales forecasting time interval is monthly (one reason for this might be because we are forecasting for inventory planning), then we will want to consider the production planning schedule for creating this inventory to determine the sales forecasting time horizon. If the production planning schedule cycle happens to be 3 months ahead, then we will want all the metrics we have discussed to measure our accuracy in forecasting 3 periods (months) in the future. The same can be said for quarterly forecasts when our purpose is to plan promotion schedules for 4 quarters ahead, yearly forecasts when we are planning 2 years ahead, and so on. All these combinations define the sales forecasting time intervals *and* the sales forecasting time horizon for measuring the accuracy metrics.

With the forecasting accuracy metric and its related issue of time horizon defined, we now turn our attention to measuring the other two dimensions of sales forecasting performance: costs and customer service.

Sales Forecasting Costs

The primary reason accuracy is the most often measured dimension of sales forecasting performance is that it is the most straightforward. The dimensions of costs and customer service have less direct relationships with forecasting, are not as easily attributed to specific sales forecasting time intervals, and, thus, are less easily quantified. Because the ambiguity of these relationships varies by company, it is not possible to put forward such universal measures of these dimensions of sales forecasting performance as we can in the dimension of accuracy. Rather, we need to discuss the impact that sales forecasting has on both costs and customer service and to leave the development of company-specific metrics to individual companies.

On the dimension of costs related to sales forecasting, we can break the discussion down into management costs, operations costs, and marketing costs.

Management Costs

The costs of managing the sales forecasting function involve the fixed and variable expenses associated with staffing the function, training the personnel involved in developing and using the sales forecasts, and providing the computer systems necessary for maintaining the relevant data, analyzing those data, and communicating the resultant information.

The size of the sales forecasting staff varies depending on the number of forecasts to be made in a given period, the accuracy required, and the degree of automatic (as opposed to qualitative) forecasting conducted. Brake Parts, Inc., a company in the automobile aftermarket, makes more than 250,000 forecasts each month and accomplishes this with a staff of 12 (Mentzer & Schroeter, 1993, 1994). This phenomenal ratio of assigning more than 20,000 forecasts per month to each forecaster can only be accomplished by the fact that most of the forecasts are developed automatically by computer, with the forecasters examining only the forecasts for those products for which the system has not automatically achieved what management considers to be acceptable accuracy levels (based on an analysis of operations costs and desired customer service levels).

Another company with which we have worked is a multi-billion-dollar chemical manufacturer with global operations that has a forecasting staff of only one person. This is accomplished through the use of the sales force to adjust quantitative forecasts for the firm's products and customers. This *decentralization* of the forecasting function allows acceptable levels of forecasting accuracy while keeping the staffing costs lower.

One of the common factors for sales forecasting effectiveness that we have found across a multitude of companies is the need for a forecasting champion—someone who is the central focus of the sales forecasting function. The personnel costs associated with this individual are the salary and training of someone who has the experience and training necessary to make informed decisions on all aspects of managing the sales forecasting function (more on the specific qualifications needed for this champion will be discussed in Chapter 7).

Training costs should be an ongoing expense to keep various personnel trained in those areas of sales forecasting most appropriate to their responsibilities. Those involved in maintaining quantitative forecasts should be trained in the correct use of time-series and regression forecasting techniques, where they do and do not work best, and how to qualitatively adjust their use. Those involved in making qualitative adjustments to these quantitative forecasts should be trained in how to take their experience and outside input to systematically make judgment forecasts and to document their thought processes, thereby developing a logical process that others involved in the forecasting process can understand and use. Those who use the sales forecasts need continued training in how the forecasts were developed, what the limitations of the forecasts are, and how all users of the forecasts apply them to their various planning processes.

Finally, computer system costs have changed dramatically over the last decade. In the 1970s and 1980s, when we talked about measuring the computer costs of sales forecasting, we had to discuss the costs of mainframe time, terminals, printing, and so on—usually a substantial part of the sales forecasting budget. In many cases today, the forecasting software is more expensive than the hardware on which it will run, and even the software can be comparatively inexpensive. In the Brake Parts example discussed earlier, the total cost of the software to make those hundreds of thousands of forecasts each month was less than $100,000. The hardware costs were even less. As we will see later in this chapter, this minimal investment resulted in dramatic operational savings and customer satisfaction improvements.

Operations Costs

Operations costs primarily involve the production and logistics costs of inaccurate forecasts. In research conducted almost 20 years ago (Bowersox, Closs, Mentzer, & Sims, 1979), it was demonstrated that production and logistics cost overages occur primarily from two sources: operations errors and forecasting errors. Operations errors include production and logistics aspects such as the raw materials arrived late or were damaged in transit, the production equipment was broken and either could not produce the final product or damaged it in process, or the product was not delivered to the correct location for sale or was damaged or delayed in transit. Our purpose here is not to detail all the problems that can arise in the operations of any organization, so these examples of operations errors will suffice.

However, considerable production and logistics costs can be incurred through sales forecasting inaccuracy:

- Although the production system may work perfectly, we may produce the wrong product based on the sales forecasts. This will cause inventory levels, and our cost of storing that inventory, to increase.
- Even if we realize our mistake and change the production schedule, changing the production schedule also will cause higher production costs. Many companies try to schedule production several months in advance based on their sales forecasts but can adjust those forecasts as the actual production dates get closer. However, the more often their production schedules are changed, the higher the costs of production personnel changes, equipment changes, and expediting raw materials.
- Inaccurate forecasts also create higher inbound materials costs. Often the raw material ordering cycle (especially for companies with global suppliers) can run into months. By forecasting inaccurately, the cost of expediting raw materials not ordered on time and the cost of storing raw materials not immediately needed can be substantial.
- Sales forecasts that cause a company to ship its product to the wrong location will cause extra logistics costs in storing the inventory in the wrong location, transshipping the product from one location to another, and discounting the price of the product to get it sold. In addition, they will cause the company to lose customers who are dissatisfied with not being able to obtain the product (more on this aspect in the later section on customer satisfaction).

To give the reader an idea of how significant the operations costs of forecasting inaccuracy can be, in one company with which we have worked, the costs incurred by production planning as a result of the inaccuracy of the forecasts generated by marketing caused the production planners to totally reject marketing's forecasts. Instead, production planning began developing their own forecasts.

Additional examples could be provided for specific companies, but the important point to realize is that any metric of sales forecasting performance should address the production and logistics costs of inaccurate forecasts. A first step in doing this is to match monthly or quarterly production overrun costs, raw material and finished goods excess inventory costs, and finished goods transshipment costs with forecasting error in the same periods. By correlating these costs with forecasting error, a clearer picture is provided of the impact of forecasting accuracy on operations costs. When this aspect of sales forecasting performance is measured, the savings from a minor expenditure on the sales forecasting function often are dramatic.

Marketing Costs

Similarly for marketing, the cost savings from improved sales forecasting accuracy can be dramatic. One manufacturer of consumer products with which we work originally spent more than $100 million each year on trade promotions on the belief that these promotions stimulated demand and took market share away from its three major competitors. In the process of analyzing the company's sales forecasting needs, we conducted a series of regression-based forecasts and discovered something interesting: There seemed to be no relationship between dollars spent on trade promotions and company sales, industry sales, or market share! From a forecasting accuracy perspective, we could have simply concluded that these were not good variables for developing a forecast and moved on. However, the metric of marketing costs led us to suggest a strategy of everyday low prices (EDLP). Can you guess what happened? The competitors also were only too happy to get rid of this drain on their balance sheets and quickly went to EDLP as well. In the aftermath of this change, industry size did not change, market share did not change (so, of course, company sales did not change), but the unnecessary marketing expense of excessive trade promotions went away.

Marketing costs of inaccurate forecasting include not only trade promotions but also the costs of the following:

- Ineffective advertising
- Development of new products without adequate demand
- Pricing at a level that does not maximize profit contribution
- Inappropriate sales quotas

The last point bears elaboration. Salespeople often have conflicting goals when they are a part of the sales forecasting process. It is in the nature of salespeople to be optimistic and set goals for themselves that they will strive to achieve. This is fine for motivation but can be detrimental to the sales forecasting process. High sales forecasts may lead to unrealistic sales quotas, which may lead to lower sales force morale.

Conversely, salespeople often are rewarded for exceeding their quotas. When such is the case, a strong motivation exists to forecast low so that quotas will be set at a low level that can easily be exceeded. This makes life easier for the sales force but may result in lost sales opportunities because the "bar has been set too low."

We actually worked with one company that explained to us its unique "quarterly seasonal pattern." This pattern clearly showed that sales always were high in the first 2 months of each quarter and low in the 3rd month. This pattern repeated each quarter, and the company wanted to know what would cause its customers to buy in such a way. Upon investigation, we found that sales quotas (which were based on sales forecasts) actually were set too low, and the salespeople received lower commissions for any sales in excess of the quota in any quarter (an interesting concept in itself given that it reduces motivation to beat the goal). Thus, members of the sales force (who were intelligent people) simply sold at normal levels until their quota was met (this usually took only 2 of the 3 months in each quarter) and would not call on customers during the 3rd month. Literally, customers could not buy from the company for 4 months each year! Of course, this caused considerable production and logistics costs to address this "seasonal" pattern and was all a marketing cost associated with an inaccurate forecast.

Putting Costs Together

As these examples illustrate, the management, operations, and marketing costs associated with sales forecasting performance measurement will vary by company. What is important here is to realize that it is not just accuracy that counts; the cost implications of that accuracy should be measured as well.

One final example on this point may help. We were asked by one company to develop a sales forecasting system for the firm to improve accuracy. Sales forecasting error at the time ranged from 20% to 30%, and management set the goal of reducing error to below 15%. This all seems like a reasonable goal when only accuracy is examined. However, when we looked at the cost aspect, several factors became important. First, the company's product line was fairly low value with few special storage needs. Thus, it was inexpensive to keep in inventory. Second, the production process was very flexible and allowed for daily changes in production schedules with little added cost. Finally, the low cost of the product and the fact that it represented a small cost component of the final product produced by the company's customers led to the fact that customers tended to carry sufficient quantities in inventory to cause few customer service problems from late deliveries. These factors led to a conclusion that the operations and marketing cost savings from improved forecasting accuracy would be minimal. In fact, the total savings from these areas would result in only an estimated savings of $50,000 per year.

However, the management costs of reducing forecasting error to 15% would include hiring a director of forecasting to champion the new process, buying new forecasting software and the hardware on which to operate it, and training for numerous personnel involved in making qualitative adjustments to the forecasts. The estimated annual costs of these activities totaled over $65,000, so, literally, improving accuracy would have cost the company money! Although this is an extreme example (albeit a true one), it illustrates the importance of examining not just sales forecasting accuracy but also its cost implications.

Customer Satisfaction

The customer satisfaction implications of inaccurate sales forecasting involve the following:

- Dissatisfying customers by designing and producing products that customers do not want
- Dissatisfying customers by not designing and producing products that customers do want
- Dissatisfying customers by not having products desired by customers in the locations and in the quantities demanded

The metrics of all three of these implications involve surveys of customers to determine their satisfaction with all the marketing activities of the company and, as such, can vary from company to company. For example, one company selling its products through grocery stores found that when loyal customers came into the stores to buy its brand and the store did not have it in stock (through either operations errors or forecasting errors), the customers typically bought the company's major competitor's brand and *permanently switched brands*. Thus, in this example, the customer satisfaction implications of inaccurate forecasts were considerable (i.e., lost customers).

Regardless of the specifics, use of this dimension of sales forecasting performance metrics involves some form of research to determine the customer satisfaction implications of inaccurate forecasts. As such, the metrics are more suited to the particular company's customer mix and the intricacies of the specific situation. The latter intricacies can involve not only market characteristics but also investigation of operational characteristics. For instance, loss of customer sales due to the product not being available on the retail shelves may lead to research on what caused this customer dissatisfying incident. We may find that forecasts of point-of-sale demand were in fact accurate but that lack of communication with production and logistics failed to alert marketing that the forecast demand for that time interval exceeded the capacity of the operations system to produce and deliver the product. Thus, the customer dissatisfaction resulting from not having the product available was caused by a problem in the forecasting information system.

Although the specific items used to measure customer satisfaction with the company's delivery system should reflect the context of that specific company, research has shown that efforts to assess delivery system customer satisfaction should evaluate customers' perceptions of the timeliness, availability, and condition of the distribution service they receive. Timeliness addresses whether or not customers receive products when they are required. Availability addresses whether products are available in inventory when customers order them. Condition taps the concepts of whether or not orders are picked accurately as well as the degree of damage to products that occurs during distribution (Bienstock, Mentzer, & Bird, 1997).

Conclusions

In this chapter, we have discussed the three dimensions of sales forecasting performance measurement: accuracy, costs, and customer satisfaction. For accuracy, we provided specific recommendations for multidimensional metrics of this aspect of sales forecasting performance. For the other two dimensions, we discussed what constitutes each dimension and made recommendations on the directions management should take in measuring each. A truly multidimensional metric of sales forecasting performance must include all three aspects. Without such multidimensional metrics, management cannot make decisions on the cost efficiency or customer satisfaction effectiveness of improving the accuracy of the sales forecasts it develops.

Perhaps the best conclusion we can provide for this chapter is to complete the example of Brake Parts (Mentzer & Shroeter, 1993) that has appeared at several places throughout the chapter. Although Brake Parts devoted considerable effort to measuring and rewarding increased accuracy of its sales forecasts, management also wanted to know the cost implications of lower inventory and the customer service implications of sales not lost due to being out of stock. The results were dramatic: Average forecast error was reduced to less than 10% per month and, more important, the savings from this improved accuracy in terms just of sales not lost due to stockouts exceeded $6 million per month. Although the additional savings in lower inventory levels cannot be reported here, the important point to remember is the increased value of measuring the improvement of sales forecasting accuracy *and* its impact on corporate costs and customer satisfaction.

References

Bienstock, C. C., Mentzer, J. T., & Bird, M. M. (1997). Measuring physical distribution service quality. *Journal of the Academy of Marketing Science, 25,* 31-44.

Bowersox, D. J., Closs, D. J., Mentzer, J. T., & Sims, J. R. (1979). *Simulated product sales forecasting.* East Lansing: Michigan State University, Bureau of Business Research.

Mentzer, J. T., & Schroeter, J. (1993, Fall). Multiple forecasting system at Brake Parts, Inc. *Journal of Business Forecasting, 12*(3), 5-9.

Mentzer, J. T., & Schroeter, J. (1994). Integrating logistics forecasting techniques, systems, and administration: The multiple forecasting system. *Journal of Business Logistics, 15,* 205-225.

Theil, H. (1966). *Applied economic forecasting.* Amsterdam: North-Holland.

CHAPTER 3

Time-Series
Forecasting Techniques

*B*ack in the 1970s, we were working with a company
in the major home appliance industry. In an
interview, the person in charge of quantitative forecasting
for refrigerators explained that the company's forecast
was based on one time-series technique (it turned out to
be the exponential smoothing with trend and seasonality
technique discussed later in this chapter). This technique
requires the user to specify three smoothing constants
called α, β, and γ (we will explain what these are later in
the chapter). The selection of these values, which must be
somewhere between 0 and 1 for each constant, can have a
profound effect on the accuracy of the forecast.

As we talked with this forecast analyst, he explained
that he had chosen the values of 0.1 for α, 0.2 for β, and
0.3 for γ. Being fairly new to the world of sales
forecasting, we envisioned some sophisticated sensitivity
analysis that this analyst had gone through to find the
right combination of the values for the three smoothing
constants to accurately forecast refrigerator demand.

However, he explained to us that in every article he
read about this technique, the three smoothing constants
always were referred to as α, β, and γ in that order. He
finally realized that this was because they are the first,

> *second, and third letters in the Greek alphabet. Once he*
> *realized that, he "simply took 1, 2, and 3, put a decimal*
> *point in front of each, and there were my smoothing*
> *constants."*
>
> *After thinking about it for a minute, he said rather*
> *sheepishly, "You know, it doesn't work worth a darn,*
> *though."*

Hopefully, over the years, we have come a long way from this type of time-series forecasting. First, it is not realistic to expect that each product in a line such as refrigerators would be accurately forecast by the same time-series technique; we probably will need to select a different time-series technique for each product. Second, there are better ways in which to select smoothing constants than our friend used in the preceding example. To understand how to better accomplish both of these, the purpose of this chapter is to provide an overview of the many techniques that are available in the general category of time-series analysis. This overview should provide the reader with an understanding of how each technique works and where it should and should not be used.

Time-series techniques all have the common characteristic that they are endogenous techniques. This means that a time-series technique looks at only the patterns of the history of actual sales (or the series of sales through time, thus, the term *time series*). If these patterns can be identified and projected into the future, then we have our forecast. Therefore, this rather esoteric term, *endogenous,* means that time-series techniques look inside (i.e., *endo-*) the actual series of demand through time to find the underlying patterns of sales. This is in contrast to regression analysis, which is an exogenous technique and will be discussed in Chapter 4. *Exogenous* means that regression analysis examines factors external (i.e., *exo-*) to the actual sales pattern to look for a relationship between these external factors (e.g., price changes) and sales patterns.

If time-series techniques look only at the patterns that are part of the actual history of sales (i.e., are endogenous to the sales history), then what are these patterns? The answer is that no matter what time-series technique we are talking about, they all examine one or more of only four basic time-series patterns: level, trend, seasonality, and noise. Figure 3.1 illustrates these four patterns broken out of a monthly time series of sales for a particular refrigerator model. The *level* is a horizontal sales history, or what the sales pattern would be if there were no trend, seasonality, or noise. For a product that is sold to a manufacturing concern as a component in another product whose demand is stable, the sales pattern for this product would essentially be level with no trend, seasonality, or noise. In our example in Figure 3.1, however, the level is simply the starting point for the time series (the horizontal line) with the trend, seasonality, and noise added to it.

Trend is a continuing pattern of a sales increase or decrease, and that pattern can be a straight line or a curve. Of course, any business person wants a positive trend that is increasing at an increasing rate, but this is not always the case. If sales are decreasing (either at a constant rate, an increasing rate, or a decreasing rate), then we need to know this for forecasting purposes. In our example in Figure 3.1, trend is expressed as a straight line going up from the level.

Seasonality is a repeating pattern of sales increases and decreases that occurs within a 1-year period or less. (*Seasonal patterns* of longer than 1 year typically are referred to as *cycles* but can be forecast using the same time-series techniques.) Examples of seasonality are high sales every summer for air conditioners, high sales of agricultural chemicals in the spring, and high sales of toys in the fall. The point is that the pattern of high sales in certain periods of the year and low sales in other periods repeats itself every year. When broken out of the time series in Figure 3.1, the seasonality line can be seen as a regular pattern of sales increases and decreases around the zero line at the bottom of the graph.

Noise is random fluctuation, or that part of the sales history that a time-series technique cannot explain. This does not mean the fluctuation could not be explained by regression analysis or some qualitative technique; rather, it means the pattern has not happened consistently in the past, so the time-series technique cannot pick it up and forecast it. In fact, one test of how well we are doing at forecasting with time series is whether the noise pattern looks random. If it does not have a random pattern like the one in Figure 3.1, then it means there still is a trend and/or seasonal pattern in the time series that we have not yet identified.

We can group all time-series techniques into two broad categories, *open-model time-series* (OMTS) techniques and *fixed-model time-series* (FMTS) techniques, based on how the techniques try to identify and project these four patterns. OMTS techniques analyze the time series to determine which patterns exist and then build a unique model of that time series to project the patterns into the future and, thus, to forecast the time series. This is in contrast to FMTS techniques, which have fixed equations that are based on a priori assumptions that certain patterns do or do not exist in the data.

In fact, when you consider both OMTS and FMTS techniques, there are more than 60 different techniques that fall into the general category of time-series techniques. Fortunately, we do not have to explain each of them in this chapter. The reason for this is that because some of the techniques are very sophisticated and take a considerable amount of data but do not produce any better results than do simpler techniques, they seldom are used in practical sales forecasting situations. In other cases, several different time-series techniques may use the same approach to forecasting and have the same level of effectiveness. In these latter cases in which several techniques work equally well, we discuss only the one that is easiest to understand. (Why make something complicated if it does not have to be?) This greatly reduces the number of techniques that need to be discussed.

Because they are generally easier to understand and use, we start with FMTS techniques and return to OMTS techniques later in the chapter.

Fixed-Model Time-Series Techniques

FMTS techniques often are simple and inexpensive to use, and they require little data storage. Many of the techniques, because they require little data storage, also adjust very quickly to changes in sales conditions and, thus, are appropriate for short-term forecasting. We can fully understand the range of FMTS techniques by starting with the concept of an average as a forecast (which is the basis on which all FMTS techniques are founded) and move through the levels of moving average, exponential smoothing, adaptive smoothing, and incorporating trend and seasonality.

The Average as a Forecast

All FMTS techniques are essentially a form of average. The simplest form of an average as a forecast can be represented by the following formula:

$$\text{Forecast}_{t+1} = \text{Average Sales}_{1 \text{ to } t} = \sum_{t=1}^{N} S_t/N, \qquad (3.1)$$

where S = sales and N = number of periods of sales data, or t.

In other words, our forecast for next month (or any month in the future, for that matter) is the average of all sales that have occurred in the past.

The advantage to the average as a forecast is that the average is designed to "dampen" out any fluctuations. Thus, the average takes the noise (which time-series techniques assume cannot be forecast anyway) out of the forecast. However, the average also dampens out of the forecast *any* fluctuations, including important ones such as trend and seasonality. This principle can be demonstrated with a couple of examples.

Figure 3.2 provides a history of sales that has only the time-series components of level and noise. The forecast (an average) does a fairly good job of ignoring the noise and forecasting only the level. However, Figure 3.3 illustrates a history of sales that has the time-series components of level and noise *plus trend*. As will always happen when the average is used to forecast data with a trend, the forecast lags behind the actual data. Because the average becomes more "sluggish" as more data are added, the lagging of the forecast behind the actual sales gets worse over time. If our example in Figure 3.3 had been a negative trend, then lagging behind would have meant that the average always would have forecast high.

As a final example, Figure 3.4 illustrates a history of sales that has the time-series components of level and noise *plus seasonality*. Notice that the average has the unfortunate effect of losing (i.e., dampening out) the seasonal pattern. Thus, we would lose this important component of any possible forecast.

The conclusion from these three illustrations is that the average should only be used to forecast sales patterns that contain only the time-series components of level and noise. Remember that FMTS techniques assume certain patterns exist in the data. In the case of the average, we are assuming there is no trend or seasonality in the data. This is why we stated earlier that the forecast for the next period also is the forecast for all future periods. Because the data are supposed to be level, there should be no pattern of sales increasing (trend) or increasing and decreasing (seasonality). Therefore, sales should be the same (level) for each period in the future. If nothing else, this demonstrates the rather naive assumption that accompanies the use of the average as a forecast.

The average as a forecasting technique has the added disadvantage of requiring an ever-increasing amount of data storage. With each successive month, an additional piece of data must be stored for the calculation. With the data storage capabilities of today's computers, this may not be too onerous a disadvantage, but it does cause the average to be sluggish to changes in level of demand. One final example should illustrate this point. Figure 3.5 shows a data series with little noise, but the level changes. Notice that the average as a forecast never really adjusts to this new level because we cannot get rid of the "old" data (i.e., the data from the previous level).

Thus, the average as a forecast does not consider trend or seasonality, and it is sluggish to react to changes in the level of sales. In fact, it does little for us as a forecasting technique other than to give us an excellent starting point.

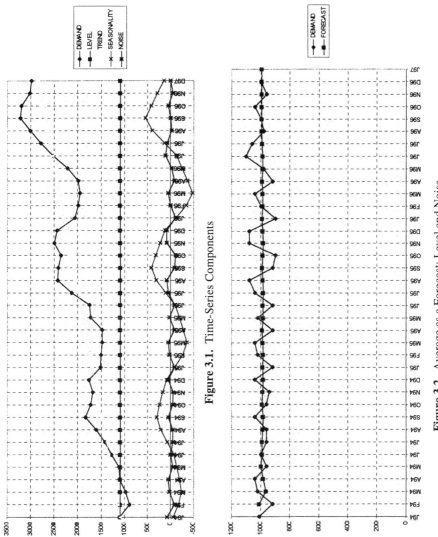

Figure 3.1. Time-Series Components

Figure 3.2. Average as a Forecast: Level and Noise

47

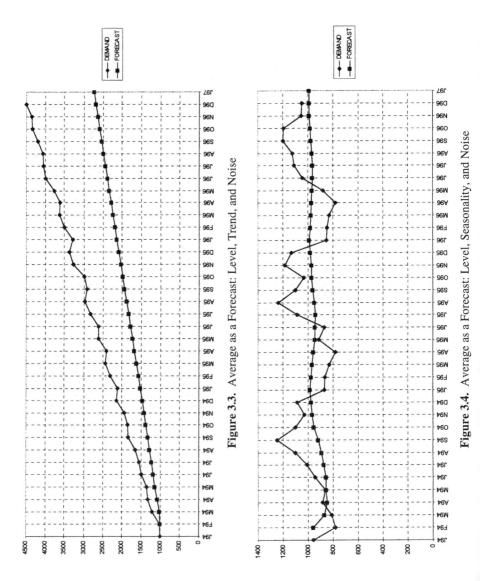

Figure 3.3. Average as a Forecast: Level, Trend, and Noise

Figure 3.4. Average as a Forecast: Level, Seasonality, and Noise

All FMTS techniques were developed to overcome some disadvantage of the average as a forecast. We next explore the first attempt at improvement, a moving average.

Moving Average

Rather than use all the previous data in the calculation of an average as the forecast, why not just use some of the more recent data? This is precisely what a moving average does with the following formula:

$$F_{t+1} = (S_t + S_{t-1} + S_{t-2} + \ldots + S_{t-N-1}) / N, \qquad (3.2)$$

where F_{t+1} = forecast for Period $t + 1$, S_{t-1} = sales for Period $t - 1$, and N = number of periods in the moving average.

So, a 3-period moving average would be

$$F_{t+1} = (S_t + S_{t-1} + S_{t-2}) / 3,$$

a 4-period moving average would be

$$F_{t+1} = (S_t + S_{t-1} + S_{t-2} + S_{t-3}) / 4,$$

a 5-period moving average would be

$$F_{t+1} = (S_t + S_{t-1} + S_{t-2} + S_{t-3} + S_{t-4}) / 5,$$

and so on for as many periods in the moving average as you would like.

The problem with a moving average is deciding how many periods of sales to use in the forecast. The more periods used, the more it starts to look like an average. The less periods used, the more reactive the forecast becomes but the more it starts to look like our naive technique from Chapter 2 (the forecast for the next period equals the sales from the last period). Applying 3-, 6-, and 12-period moving averages to each of the demand patterns in Figures 3.2 through 3.5 (see Figures 3.6 through 3.9, respectively) should illustrate some of these points.

For a time series that has only level and noise (Figure 3.6), our three moving averages work equally well. This is because all dampen out the relatively small amount of noise, and there is no change in level to which to react. Because it uses the least data, the 3-period moving average is superior in this case.

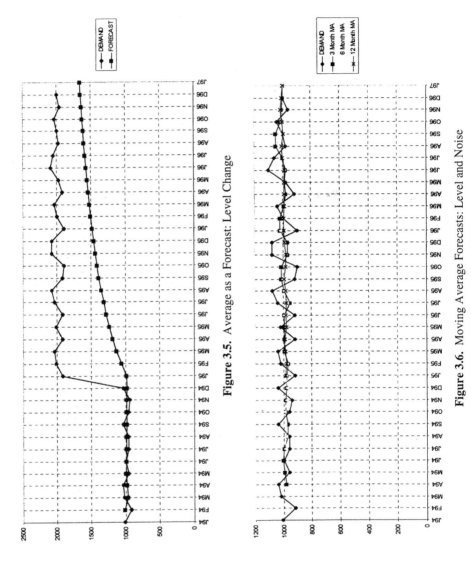

Figure 3.5. Average as a Forecast: Level Change

Figure 3.6. Moving Average Forecasts: Level and Noise

However, for the time series with trend added (Figure 3.7), very different results are obtained. The longer the moving average, the less reactive the forecast and the more the forecast lags behind the trend (because it is more like the average). Again, this is because moving averages were not really designed to deal with a trend, but the shorter moving averages adjust better (are more reactive) than the longer ones in this case.

An interesting phenomenon occurs when we look at the use of moving averages to forecast time series with seasonality (Figure 3.8). Notice that both the 3- and 6-period moving averages lag behind the seasonal pattern (forecast low when sales are rising and forecast high when sales are falling) and miss the turning points in the time series. Notice also that the more reactive moving average (3 periods) does a better job of both of these. This is because in the short run (defined here as between turning points) the seasonal pattern simply looks like trend to a moving average.

However, the 12-period moving average simply ignores the seasonal pattern. This is due to the fact that any average dampens out random fluctuations (i.e., noise) *and* any patterns that are the same length as the average. Because this time series has a 12-month seasonal pattern, a 12-month moving average completely loses the seasonal component in its forecast. This is particularly dangerous when you consider how many sales managers use a simple 12-month moving average to generate forecasts; they are inadvertently dampening out the seasonal fluctuations from their forecasts.

Finally, let us look at the time series in which the level changes (Figure 3.9). Again, the longer moving average tends to dampen out the noise better than does the shorter moving average, but the shorter moving average reacts more quickly to the change in level.

Thus, what we need in a moving average is one that acts like an average when there is only noise in the time series (dampens out the noise but uses less data than an average) but acts like a naive forecast when the level changes (puts more weight on what happened very recently). The problem with this is how to recognize the difference in a change that is noise as opposed to a change in level, a trend, or a seasonal pattern.

A final problem with the moving average is that the same weight is put on all past periods of data in determining the forecast. It is more reasonable to put greater weight on the more recent periods than on the older periods (especially when a longer moving average is being used). Therefore, the question when using a moving average becomes one of how many periods of data to use and how much weight to put on each of those periods. To answer this question about moving averages, a technique called exponential smoothing was developed.

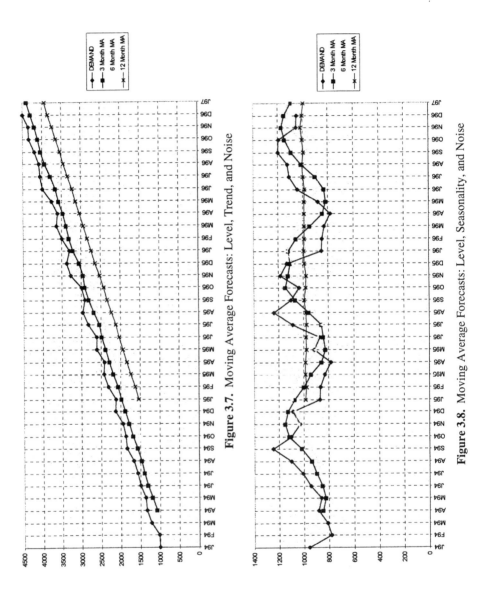

Figure 3.7. Moving Average Forecasts: Level, Trend, and Noise

Figure 3.8. Moving Average Forecasts: Level, Seasonality, and Noise

Exponential Smoothing

Exponential smoothing is the basis for almost all FMTS techniques in use today. It is easier to understand this technique if we acknowledge that it originally was called an *exponentially weighted moving average.* Obviously, the original name was too much of a mouthful for everyday use, but it helps us to explain how this deceptively complex technique works. We are going to develop a moving average, but we will weight the more recent periods of sales more heavily in the forecast, and the weights for the older periods will decrease at an exponential rate (which is where the *exponential smoothing* term came from).

Regardless of that rather scary statement, we are going to accomplish this with a very simple calculation (Brown & Meyer, 1961):

$$F_{t+1} = \alpha S_t + (1 - \alpha) F_t, \qquad (3.3)$$

where F_t = forecast for Period t, S_t = sales for Period t, and $0 < \alpha < 1$.

In other words, our forecast for next period (or, again, for any period in the future) is a function of last period's sales and last period's forecast with this α thing thrown in to confuse us.

What we actually are doing with this exponential smoothing formula is merely a weighted average. Because α is a positive fraction (i.e., between 0 and 1), $1 - \alpha$ also is a positive fraction, and the two of them add up to 1. Any time we take one number and multiply it by a positive fraction, take a second number and multiply it by the reciprocal of the positive fraction (another way of saying 1 minus the first fraction), and add the two results together, we have merely performed a weighted average. Several examples should help.

1. When we want to average the sales of 2 periods (e.g., Period 1 was 50 and Period 2 was 100) and not put more weight on one than the other, we actually are calculating it as $[(.5 * 50) + (.5 * 100)] = 75$. We simply placed the same weight on each period. Notice that this gives us the same result as if we had done the simpler equal-weight average calculation of $(50 + 100) / 2$.

2. When we want the same 2 periods of sales but want to put three times as much weight on Period 2 (for reasons we will explain later), the calculation would now be $[(.25 * 50) + (.75 * 100)] = 87.5$. Notice that in this case α would be .25 and that $1 - \alpha$ would be .75.

3. Finally, when we want nine times as much weight on Period 2, the resultant calculation would be $[(.1 * 50) + (.9 * 100)] = 95$. Again, notice that in this case α would be .1 and that $1 - \alpha$ would be .9.

Therefore, we can control how much emphasis in our forecast is placed on what sales actually were last period. But what is the purpose of using last period's forecast as part of next period's forecast? This is where exponential smoothing is deceptively complex and requires some illustration.

For the purpose of this illustration, let us assume that on the evening of the final day of each month, we make a forecast for the next month. Let us also assume that we have decided to use exponential smoothing and to put 10% of the weight of our forecast on what happened last month. Furthermore, let us assume that this is the evening of the final day of June. Thus, our value for α would be .1 and our forecast for July would be

$$F_{\text{July}} = .1\ S_{\text{June}} + .9\ F_{\text{June}}.$$

But where did we get the forecast for June? In fact, a month ago on the evening of the final day of May, we made this forecast:

$$F_{\text{June}} = .1\ S_{\text{May}} + .9\ F_{\text{May}}.$$

Again, where did we get the forecast for May? And again, a month ago on the evening of the final day of April, we made this forecast:

$$F_{\text{May}} = .1\ S_{\text{April}} + .9\ F_{\text{April}}.$$

We could keep this up forever, but suffice it to say that each month the forecast from the previous month has in it the forecasts (and the sales) from all previous months. Thus, 10% of the forecast for July is made up of sales from June, but the other 90% is made up of the forecast for June. However, the forecast for June was made up of 10% of the sales from May. Thus, 90% times 10% (or 9%) of the July forecast is made up of the sales from May. The rest of the forecast for June was made up of 90% of the forecast for May, which, in turn, was made up of 10% of the sales from April (so April sales make up 90% times 90% times 10%, or 8.1%, of the July forecast) and 90% of the forecast from April, and so on back to where we made our first forecast. This leads us to the fact that the forecast for July actually is made up of the following rather complicated formula:

$$F_{\text{July}} = .1\ S_{\text{June}} + (.9)\ (.1)\ S_{\text{May}} + (.9)^2\ (.1)\ S_{\text{April}} + (.9)^3\ (.1)\ S_{\text{March}} + \ldots + (.9)^N\ (.1)\ S_{\text{July}-(N+1)}.$$

If we take a second to study this formula, we see that sales from June make up 10% of our forecast, sales from May make up 9% (.9 * .1) of our forecast, sales from April make up 8.1% (.9 * .9 * .1) of our forecast, sales from March make up 7.2% (.9 * .9 * .9 * .1) of our forecast, and so on back to the 1st month we used this technique.

What is happening with the rather simple-looking exponential smoothing formula is that we are putting α weight on last period's sales, putting α times $(1 - \alpha)$ weight on the previous period's sales, and changing the weight for each previous period's sales by multiplying the weight by $(1 - \alpha)$ for each successive period we go into the past.

For $\alpha = .1$, this causes the weights for previous period sales to decrease at the following exponential rate: .1, .09, .081, .072, .063, . . .; for $\alpha = .2$, the weights for previous period sales decrease at the following exponential rates: .2, .16, .128, .1024, .08192, . . .

We could try to develop similar series for every value of α (the possible values of α between 0 and 1 are infinite, so our attempt might take a while), but it is not necessary; the simple exponential smoothing formula does it for us. We do need to remember, however, that the higher the value of α, the more weight we are putting on last period's sales and the less weight we are putting on all the previous periods combined. In fact, as α approaches 1, exponential smoothing puts so much weight on the past period sales and so little on the previous periods combined that it starts to look like our naive technique ($F_{t+1} = S_t$). Conversely, as α approaches 0, exponential smoothing puts more equal weight on all periods and starts to look much like the average as a forecast.

This leads us to some conclusions about what the value of α should be:

1. The more the level changes, the larger α should be so that exponential smoothing can quickly adjust.
2. The more random the data, the smaller α should be so that exponential smoothing can dampen out the noise.

Several examples should help illustrate these conclusions. For our first illustration, we can use the data pattern from Figure 3.9 for the moving average to illustrate Figure 3.10 for exponential smoothing. In Figure 3.10, we can see three exponential smoothing forecasts of the time series. All three do a fairly good job when the level is stable, but the higher the value of α in the forecast, the quicker it reacts to the change in level. Because a low value of α is much like an average, the forecast for the low α never quite reaches the new level.

However, a very different result is found when we observe the forecasts of the time series in Figures 3.11 and 3.12. Figure 3.11 is a reproduction of

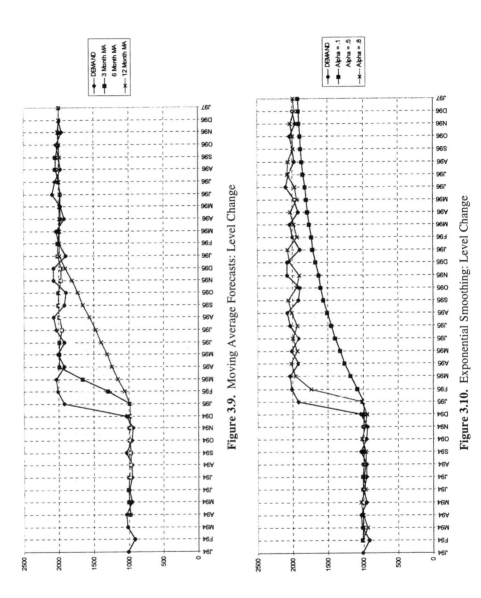

Figure 3.9. Moving Average Forecasts: Level Change

Figure 3.10. Exponential Smoothing: Level Change

the data series used in Figures 3.2 and 3.6 and represents a time series with stable trend and a low amount of noise. In this series, the exponential smoothing forecasts with various levels of α all perform fairly well. However, in the time series of Figure 3.12, which has a stable level but a high amount of noise, the forecasts with the higher values of α overreact to the noise and, as a result, jump around quite a bit. The forecast with the lower level of α does a better job of dampening out the noise.

Given these illustrations of our conclusions about the value of α that should be used, we have in exponential smoothing a technique that overcomes many of the problems with the average and the moving average as forecasting techniques. Exponential smoothing is less cumbersome than the average because exponential smoothing requires only the values of last period's sales and forecast and the value of α. Exponential smoothing solves the problems with the moving average of how much data to use and how to weight it by using an exponentially decreasing weight for all previous periods.

However, with exponential smoothing, we still are faced with a dilemma: How do we determine whether the level is changing or whether it is simply noise and, thus, what the value of α should be? To answer this dilemma, the next group of techniques (called adaptive smoothing) were developed.

Adaptive Smoothing

Although a number of adaptive smoothing techniques exist, they all have one thing in common: Each is an attempt to automatically select the value of α. Because there are so many adaptive smoothing techniques and they all essentially work equally well, we only discuss the simplest of this group of techniques here. This adaptive smoothing approach uses the absolute value of the percentage error from the previous period's forecast to adjust the value of α for the next period's forecast (Trigg, 1967). Thus, the original exponential smoothing formula still is used:

$$F_{t+1} = \alpha S_t + (1 - \alpha) F_t. \tag{3.4}$$

However, after each period's sales are recorded, the value of α is adjusted for the next period by the following formula:

$$\alpha_{t+2} = |(F_{t+1} - S_{t+1}) / S_{t+1}| = |PE_{t+1}|. \tag{3.5}$$

Because Equation 3.5 can produce values outside the range of α, this calculation is adjusted by the following rules:

TABLE 3.1 Adaptive Smoothing Forecast Calculations

Month	Demand	Forecast	Percent Error	Absolute Percent Error or α_{t+1}
January 1994	1,010			
February 1994	920	1,010	.098	.098
March 1994	1,020	1,002	−.018	.018
April 1994	1,040	1,002	−.037	.037
May 1994	960	1,003	.045	.045
June 1994	1,000	1,002	.001	.001
July 1994	960	1,002	.043	.043
August 1994	960	1,000	.041	.041
September 1994	1,040	998	−.041	.041
October 1994	960	1,000	.041	.041
November 1994	940	998	.061	.061
December 1994	1,040	995	−.044	.044
January 1995	1,920	997	−.481	.481
February 1995	2,020	1,441	−.287	.287
March 1995	1,920	1,607	−.212	.212
April 1995	2,040	1,699	−.115	.115
May 1995	2,080	1,725	−.146	.146
June 1995	1,920	1,768	−.079	.079
July 1995	2,040	1,780	−.128	.128
August 1995	2,080	1,813	−.128	.128
September 1995	1,920	1,848	−.038	.038
October 1995	1,900	1,850	−.026	.026
November 1995	2,080	1,852	−.110	.110
December 1995	2,080	1,877	−.098	.098
January 1996	1,900	1,897	−.002	.002
February 1996	2,000	1,897	−.052	.052
March 1996	2,040	1,902	−.068	.068
April 1996	1,920	1,912	−.005	.005
May 1996	1,980	1,912	−.035	.035
June 1996	2,100	1,914	−.089	.089
July 1996	2,060	1,931	−.063	.063
August 1996	1,980	1,939	−.021	.021
September 1996	2,000	1,940	−.030	.030
October 1996	2,040	1,942	−.049	.049
November 1996	1,960	1,946	−.007	.007
December 1996	2,000	1,946	−.027	.027
January 1997		1,947		

If $|PE_{t+1}|$ is equal to or greater than 1, then $\alpha_{t+2} = 0.99999$.
If $|PE_{t+1}|$ is equal to 0, then $\alpha_{t+2} = 0.00001$.

We can illustrate the adaptability of this technique by forecasting the time series with level change in Figure 3.10 to give us Figure 3.13 for adaptive smoothing. To illustrate the changes in α that result in this technique, the calculations also are reproduced in Table 3.1.

To get the process started, we used the usual convention of setting the initial value of α at .1, although any value can be chosen without changing the resultant forecasts. The reason for this is that we also assume that the initial forecast was equal to the first period demand, and so the first forecast becomes

$$F_2 = \alpha \, S_1 + (1 - \alpha) \, S_1.$$

So, regardless of the initial value of α that is chosen, the forecast for Period 2 always is equal to sales from Period 1. The true calculation of a forecast and the adapted values of α begin at that point.

Notice that the value of α stays low (well below .1) while the time series is level (a low value of α dampens out the noise), but as soon as the level changes, the value of α jumps dramatically to adjust. Once the time series levels off, the value of α again returns to a low level.

This adaptive smoothing technique overcomes one of the major problems with exponential smoothing: What should be the value chosen for α? However, all the techniques we have discussed so far have a common problem: None of them considers trend or seasonality. Because this technique assumes that there is no trend or seasonality, our forecast of January 1997 is 1,947, which also is our forecast for *every month* in 1997; we assume that there will be no general increase or decrease in sales (trend) or any pattern of fluctuation in sales (seasonality). Because this is unrealistic for many business demand situations, we need some way in which to incorporate trend and seasonality into our FMTS forecasts. To do so, we temporarily set aside the concept of smoothing constant adaptability and introduce first trend and then seasonality into our exponential smoothing calculations.

Exponential Smoothing With Trend

Although we tend to think of trend as a straight or curving line going up or down, for the purposes of exponential smoothing, it is helpful to think of trend as a series of changes in the level. In other words, with each successive period, the level either "steps up" or "steps down." This *step function* (or changing level pattern) of trend is conceptually illustrated in Figure 3.14. Although demand is going up in a straight line, we can conceive of it as a series of increases in the level (the dashed horizontal lines). This is much like climbing a set of stairs. Although we make steady progress up the stairs, we actually are stepping up one step each period (the amount we step up, or the height of each step, on a set of stairs is called the *riser*). The height of each step (the riser) is what we call *trend* in exponential smoothing, and that trend is designated in Figure 3.14 as T. For period $t + 1$, the trend is the amount the level changed from Period t to Period $t + 1$ ($L_{t+1} - L_t$), or T_{t+1}. Similarly for Period $t + 2$, the trend is the amount the level changed from Period $t + 1$ to Period $t + 2$ ($L_{t+2} - L_{t-1}$), or T_{t+2}.

To understand the calculation of trend in exponential smoothing, we also must understand that an exponential smoothing calculation is just a weighted average of two measures of the same thing. Our original exponential smoothing formula (Equation 3.4) was

$$F_{t+1} = \alpha\, S_t + (1 - \alpha)\, F_t.$$

In this calculation, S_t is one measure of past sales (last period's sales), and F_t is another measure of past sales (a weighted average of sales in all periods prior to t). Thus, we were taking a weighted average of two measures of the same thing. We are now going to do the same thing for level and trend with the following formulas (Holt, Modigliani, Muth, & Simon, 1960):

$$L_t = \alpha\, S_t + (1 - \alpha)\, (L_{t-1} + T_{t-1}) \tag{3.6}$$

$$T_t = \beta\, (L_t - L_{t-1}) + (1 - \beta)\, T_{t-1}, \tag{3.7}$$

where L = level, T = trend, $0 < \alpha < 1$, and $0 < \beta < 1$.

Notice that Equation 3.6 looks very similar to our earlier exponential smoothing forecast calculation; we still use α in the same way, and we still use last period's sales. This difference is the addition of trend into the second part of Equation 3.6 and the fact that it is not a forecast for next period (F_{t+1}) but rather a measure of level for this period (L_t). In fact, in our original exponential smoothing formula (Equation 3.4), we did not include trend because we assumed it did not exist. Because trend was assumed not to exist, our estimate of level this period *was* our forecast of next period.

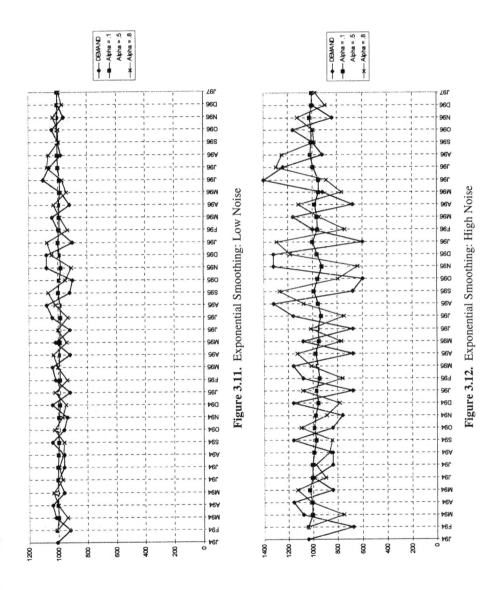

Figure 3.11. Exponential Smoothing: Low Noise

Figure 3.12. Exponential Smoothing: High Noise

61

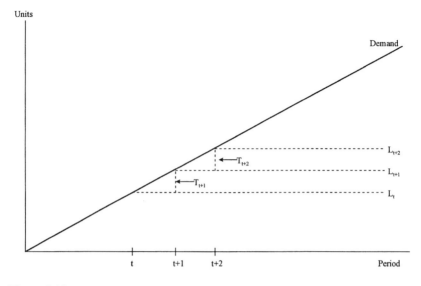

Figure 3.14. Trend in a Time Series

What we need are two estimates of level for this period so that we can exponentially smooth them. The first estimate is simply sales for this period. Because we assume there is no seasonality in the time series (an assumption that we discard in the next section), this sales value has no seasonality in it. Because the trend is a change in level from one period to the next, any given value of sales does not have trend in it (i.e., trend is in the *change* in sales from one period to the next, not any single sales value). Finally, when we perform the weighted averaging of the exponential smoothing calculation in Equation 3.6, we get rid of the noise (recall that averaging removes noise). Because this logic says that there is no trend or seasonality in the sales value and we will get rid of this noise when we do our exponential smoothing calculation, we are left with only one time-series component in the sales value, and that component is level.

The second estimate of level is our estimate of level from last period plus the estimate of how much level would change from last period to this period (i.e., the trend). This gives us two measures of level to exponentially smooth with α.

Our two estimates of trend in Equation 3.7 are how much the level changed from last period to this period and our estimate of trend from last period. These two measures of trend are exponentially smoothed with our new smoothing constant, β, which is just like α in that it is a positive fraction (i.e., between 0 and 1). It is designated by a different Greek symbol to indicate that α and β can have different values.

Once we have our new estimates of level (L) and trend (T), we can forecast as far into the future as we want by taking the level and adding to it the trend per period times as many periods into the future as we want the forecast. This can be represented by the following formula:

$$F_{t+m} = L_t + (T_t * m),\qquad(3.8)$$

where m = number of periods into the future to forecast.

To illustrate this technique, consider the time series with trend introduced in Figure 3.3, now given in Figure 3.15 for exponential smoothing with trend. To illustrate the calculations involved in this technique, Table 3.2 provides the calculations of level and trend and a forecast forward for 1 period throughout the time series (also provided in Figure 3.15). For purposes of illustration, we arbitrarily chose the values of .1 for α and .2 for β. Notice that to get the process started, we used the usual convention of assuming that the level for the 1st period equaled 1st-period demand and that the trend for the 1st period equaled the change in demand from the 1st period to the 2nd period.

To provide a forecast for any period more than 1 in the future (e.g., April 1997), it is merely a task of taking the most recent value of level that has been calculated (in this case, December 1996) and adding to it the most recent value of trend that has been calculated (also in this case, December 1996) times the number of months into the future we wish to forecast (because April is 4 months past December, it would be times 4). For April 1997, the calculations are

$$F_{\text{Apr97}} = L_{\text{Dec96}} + (T_{\text{Dec96}} * m)$$
$$F_{\text{Apr97}} = 4{,}614 + (106 * 4)$$
$$F_{\text{Apr97}} = 5{,}038.$$

Now that we have the logic for introducing trend into the exponential smoothing calculations, it is fairly easy to also bring in seasonality.

Exponential Smoothing With Trend and Seasonality

To introduce seasonality, let us first think of a simple demand example in which we sell 12,000 units of a product every year. If there is no trend, no noise, and no seasonality, then we would expect to sell 1,000 units every month (i.e., the level). If, however, we noticed that every January we sold, on

TABLE 3.2 Exponential Smoothing With Trend Forecast Calculations

Month	Demand	Level ($\alpha = .1$)	Trend ($\beta = .2$)	Forecast
January 1994	1,010	1,010	10	
February 1994	1,020	1,020	10	
March 1994	1,220	1,049	14	1,030
April 1994	1,340	1,091	19	1,063
May 1994	1,360	1,135	24	1,110
June 1994	1,500	1,193	31	1,159
July 1994	1,560	1,258	38	1,224
August 1994	1,660	1,332	45	1,296
September 1994	1,840	1,424	54	1,377
October 1994	1,860	1,516	62	1,478
November 1994	1,940	1,615	69	1,578
December 1994	2,140	1,729	78	1,684
January 1995	2,120	1,839	85	1,808
February 1995	2,320	1,963	93	1,924
March 1995	2,440	2,094	100	2,056
April 1995	2,420	2,217	105	2,195
May 1995	2,620	2,352	111	2,322
June 1995	2,620	2,478	114	2,462
July 1995	2,840	2,617	119	2,592
August 1995	2,980	2,760	124	2,736
September 1995	2,920	2,887	124	2,884
October 1995	3,000	3,011	124	3,012
November 1995	3,280	3,149	127	3,135
December 1995	3,380	3,287	129	3,277
January 1996	3,300	3,404	127	3,416
February 1996	3,500	3,528	126	3,531
March 1996	3,640	3,653	126	3,654
April 1996	3,620	3,763	123	3,779
May 1996	3,780	3,875	121	3,886
June 1996	4,000	3,996	121	3,996
July 1996	4,060	4,111	120	4,117
August 1996	4,080	4,216	117	4,231
September 1996	4,200	4,319	114	4,332
October 1996	4,340	4,424	112	4,433
November 1996	4,360	4,518	109	4,536
December 1996	4,500	4,614	106	4,627
January 1997				4,720

average, 1,150 units, then there clearly is a pattern here of selling more than the level in January. In fact, we are selling 1,150/1,000, or 1.15, times the level.

This value of 1.15 is called a *multiplicative seasonal adjustment* and means that sales in that month are 15% higher than they would be without a seasonal pattern. Similarly, a seasonal adjustment of 1.00 means that sales are right at the nonseasonal level, and a seasonal adjustment of 0.87 means that sales are 13% below what we would expect if there were no seasonal pattern.

We are now going to use this concept of a multiplicative seasonal adjustment to introduce seasonality into the exponential smoothing calculations. Again, we will develop two different measures of each seasonal adjustment and take a weighted average of them (through exponential smoothing) to come up with our new estimate. To do this, however, we also need to update our formulas for exponential smoothing with trend (Equations 3.6 and 3.7) to take into account the fact that seasonality is now assumed to exist. This leads us to the following formulas (Winters, 1960):

$$L_t = \alpha \, (S_t \, / \, SA_{t-C}) + (1 - \alpha) \, (L_{t-1} + T_{t-1}) \tag{3.9}$$

$$T_t = \beta \, (L_t - L_{t-1}) + (1 - \beta) \, T_{t-1} \tag{3.10}$$

$$SA_t = \gamma \, (S_t \, / \, L_t) + (1 - \gamma) \, (SA_{t-C}), \tag{3.11}$$

where L = level, T = trend, SA_t = seasonal adjustment for Period t, C = cycle length of the seasonal pattern (e.g., cycle length for a 12-month pattern is $C = 12$), $0 < \alpha < 1$, $0 < \beta < 1$, and $0 < \gamma < 1$.

We have revised our calculation for level to take seasonality into account in our first estimate of level. Recalling our previous example of annual sales of 12,000, how would we take the seasonality out of January sales? If sales were 1,150 and our previous estimates of the seasonality adjustment for January were 1.15, we can deseasonalize January sales simply by dividing the sales value of 1,150 by the seasonal adjustment of 1.15. This give us a deseasonalized value of 1,00—precisely the value we said would be the expected level if there were no seasonality.

Thus, by dividing sales for any period by the seasonal adjustment for the same period last year (e.g., dividing sales for January 1997 by the seasonal adjustment for January 1996), we have an estimate in the first formula of level with the seasonality taken out (recall that the original formula already took out the trend and the noise). Because the second part of this formula contains the level from the last period, which was deseasonalized at that time, we now have two estimates of level to exponentially smooth.

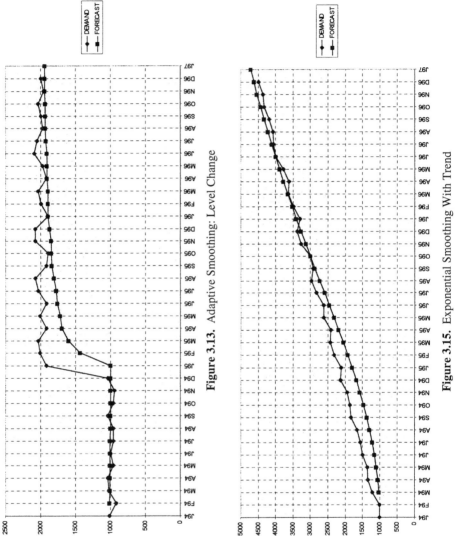

Figure 3.13. Adaptive Smoothing: Level Change

Figure 3.15. Exponential Smoothing With Trend

Thankfully, the formula for trend (Equation 3.10) does not change. Therefore, we do not have to revisit it here.

However, we now have added a formula to calculate the seasonal adjustments (Equation 3.11). Again, we need two estimates of the seasonal adjustment for each period, so we can exponentially smooth each. This means that we would have 12 of these calculations per year if we are forecasting monthly sales, 52 if we are forecasting weekly sales, and 4 if we are forecasting quarterly sales.

The first part of Equation 3.11 is, again, a throwback to our initial example. If we take the sales value for this period and divide it by the most recently calculated level (which was just done two formulas before and is L_t), we have one estimate of the seasonal adjustment for this period. In our initial example, we did the same thing when we divided 1,150 by 1,000 to obtain 1.15 as our estimate of the seasonal adjustment for January.

For our second estimate of the seasonal adjustment for this period, we need to look back 1 year to the same period last year. We can now exponentially smooth these two estimates of the seasonal adjustment for this period using the smoothing constant, γ. Again, γ is just like α and β in that it is a positive fraction (i.e., between 0 and 1). It is designated by a different Greek symbol to indicate that α, β, and γ all can have different values.

Once we have our new estimates of level (L), trend (T), and seasonal adjustments (SA), we can forecast as far into the future as we want by taking the level, adding to it the trend per period times as many periods into the future as we want the forecast, and multiplying that result by the most recent seasonal adjustment for that period. This can be represented by the following formula:

$$F_{t+m} = [L_t + (T_t * m)] * SA_{t-C+m}, \tag{3.12}$$

where m = number of periods into the future to forecast.

The final component of Equation 3.12 probably needs a little illustration. If we have just received sales for December 1996 and want to forecast April 1997, we will use the values of L and T calculated in December 1996 (in this case, December 1996 is t) for the first part of the forecast. However, our most recent estimate of the seasonal adjustment for April was calculated back in April 1996. The symbol to represent using this value is to take t (December 1996), subtract C (or 12) months from it (placing us in December 1995), and add to it m (or 4) months to bring us to the seasonal adjustment for April 1996.

To illustrate this technique, we go all the way back to our original time series with trend and seasonality introduced in Figure 3.1, now given in Figure 3.16 for exponential smoothing with trend and seasonality. To illustrate the

TABLE 3.3 Exponential Smoothing With Trend and Seasonality Forecast Calculations

Month	Demand	Level ($\alpha = .1$)	Trend ($\beta = .2$)	Seasonality ($\gamma = .15$)	Forecast
January 1994	1,104	1,104	−219	1.00	
February 1994	885	885	−219	1.00	885
March 1994	976	697	−213	1.06	666
April 1994	1,101	546	−200	1.15	484
May 1994	1,120	423	−185	1.25	345
June 1994	1,276	342	−164	1.41	238
July 1994	1,419	302	−139	1.56	178
August 1994	1,615	308	−110	1.64	162
September 1994	1,836	361	−78	1.61	197
October 1994	1,730	428	−49	1.46	284
November 1994	1,686	510	−22	1.35	380
December 1994	1,769	616	3	1.28	488
January 1995	1,521	709	21	1.17	619
February 1995	1,504	808	37	1.13	730
March 1995	1,478	899	48	1.15	895
April 1995	1,480	981	54	1.21	1,091
May 1995	1,726	1,070	61	1.30	1,291
June 1995	1,759	1,143	64	1.43	1,595
July 1995	2,137	1,223	67	1.58	1,877
August 1995	2,436	1,310	71	1.67	2,113
September 1995	2,425	1,393	73	1.63	2,227
October 1995	2,355	1,482	76	1.48	2,136
November 1995	2,499	1,588	82	1.38	2,097
December 1995	2,442	1,694	87	1.30	2,140
January 1996	2,069	1,780	87	1.17	2,087
February 1996	1,992	1,856	85	1.12	2,108
March 1996	1,958	1,918	80	1.13	2,227
April 1996	1,990	1,963	73	1.18	2,409
May 1996	2,222	2,003	67	1.27	2,651
June 1996	2,525	2,039	60	1.40	2,958
July 1996	2,789	2,066	54	1.55	3,327
August 1996	3,017	2,088	47	1.64	3,542
September 1996	3,232	2,120	44	1.62	3,485
October 1996	3,198	2,165	44	1.48	3,195
November 1996	3,028	2,207	44	1.38	3,048
December 1996	2,985	2,255	45	1.31	2,938
January 1997					2,692

calculations involved in this technique, Table 3.3 provides the calculation of level, trend, seasonality, and a forecast forward for 1 period throughout the time series (also provided in Figure 3.16). For purposes of illustration, we arbitrarily chose the values of .1 for α, .2 for β, and .15 for γ. Notice that to get the process started, we used the usual convention of assuming that the level for the 1st period equaled 1st-period demand, that the trend for the 1st period equaled the change in demand from the 1st period to the 2nd period, and that the initial 12 seasonal adjustment values were equal to 1.00. Notice also that this technique does a pretty terrible job of forecasting until at least 1 year of the seasonal pattern is available. Thus, exponential smoothing with trend and seasonality needs at least 1 complete year of data before it is "warmed up" and can start to forecast fairly effectively.

To provide a forecast for any period more than 1 in the future (e.g., April 1997), it is merely a task of taking the most recent value of level that has been calculated (in this case, December 1996), adding to it the most recent value of trend that has been calculated (also in this case, December 1996) times the number of months into the future we wish to forecast (because April is 4 months past December, it would be times 4), and multiplying this value by the seasonal adjustment for April of last year (1996). For April 1997, the calculations are

$$F_{Apr97} = [L_{Dec96} + (T_{Dec96} * m)] * SA_{Apr96}$$
$$F_{Apr97} = [2,255 + (45 * 4)] * 1.18$$
$$F_{Apr97} = 2,874.$$

Now that we have introduced the components of trend and seasonality into our basic exponential smoothing formula, we can return to the idea of how to set the value of the smoothing constants. However, now it is not simply a matter of choosing a value for α but rather one of choosing values for β and γ as well. In fact, the accuracy of exponential smoothing with trend and seasonality is very sensitive to the values chosen for the smoothing constants, so this is no small matter.

Adaptive Exponential Smoothing With Trend and Seasonality

As with regular adaptive smoothing, there are several techniques that are adaptive and consider trend and seasonality. One of the most complex computationally is called the self-adaptive forecasting technique (SAFT) and was developed more than 25 years ago (Roberts & Reed, 1969). SAFT is a heuristic technique that examines different combinations of α, β, and γ to arrive at the

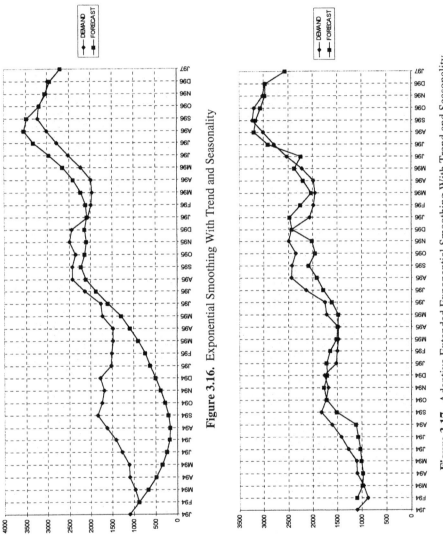

Figure 3.16. Exponential Smoothing With Trend and Seasonality

Figure 3.17. Adaptive Extended Exponential Smoothing With Trend and Seasonality

most accurate forecast. For each forecast each period, SAFT tries each combination of α, β, and γ starting with a value of .05 for each and incrementally increasing the values by .05 until a value of .95 for each is reached. For each of these 6,859 (19 * 19 * 19, where 19 is the number of values between 0 and 1, incrementing by .05 at a time) combinations, SAFT starts at the beginning of the time series and forecasts using exponential smoothing with trend and seasonality and records the resultant value of mean absolute percent error (*MAPE*). Once the lowest *MAPE* value combination of α, β, and γ is determined, a local search for a lower *MAPE* is implemented by examining the values of α, β, and γ above and below each value at a rate of change of .01.

For example, if the first search found the lowest value of *MAPE* to come from the combination of α = .15, β = .20, and γ = .30, then SAFT would try all the combinations of α = .11, .12, .13, .14, .16, .17, .18, and .19; β = .16, .17, .18, .19, .21, .22, .23, and .24; and γ = .26, .27, .28, .29, .31, .32, .33, and .34. These 512 (8 * 8 * 8) combinations are compared to the original best *MAPE* combination, and, again, the lowest combination is chosen.

It should be clear by now that SAFT is a very computationally cumbersome technique. (After all, it requires 7,371 trial forecasts for each product each period before it actually makes a forecast.) As a result, it is in little use today. More computationally efficient versions of SAFT try to calculate values of α, β, or γ and use a heuristic similar to SAFT for the smoothing constants that are not directly calculated.

As with adaptive smoothing, because these adaptive exponential smoothing techniques with trend and seasonality essentially all work equally well, we only discuss the simplest of this group of techniques here. This adaptive smoothing approach, called adaptive extended exponential smoothing (AEES), uses the absolute value of the percent error from the previous period's forecast to adjust the value of α for the next period's forecast and uses the SAFT heuristic to adjust the values of β and γ (Mentzer, 1988). Thus, the exponential smoothing with trend and seasonality formulas (Equations 3.9-3.12) still are used:

$$L_t = \alpha \, (S_t \, / \, SA_{t-C}) + (1 - \alpha) \, (L_{t-1} + T_{t-1})$$

$$T_t = \beta \, (L_t - L_{t-1}) + (1 - \beta) \, T_{t-1}$$

$$SA_t = \gamma \, (S_t \, / \, L_t) + (1 - \gamma) \, (SA_{t-C})$$

$$F_{t+m} = [L_t + (T_t * m)] * SA_{t-C+m}.$$

TABLE 3.4 Fixed-Model Time-Series Technique Selection Guidelines

Time-Series Component Characteristics	Fixed-Model Time-Series Technique
Stable level with no trend or seasonality	Exponential smoothing
Changing level with no trend or seasonality	Adaptive smoothing
Level and trend	Exponential smoothing with trend
Level, trend, and seasonality	Exponential smoothing with trend and seasonality
Changing level, trend, and seasonal patterns	Adaptive extended exponential smoothing

However, after each period's sales are recorded, the value of α is adjusted for the next period by Equation 3.5:

$$\alpha_{t+2} = |(F_{t+1} - S_{t+1}) / S_{t+1}| = |PE_{t+1}|.$$

Because this calculation still can produce values outside the range of α, this calculation is adjusted by the following rules:

If $|PE_{t+1}|$ is equal to or greater than 1, then $\alpha_{t+2} = 0.99999$.
If $|PE_{t+1}|$ is equal to 0, then $\alpha_{t+2} = 0.00001$.

Once the new value of α has been calculated, AEES tries each combination of β and γ starting with a value of .05 for each and incrementally increasing the values by .05 until a value of .95 for each is reached. For each of these 361 (19 * 19, where 19 is the number of values between 0 and 1, incrementing by .05 at a time) combinations, AEES starts at the beginning of the time series and forecasts using exponential smoothing with trend and seasonality and records the resultant value of *MAPE*. Once the lowest MAPE value combination of the calculated value of α and the heuristic values of β and γ is determined, a local search for a lower *MAPE* is implemented by examining the values of β and γ above and below each value at a rate of change of .01.

For example, if the first search found the lowest value of *MAPE* to come from the calculated value of $\alpha = .15$ and the combination of $\beta = .20$ and $\gamma = .30$, then AEES would try all the combinations of $\beta = .16, .17, .18, .19, .21, .22, .23,$ and $.24$ and $\gamma = .26, .27, .28, .29, .31, .32, .33,$ and $.34$. These 64 (8 * 8) combinations are compared to the original best *MAPE* combination, and, again, the lowest combination is chosen.

It should be clear by now that AEES is a much less computationally cumbersome technique than SAFT. AEES requires 425 trial forecasts for each product each period before it actually makes a forecast as opposed to the 7,371

TABLE 3.5 Decomposition Analysis

Month	Demand	Level and Trend	Trend	Seasonality and Noise	Seasonality	Forecast
January 1994	1,104					
February 1994	885					
March 1994	976					
April 1994	1,101					
May 1994	1,120					
June 1994	1,276	1,376		−100	−140	
July 1994	1,419	1,411	35	8	60	
August 1994	1,615	1,463	52	152	261	
September 1994	1,836	1,505	42	331	325	
October 1994	1,730	1,536	32	194	200	
November 1994	1,686	1,587	51	99	204	
December 1994	1,769	1,627	40	142	165	
January 1995	1,521	1,687	60	−166	−203	
February 1995	1,504	1,755	68	−251	−308	
March 1995	1,478	1,804	49	−326	−396	
April 1995	1,480	1,856	52	−376	−440	
May 1995	1,726	1,924	68	−198	−258	
June 1995	1,759	1,980	56	−221	−140	
July 1995	2,137	2,026	46	111	60	
August 1995	2,436	2,067	41	370	261	
September 1995	2,425	2,107	40	319	325	
October 1995	2,355	2,149	43	206	200	
November 1995	2,499	2,190	41	309	204	
December 1995	2,442	2,254	64	188	165	
January 1996	2,069	2,309	54	−240	−203	
February 1996	1,992	2,357	48	−365	−308	
March 1996	1,958	2,424	67	−466	−396	
April 1996	1,990	2,494	70	−504	−440	
May 1996	2,222	2,539	44	−317	−258	
June 1996	2,525	2,584	45	−59	−140	
July 1996	2,789		45		60	
August 1996	3,017		90		261	
September 1996	3,232		135		325	
October 1996	3,198		180		200	
November 1996	3,028		225		204	
December 1996	2,985		270		165	
January 1997			315		−203	2,696

TABLE 3.6 Decomposition of Seasonality

Month	1994	1995	1996	Average
January		−166	−240	−203
February		−251	−365	−308
March		−326	−466	−396
April		−376	−504	−440
May		−198	−317	−258
June	−100	−221	−59	−140
July	8	111		60
August	152	370		261
September	331	319		325
October	194	206		200
November	99	309		204
December	142	188		165

trial forecasts of SAFT. Furthermore, the exact value of α is calculated rather than the approximation obtained from the SAFT heuristic.

We can illustrate the adaptability of AEES by forecasting the time series with trend and seasonality used in the last section (see Figure 3.17). Notice that the forecast in Figure 3.17 "tracks" the demand better than that in Figure 3.16. This is due to the adaptability of α, β, and γ. Also, the year-to-date *MAPE* for exponential smoothing with trend and seasonality (Figure 3.16) at the end is 9.73%, whereas the same calculation for AEES (Figure 3.17) is 7.00%.

Fixed-Model Time-Series
Techniques: Summary

Considerable effort has been devoted over time to testing the various FMTS techniques discussed here (and variations on these techniques) over a wide variety of time series and forecasting horizons and intervals (for a summary, see Mentzer & Gomes, 1994). To date, no FMTS technique has shown itself to be clearly superior to any of the other FMTS techniques across a wide variety of forecasting levels and time horizons. For this reason, it is recommended that users of FMTS keep in mind where the general category of techniques works well and the time-series scenario for which each technique was designed.

In general, FMTS techniques should be used when a limited amount of data is available on anything other than an actual history of sales (i.e., little data on outside factors such as price changes, economic activity, or promotional programs). This lack of outside (exogenous) data precludes the use of regression (discussed in the next chapter). Furthermore, FMTS techniques are useful when the time-series components change fairly regularly, that is, when the trend rate changes, the seasonal pattern changes, or the overall level of demand changes. FMTS is much more effective at adjusting to these changes in time-series components than are OMTS techniques, which require more data with stable time-series components over a long period of time.

In terms of which FMTS techniques to use in which situations, a general guideline is provided in Table 3.4. However, it should be remembered that these are only general guidelines and that it is best to incorporate these techniques into a system (such as the one discussed in Chapter 9) that allows the system to try each FMTS technique on each forecast to be made and select the one that works best in terms of accuracy.

With these general guidelines established, we now move on to a discussion of OMTS techniques.

Open-Model Time-Series Techniques

OMTS techniques assume that the same components exist in any time series—level, trend, seasonality, and noise—but take a different approach to forecasting these components. Whereas FMTS techniques assume that certain components exist in the time series and use one set of formulas to forecast this series (i.e., the formulas are fixed), OMTS techniques first analyze the components in the time series to see which ones exist and what their nature is. From this information, a set of forecasting formulas unique to that time series is built (i.e., the formulas are open until the time-series components are analyzed).

Various forms of OMTS techniques exist including decomposition analysis (Shiskin, 1961a, 1961b), spectral analysis (Nelson, 1973), Fourier analysis (Bloomfield, 1976), and autoregressive moving average (or Box-Jenkins) analysis (Box & Jenkins, 1970). All of these OMTS techniques have in common the fact that they first try to analyze the time series to determine the components and, as a result, require a considerable amount of past history before any forecasts can be made. For instance, many OMTS techniques recommend no less than 48 periods of data prior to using the techniques. Obviously, this is a disadvantage for situations in which a limited amount of past history is available.

OMTS techniques also have in common the need for considerable understanding of quantitative methods to properly use the techniques. The analysis with OMTS techniques can become quite complex and require considerable input from the forecaster. For these reasons (large data requirements and considerable user experience), OMTS techniques have seen limited use in practice (Mentzer & Cox, 1984; Mentzer & Kahn, 1995). Improvements in systems technology has made OMTS techniques easier to use (as we will see in Chapter 9), but the data requirements still limit their use.

As with FMTS techniques, there is no evidence that the performance of one of these various OMTS techniques is clearly superior to any of the others. Thus, we again discuss only the simplest of the OMTS techniques here. This technique is called decomposition analysis. To demonstrate decomposition analysis, we use the time series presented at the beginning of the chapter in Figure 3.1.

Like all OMTS techniques, the purpose of decomposition analysis is to decompose the data into their time-series components. The first step in doing this is to remove noise and seasonality from the original time series. As we discussed earlier in the chapter, one of the characteristics of a moving average is that it dampens out any noise and dampens out any regular pattern of fluctuation that has a pattern length that is equal to the number of periods in the moving average. Thus, one of the first things we have to do in decomposition analysis is to make a judgment about how long the seasonal pattern is.

Hopefully, visual examination of Figure 3.1 will lead us to conclude that the seasonal pattern takes 12 months. Therefore, a 12-month moving average should remove noise and seasonality from the time series. As in the discussion earlier in the chapter, the value of the moving average in any given period is our estimate of level, and how much that level estimate changes from one period to the next is our estimate of trend. However, because our purpose here is not to forecast but rather to decompose the data, we perform this moving average calculation in a slightly different way than discussed previously. This calculation is as follows:

$$MA_t = (S_{t-5} + S_{t-4} + S_{t-3} + S_{t-2} + S_{t-1} + S_t + S_{t+1} + S_{t+2} + S_{t+3} + S_{t+4} + S_{t+5} + S_{t+6}) / 12.$$

Notice that this is a *centered moving average,* which means that we take an average of 12 months and assign that value to the month in the center. The purpose of this is to find a more accurate estimate of the level. If we placed the moving average value at the end of the 12 months used in the calculation, then it would have too much old data (lower trend) to accurately represent the level for that period. Conversely, if we placed the moving average value at the beginning of the 12 months used in the calculation, then it would have too much new data (higher trend) to accurately represent the level for that period. Thus, the best place to position this estimate of level is in the center of the periods used in its calculation.

Because this moving average contains the level and the trend, we can simply take the difference between each period to determine the trend. Similarly, because the moving average contains the level and the trend, if we subtract it from the original time series (which contained level, trend, seasonality, and noise), the result is a series of data that contains only the seasonality and the noise. These calculations are demonstrated in Table 3.5.

We now have decomposed the original time series into the level and the trend. All that is left is to remove the noise from the data series containing seasonality and noise, and we will have our final component—seasonality. Again, to remove noise, we will use an average. However, because each month of the year represents a different season, we want to perform this average calculation within each season. Thus, we will take all the January values and average them, then an average of all the February values, and so on for all 12 months. This calculation is shown in Table 3.6, and the resultant values are added to Table 3.5 in the "seasonality" column. Notice that this is not a multiplicative seasonal adjustment as we used in FMTS techniques; rather, it is an *additive seasonal adjustment*; to determine the seasonal adjustment, we add it to (not multiply it by) the level plus trend.

We now have our most recent estimate of level (2,584 in June 1996), our most recent estimate of trend (45 units per month from June 1996), and our most recent estimates of the additive seasonal adjustments for the last 12 months. To forecast a future period (e.g., January 1997), we take the last estimate of level and add to it the trend times the number of periods into the future. To this value, we add the seasonal adjustment. For January 1997, the calculation is

$$\text{Forecast}_{Jan97} = \text{Level}_{June96} + (7 * \text{Trend}_{June96}) + \text{Seasonality}_{Jan96}$$
$$= 2{,}584 + (7 * 45) - 203 = 2{,}696.$$

This example illustrates just how much data are required to complete OMTS analysis. Although we have 3 years of monthly data in this example, for all but June, only two values were available to estimate the seasonality adjustment for each season (month). With another year's data, three values would be available for each season, which should improve the seasonality adjustment estimates. However, one of the primary drawbacks to OMTS techniques is this dependency on a large amount of data.

Summary

In this chapter, we have covered a number of time-series techniques. All have in common a recognition of the time-series components—level, trend, seasonality, and noise. FMTS techniques deal with these components by assuming that certain components are (and are not) in the data, whereas OMTS techniques analyze the data to determine which components exist. This greater level of sophistication in OMTS techniques is somewhat ameliorated by the considerable data requirements for analysis.

Another characteristic of all the techniques included in this chapter is the fact that they ignore other factors that might have influenced demand such as price changes, advertising, trade promotions, sales programs, competitive actions, and economic activity. In many cases, much of what time-series techniques classify as noise can be explained by looking at these exogenous factors. In the next chapter, our attention turns to a technique that considers these exogenous factors—regression analysis.

References

Bloomfield, P. (1976). *Fourier analysis of time series: An introduction*. New York: John Wiley.

Box, G. E. P., & Jenkins, G. W. (1970). *Time series analysis: Forecasting and control*. San Francisco: Holden-Day.

Brown, R. G., & Meyer, R. F. (1961). The fundamental theorem of exponential smoothing. *Operations Research, 9*(5), 673-685.

Holt, C. C., Modigliani, F., Muth, J. F., & Simon, H. A. (1960). *Planning production inventories and work force*. Englewood Cliffs, NJ: Prentice Hall.

Mentzer, J. T. (1988). Forecasting with adaptive extended exponential smoothing. *Journal of the Academy of Marketing Science, 16*(4), 62-70.

Mentzer, J. T., & Cox, J. E., Jr. (1984). Familiarity, application, and performance of sales forecasting techniques. *Journal of Forecasting, 3*, 27-36.

Mentzer, J. T., & Gomes, R. (1994). Further extensions of adaptive extended exponential smoothing and comparison with the M-competition. *Journal of the Academy of Marketing Science, 22*, 372-382.

Mentzer, J. T., & Kahn, K. B. (1995). Forecasting technique familiarity, satisfaction, usage, and application. *Journal of Forecasting, 14*, 465-476.

Nelson, C. R. (1973). *Applied time series analysis*. San Francisco: Holden-Day.

Roberts, S. D., & Reed, R. (1969). The development of a self-adaptive forecasting technique. *AIIE Transactions, 1*, 314-322.

Shiskin, J. (1961a). *Electronic computers and business indicators*. Occasional Paper No. 56, National Bureau of Economic Research.

Shiskin, J. (1961b). *Tests and revisions of Bureau of the Census methods of seasonal adjustments*. Technical Paper No. 5, Bureau of the Census.

Trigg, D. W., & Leach, A. G. (1967). Exponential smoothing with an adaptive response rate. *Operations Research Quarterly, 18*, 53-59.

Winters, P. R. (1960). Forecasting sales by exponentially weighted moving averages. *Management Science, 6*, 324-342.

CHAPTER 4

Regression Analysis

*D*uring a visit to one company, we asked a sales
forecasting analyst what modeling techniques were
used to generate the company's forecasts. His reply was
that he used regression analysis. When we asked what
predictor variables were in the model, however, he said
he did not know. He was equally uninformed about how
the predictor variables were selected, whether they ever
changed, and how the forecast model was calculated. In
fact, after a number of questions about the specifics of the
model, his reply was, "It's just—you know—regression
analysis." It probably comes as no surprise that both he
and management were not very pleased with the
forecasting results obtained from this rather uninformed
approach to forecasting.

When used properly, regression analysis can provide
considerable insight into the various factors that affect
demand and, as a result, can be very useful in forecasting
demand. However, regression models must be created and
evaluated in an informed way to make certain they
accomplish what they were intended to do—to accurately
forecast product demand. Once evaluated, they must be
assessed for generalizability, that is, their ability to
continue to accurately forecast demand in the future.

As we discussed in Chapter 3, what regression analysis provides that time series does not is an assessment of how outside factors are related to fluctuations in demand. This assessment is called a *correlation,* meaning how demand (which is called the dependent variable because it is dependent on the values of the other factors) and these outside factors (called the independent, or predictor, variables) are correlated (or co-related). If we can find factors that are highly correlated to demand, then we can use the future values of these factors to forecast future demand.

Regression analysis accomplishes this assessment by building a regression model, which represents the relationship between the dependent variable (y) and a set of independent variables (x_i). This model is a mathematical equation of the general form

$$y = \beta_0 + \beta_1 x_1 + \beta_2 x_2 + \ldots + \beta_k x_k \qquad (4.1)$$

The values of the β_i, the model parameters, are assumed to describe the "true" relationship (i.e., the correlation) between the dependent variable (y) and each of the independent variables (x_i). Because we do not have perfect information, it is assumed that we cannot find the true values in Equation 4.1; rather, we will come up with an estimated model of the "true" model using the data that are available to us. Using past data on the values of y and x_i, regression analysis generates estimates of the "true" model parameters. These estimates are designated as b_i:

$$\hat{y} = b_0 + b_1 x_1 + b_2 x_2 + \ldots + b_k x_k \qquad (4.2)$$

Regression analysis has a number of applications. Regression models may be used (a) to explain the behavior of a system (understanding which factors are related to demand helps explain why demand fluctuates), (b) to discover the importance of certain factors within a system (of all the marketing inputs on which we can spend our money, which has the most effect on demand?), or (c) for forecasting (Myers, 1990). When used in sales forecasting, the primary purpose of a regression model is prediction, not explanation.

Using regression analysis for forecasting demand requires an understanding of the process of creating and evaluating regression models. Using regression analysis without an understanding of these concepts is frustrating for the analyst and can lead to some costly mistakes. The forecaster in the example described at the beginning of this chapter was certainly frustrated with his inability to answer our questions about his regression model, but more important, he was frustrated with trying to employ a technique blindly. He also knew the model was leading to some decisions that were flawed.

The purpose of this chapter is to discuss how to create and evaluate regression models used for forecasting demand. Our objective is to provide a general understanding of the technique and to recommend guidelines and criteria for the evaluation of regression models that are meant to be used in sales forecasting. To accomplish this, we start with a straightforward discussion of how regression analysis works and the concept of R^2 as a measure of correlation. This is followed by a three-step procedure to develop regression analysis forecasting models. We conclude with a description of how regression analysis can be used to place a *confidence interval* around the forecast.

How Regression Analysis Works

Conceptually, regression analysis is simply trying to find the best line to draw through a set of data. For instance, if we take the data in Figure 4.1a, we see that for each month's expenditures on promotions, we also have noted the sales that resulted. Figure 4.1a represents a set of what are called *matched pairs* data; that is, we have matched the promotional expenditures in a given month with the sales that resulted from those expenditures. Which months we match is a function of how long it takes the promotional expenditures to have an effect. If, for example, we think that promotional expenditures this month affect sales next month, then we will "lag" the data by 1 month, meaning we match promotional expenditures in each month with sales from the next month (i.e., 1-month lag).

What regression analysis does mathematically is represented graphically in Figure 4.1b; regression analysis tries to find the one line that most closely "fits" the data. In the case of regression analysis, *fit* is defined as finding the one line through the data that minimizes the mean squared error or minimizes the sum total of the distance of each data point from the line.

But how does this tell us anything about the correlation between sales and promotional expenditures? The answer to this is in a statistic called the *coefficient of determination*, or R^2. If we knew nothing about the relationship between sales and promotional expenditures (and have no other information, for that matter), then the best forecast of any future value of sales would be the average (just like it was our starting point in Chapter 3). This best forecast of sales, regardless of the level of promotional expenditures (given that we start off believing that sales and promotional expenditures are not related), is the average and is represented graphically by the horizontal line in Figure 4.2.

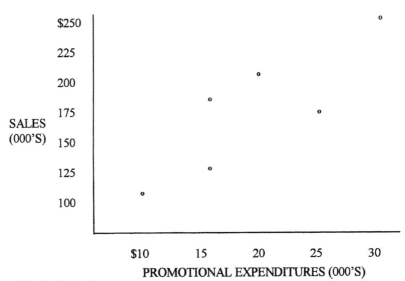

a. Matched Pairs Data

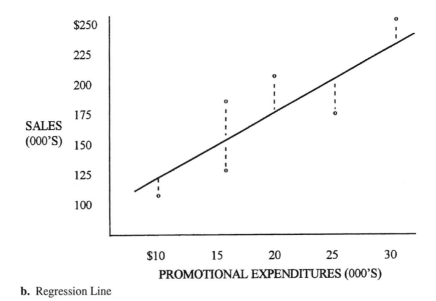

b. Regression Line

Figure 4.1. How Regression Analysis Works

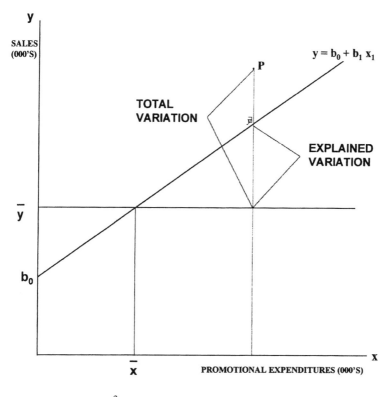

Figure 4.2. Concept of R^2

However, once we have conducted regression analysis and found the line that was illustrated in Figure 4.1b (now shown graphically as the line $y = b_0 + b_1 x_1$ in Figure 4.2), we see that increases in promotional expenditures lead to increases in sales. Notice also that the regression line goes through the point that is the average of both sales (y) and promotional expenditures (x). Mathematically, this has to happen because regression analysis is designed to determine whether y is above or below its average when x is above or below its average. In other words, regression analysis tells you whether the relationship between x and y is positive (when x is above its average, y is above its average; when x is below its average, y is below its average) or negative (when x is above its average, y is below its average; when x is below its average, y is above its average).

For any given observation (Point P in Figure 4.2), we can observe what sales were given the matched value of promotional expenditures. The difference between this point and the average value of y is called the *total variation,* or the total amount the actual value varies from the simple average as the forecast. The distance from the average to the regression model forecast value of y ($\hat{y}$) is called the *explained variation,* or the amount of the variation of the actual sales value from the average that is explained by the relationship between sales and promotional expenditures (i.e., the regression model). If we take the average of the explained variation divided by the total variation for each sales value, then we have a good estimate of the mathematical value of R^2.

The mathematical value of R^2 is between 0 and 1 and tells us the percentage of fluctuation in the dependent variable (sales) that is explained by the predictor variable (promotional expenditures). Incidentally, the sign of R (the square root of R^2) tells us whether the correlation between x and y is positive (as x goes up, y goes up) or negative (as x goes up, y goes down).

We discuss later how to test whether the value of R^2 is significant enough to use promotional expenditures to forecast sales. Conceptually, however, this significance means how different the regression equation in Figure 4.2 is from the horizontal line. If the line, $\hat{y} = b_0 + b_1 x_1$, is not significantly different from a horizontal line, then there is no reason to conclude that the best estimate of y is not still its average, regardless of the value of x. This means that there is no co-relation between x and y and that x should not be used to forecast y.

Before we go on, we must introduce the concept of *multiple regression.* The illustrations in Figures 4.1 and 4.2 are *simple regression,* meaning that only one independent variable is used to forecast the dependent variable. In multiple regression, we use two or more independent variables to forecast the dependent variable (as in Equation 4.2). The concepts just discussed are the same for multiple regression as they are for simple regression, but it gets a bit difficult to provide an illustration.

The only additional concept that needs to be introduced for multiple regression is *multicollinearity.* This rather daunting term simply means that the independent variables are not only correlated to the dependent variable but also correlated to each other. Because the purpose of regression analysis is to explain the variation in the dependent variable with the independent variables, we do not want independent variables that are correlated to each other. If this multicollinearity exists, then the independent variables all may be explaining the same part of the fluctuation in sales, and each independent variable adds little to the overall accuracy of the regression model after the first independent variable. If each new independent variable is not correlated to the other independent variable, then whatever part of the fluctuation in sales it explains is new to the forecast model and should improve forecasting accuracy. Thus, we want to minimize multicollinearity.

As with the significance of R^2, how to test for multicollinearity is discussed later in the recommended process for using regression analysis for forecasting.

The Process of Regression Analysis for Forecasting

Creation and evaluation of regression models for use in sales forecasting involves three steps: generating a set of potential predictor variables (variable selection), constructing a regression model by assessing subsets of the selected predictor variables (model construction), and validating the final model by evaluating the generalizability of its predictive ability (model validation).

During variable selection, factors (predictor variables) are chosen for their presumed usefulness in forecasting demand. Model construction consists of evaluating subsets of potential predictor variables and selecting the subset we believe comprises the "best" regression model. Model validation involves evaluating a model for its generalizability (Myers, 1990; Stevens, 1992). In a forecasting context, a generalizable or valid model will accurately forecast demand when new data on the predictor variables are used in the model (i.e., data other than those used to formulate the model). Figure 4.3 contains a flowchart summarizing these three steps.

Although this discussion on predictor variable selection, model construction, and model validation may give the impression that these three procedures are conducted in a sequential fashion, this is not necessarily the case. In the first place, the problems that variable selection, model construction, and model validation procedures are meant to detect do not always fit neatly into these three categories. For example, we may learn something about the forecasting environment during model validation that highlights requirements for additional predictor variables that are different from those we first chose.

In addition, the various criteria used for predictor variable selection, model construction, and model validation will not always agree on what constitutes the "best" model. Because of the relationships among the criteria used for these three procedures, the process of creating and evaluating a regression model may not always proceed sequentially. For instance, a set of potential predictor variables may be generated and a model constructed consisting of a subset of those predictors. However, the model may encounter difficulties during model validation procedures (e.g., the model construction

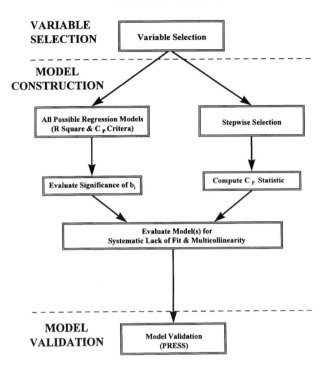

Figure 4.3. Process of Regression Analysis

went well but the model does not work well with new data), causing the predictor variable selection procedure or the model construction procedure to be reexamined.

Variable Selection

If we wanted to use regression analysis to generate a demand forecast, then how would we come up with the factors that the model will use to forecast (or predict) demand, that is, the predictor variables?

Although criteria for model construction and model validation are largely quantitative, guidelines for generating a set of potential predictor variables for forecasting demand are, of necessity, qualitative. That is because the single most important tool available to us as we begin the process of creating a regression model is our own expertise (Stevens, 1992), that is, our knowledge of the factors that we believe influence the demand for our products. Statistical techniques used during model construction and model validation cannot replace this understanding for the simple reason that it is up to you to initially produce a set of variables from which to select a subset that will comprise your model. Quantitative techniques cannot generate these initial variables; they can only evaluate the subsets and combinations of them.

As you begin to think about which variables should be in your regression model, you should constantly ask yourself, "Given what I know about the demand for this product line or brand, what factors are likely to affect that demand?" The primary source of information on variables that should be included in your model is the experience of people familiar with the nature of the demand for the product(s). Other possible sources include models that have been constructed previously for the product(s), models constructed to predict demand for similar products, and information on predictor variables used by other firms or trade groups in your industry.

When attempting to predict product demand, do not ignore the possibility of using *dummy variables.* These are predictor variables that are qualitative or categorical, rather than quantitative, in nature. Dummy variables, such as the presence (denoted by a value of 1) or absence (denoted by a value of 0) of a sales promotion, can be effective when combined with quantitative variables to model product demand.

Finally, after you have selected the predictor variables that you want to use in constructing your model, you must determine whether data on this variable are actually available. Without complete data on a predictor variable, it is unlikely it will survive the next step—model construction.

Model Construction

Once you have generated a set of potential predictors for your proposed regression model, you must determine which subset of those predictors yields the "best" model. An important point to remember, however, is that there are likely to be a number of models that will do an adequate job (Myers, 1990; Stevens, 1992). Our job is to pick the best of these adequate models. An effective strategy to use to do this during model construction is the following two-step procedure:

- Use a computer routine to generate a candidate model or a set of candidate models.
- Evaluate the candidate model(s) through the use of additional regression diagnostics to yield a preliminary model (Stevens, 1992).

Once these two steps are completed, the preliminary model can be subjected to model validation procedures to ascertain the generalizability of its predictive ability.

Generating Candidate Models

There are two procedures recommended for generating a set of candidate models: *all possible regression models* and *stepwise selection*. Because each works equally well, we present both here so that the reader can pick the procedure with which he or she is most comfortable.

All Possible Regression Models

This procedure consists of examining all the possible models for a set of predictor variables. For example, if we identified Variables *A, B, C,* and *D* as possible predictor variables, then we would test the following variable combinations as potential regression models:

1. *A*
2. *B*
3. *C*
4. *D*
5. *AB*
6. *AC*
7. *AD*
8. *BC*
9. *BD*
10. *CD*
11. *ABC*
12. *ABD*
13. *ACD*
14. *BCD*
15. *ABCD*

When using a computer routine, the output obtained generally presents models sorted from best to worst on the specified criteria.[1] Usually, there will be a small number of models that appear near the top of each set of sorted models (Stevens, 1992). Although there are a number of criteria that can be used to examine (and sort) all of the possible models that can be formed from a given set of predictors, the criteria discussed below are good choices because they enable a range of model attributes to be evaluated.

The first criterion that is useful for model evaluation is R^2, or the *coefficient of determination,* which indicates the proportion of variation in the dependent variable that is explained by the regression model. For example, if you are trying to predict product demand,

$$R^2 = \frac{\text{Variation in Product Demand Explained by the Model}}{\text{Total Variation in Product Demand around the Average}} . \quad (4.3)$$

The value of R^2 varies between 0 and 1; the closer the value is to 1, the greater the proportion of the variation in product demand the regression model explains. Obviously, the more variation in product demand you are able to explain with your model, the better. However, one problem with using only R^2 to select which predictor variables belong in your model is that adding predictor variables to a model always increases the R^2, even if the additional predictor variables do not add significantly to the ability of the model to forecast demand.

An additional consideration regarding R^2 is that this statistic tends to overestimate the proportion of variation in product demand explained by a regression model. The reason for this overestimation is that the proportion of variance explained (R^2) is computed using the model that has been fitted to a specific data set, that is, the data set that was used to construct the regression model (Pedhazur, 1982; Stevens, 1992). However, once you have constructed a regression model, you want to be able to forecast demand using new, perhaps more accurate or more timely, data. The adjusted R^2 (which is calculated and printed by most computer programs) attempts to correct the overly optimistic estimation of the proportion of variance explained by R^2; that is, the adjusted R^2 is an attempt to more closely represent the proportion of variation in product demand that would be explained if data other than those used to construct the model were used to forecast demand.

Although both R^2 and adjusted R^2 are useful criteria for evaluating regression models, they need to be combined with additional criteria for model evaluation because the proportion of variance in product demand is not the only consideration when constructing a model to forecast the dependent variable (Myers, 1990; Ott, 1988). Two additional model evaluation issues are whether or not the model is generating unbiased forecasts and the stability of the forecasts generated by the model.

Mallow's C_P (also known as Mallow's C and Mallow's C_k) makes it possible to evaluate both these aspects of the model's ability to accurately forecast demand: *model bias* and *model stability* (Myers, 1990; Stevens,

1992). The value of C_P indicates the degree to which the model tends to overforecast or underforecast demand, that is, the extent of *model bias.* An important source of bias in regression models is underfitting the model, that is, not including a sufficient number of predictor variables in the model. If a regression model is biased, then it lacks accuracy, which will limit its usefulness in forecasting demand.

The C_P statistic also gives an indication of *model stability.* Model stability addresses the consistency or precision of the model's forecasts. Including too many predictor variables in a regression model causes the model's forecasts to be unstable or imprecise. Like model bias, lack of model stability can limit the value of a regression model that is used for forecasting. The C_P statistic increases as the amount of bias and/or variability in the regression model increases. Models that have C_P values that are approximately equal to the number of predictor variables (k) in the model $(C_P \approx k)$ are preferred over models that have C_P values greater than the number of predictor variables in the model $(C_P > k)$ (Stevens, 1992). For example, consider the following two regression models:

$$\text{Model A: } \hat{y} = 153.39 + 5.29x_1 + 0.98x_2 - 3.25x_3 \; C_P = 2.92$$

$$\text{Model B: } \hat{y} = 293.31 + 1.30x_1 + 2.84x_2 - 5.88x_3 + 37.53x_4 \; C_P = 8.16.$$

Model A would be preferred over Model B because Model A's C_P (2.92) is closer to the number of predictor variables (k) in the model. For Model A, $k = 3$ and $C_P = 2.92$; consequently, $C_P \approx k$. However, for Model B, $k = 4$ and $C_P = 8.16$, making $C_P > k$ and making Model B less useful as a forecasting model.[2]

The third criterion used to evaluate candidate models generated using the all possible regression models procedure is *statistical significance* of the regression estimates. Statistical significance of the regression estimates (b_i in Equation 4.2) for each candidate model can be evaluated by testing how much this value of b_i differs from zero. Referring back to Figure 4.2, we can see that the value of b_i (the slope) in the horizontal line is zero. The value of b_1 takes on a value other than zero only when there is a relationship between x_1 and y. We can test whether each b_i is sufficiently different from zero to believe there is a relationship between x_i and y. We do this by entering the predictor variables for each model into a regression procedure and checking the "t" value[3] for the estimate of the regression coefficient of that predictor variable. The t value for each variable will be zero if the value of b_i is zero, and the t value gets larger as b_i gets larger. Thus, the t value for each variable tells us whether or not that predictor variable is sufficiently important for the prediction of the dependent variable in the model. As a general rule, any variable whose t value is not greater than 1.65 should be deleted as a predictor variable (Ott, 1988).

Stepwise Selection

Stepwise selection is one of a group of sequential procedures for automatically selecting the best model for forecasting a dependent variable (e.g., demand). These sequential procedures were designed to explore sets of possible predictor variables using the most efficient computation techniques (Myers, 1990). Although there are several sequential selection procedures available, stepwise selection is the only one of these procedures that considers the effects of multicollinearity[4] in selecting which predictor variables to include in the regression model (Myers, 1990; Stevens, 1992), so it is the one discussed here.

Stepwise selection[5] sequentially enters predictor variables into the regression model based on each variable's ability to contribute to the prediction of the dependent variable (e.g., demand). At each stage in the analysis (i.e., as each new predictor variable enters the model), variables currently in the model are reevaluated for their contribution to the prediction of the dependent variable. Due to this reevaluation at each stage of the analysis, the possibility exists for variables in the model to be deleted. The ability of variables to enter and leave the model is an important advantage of the stepwise technique. Different combinations of predictor variables behave differently in their ability to predict the dependent variable. Therefore, it is important to be able to delete variables that lose their effectiveness in the model (Cohen & Cohen, 1983; Ott, 1988; Stevens, 1992).

Although it is widely available in computer programs, the limitations of stepwise selection are threefold:

1. Stepwise selection proposes a "best" candidate model when, in fact, there are likely to be a set of good models instead of just one "best" model.
2. Stepwise selection does not consider predictor variables on criteria other than their ability to explain variance in the dependent variable (i e , their contribution to R^2).
3. Stepwise selection tends to result in a model that is data specific, that is, a model that will work well with the data set that is used to estimate the model's parameters (Myers, 1990; Ott, 1988; Stevens, 1992) but not necessarily a model that will work well in the future.

The third limitation is especially problematic if the regression model is to be used with different data sets for forecasting demand. For this reason, it is particularly important to validate stepwise regression models to ensure that these models can predict accurately and consistently using data other than the data used to estimate the model.

As a step toward this assurance, if a stepwise selection technique is used to generate a candidate model, then the C_P statistic for the model still should be computed and compared to the value for k (the number of predictor variables in the model) to verify that $C_P \approx k$ before proceeding with further evaluation of the model.

Once a "best" model is selected using a stepwise selection technique or a set of candidate models is selected using all possible regression models, additional evaluation is required to investigate the model formulation and the relationships among the predictor variables.

Further Evaluation of Candidate Models

Regardless of whether the all possible regression models or the stepwise approach was taken to this point in model construction, there are two additional issues that, due to their potential impact on the predictive ability of the regression model, should be investigated prior to validating the candidate model(s). This section discusses how to evaluate candidate models for the following:

- The presence of systematic lack of fit between the model and the data
- The presence of large and/or multiple intercorrelations among the predictor variables

Systematic Lack of Fit

The first issue, a systematic lack of fit between the model and the data, is important to investigate because this suggests that the model may not be formulated correctly. Problems with model formulation are caused by the following:

- Assuming an incorrect model formulation for the relationship between the dependent variable and the predictor variables
- The presence of nonconstant variance

The first source of systematic lack of fit arises as a result of the form of the equation assumed to represent the relationship between the dependent variable (what is being predicted) and the predictor variables. The general form of a multiple regression model assumes that the relationship between what is being predicted (the dependent variable, y) and the predictor variables (the independent variables, the x_i) can be represented by a first-order (or linear) equation (Equation 4.1), described as follows and graphically represented in Figure 4.4a:

$$y = \beta_0 + \beta_1 x_1 + \beta_2 x_2 + \ldots + \beta_k x_k.$$

However, the relationship between the dependent variable and the predictor variables may be more appropriately represented by a different model formulation. For example, a second-order (or curvilinear) model (i.e., a regression model with a polynomial expression such as the one in Equation 4.4 and graphically represented in Figure 4.4b) could more suitably represent the relationship. By the way, this is a relationship that often exists between demand and advertising expenditures.

$$y = \beta_0 + \beta_1 x_1 + \beta_2 x^2. \tag{4.4}$$

Using a model formulation that is inappropriate to forecast demand means that the model will not be able to accurately forecast some values of the dependent variable (e.g., high or low values) (Cohen & Cohen, 1983; Stevens, 1992). The simplest way in which to evaluate models for incorrect formulation is to produce graphs or plots of the forecast value of the dependent variable versus the standardized residuals. Residuals are simply the differences between the actual values of the dependent variable in the data (y) and the forecast value of the dependent variable (i.e., the value predicted by the regression model ($\hat{y}$)). For example, the residual for y_i would be

$$r_i = (y_i - \hat{y}_i). \tag{4.5}$$

Standardizing the residuals means taking each r_i and converting it to a "standardized" value by the following equation:

$$sr_i = (r_i - A_r) / \sigma_r, \tag{4.6}$$

where sr_i = standardized value of r_i, A_r = average of all r_i, and σ_r = standard deviation of all r_i.

This standardization calculation makes the majority of the values of r_i fall between -3 and $+3$, regardless of the units in which the dependent variable is measured. This makes it easier to spot any large differences (< -2 or $> +2$)

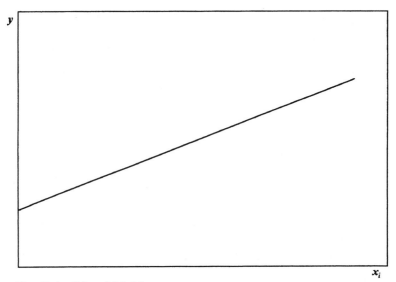

a. First-Order (Linear) Model

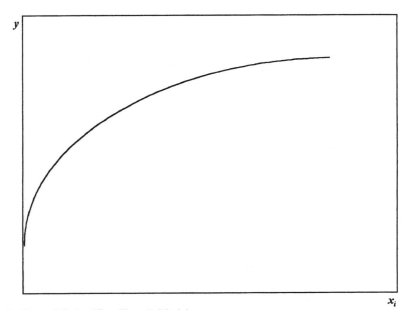

b. Second-Order (Curvilinear) Model

Figure 4.4. Illustration of First- and Second-Order Relationships

between the actual and the predicted values for the dependent variable (Stevens, 1992).

Plots of the predicted values of the dependent variable versus the standardized residuals, called *residual plots,* are available in most computer software packages that perform regression analysis.[6] Figure 4.5a depicts a residual plot for a regression model with no model formulation problems. The standardized residuals are scattered randomly around the line passing though 0 (i.e., there is no pattern related to the value of y), and all values are between -2 and $+2$. Figure 4.5b depicts a residual plot for a regression model that portrays a systematic pattern, indicating that the model is doing a poor job of forecasting the dependent variable. This suggests that the model should be reformulated, perhaps using a curvilinear (i.e., second-order) model.

If an examination of the residual plots of any candidate model reveals such systematic patterns, suggesting that forecasting demand with this model may be very inaccurate for certain values, then an exploration of a curvilinear model formulation[7] may be worth considering (Pedhazur & Schmelkin, 1991; Ott, 1988), which puts us back at the beginning of the model construction stage for this new curvilinear model.

The second source of systematic lack of fit for a regression model is the presence of nonconstant variance in the data used to estimate the regression coefficients. This means that the degree of variability in the residuals changes, depending on the value of the dependent variable (y). The degree of variability in the residuals should be the same, no matter what the value of y (Myers, 1990; Stevens, 1992). The rather intimidating term for this constant variability is homoscedasticity.

The way to detect the presence of nonconstant variance (or heteroscedasticity) is, again, by examining the residual plots already discussed. Figure 4.6a shows a residual plot with constant variance; that is, the residual terms are spread out equally around the 0 line. Figure 4.6b shows a residual plot with nonconstant variance; in this case, the variance increases as the value of the predicted dependent variable increases.

If nonconstant variance is present, then the consequences will be similar to the consequences of incorrect model formulation. At certain values of the dependent variable (e.g., for high or low levels of demand), the model will not accurately forecast the dependent variable. If the residual plot of the candidate model shows a pattern of nonconstant variance, then transforming the data (e.g., converting data values to their logarithm or square root) could be a solution to the problem, facilitating the model's predictive ability (for a discussion of alternative model formulations and suggestions for data trans-

(Text continues on p. 96)

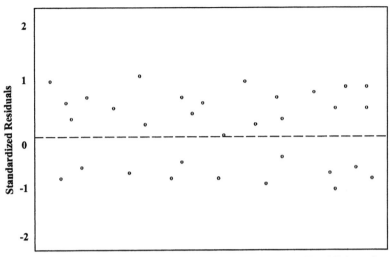

a. Residual Plot of Valid Model Formulation

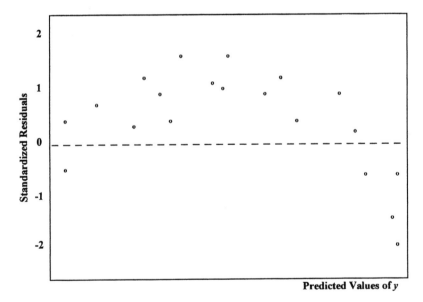

b. Residual Plot of Invalid Model Formulation

Figure 4.5. Plots of Standardized Residuals Versus Predicted Values of *y*

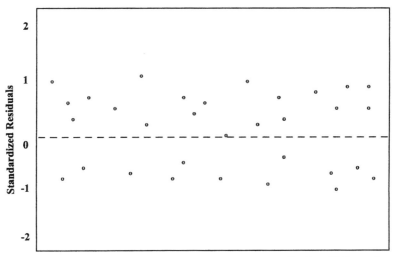

a. Residual Plot of Constant Variances

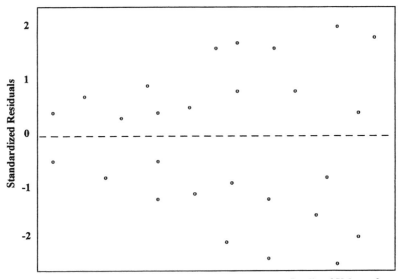

b. Residual Plot of Nonconstant Variances

Figure 4.6. Plots of Standardized Residuals Versus Predicted Values of *y*

formations, see Weisberg, 1985). Alternatively, we may simply want to turn to a different candidate model that does not exhibit heteroscedasticity.

Intercorrelations Among
Predictor Variables

The second issue for which candidate models should be evaluated is the presence of intercorrelations among the predictor variables. As we introduced earlier, the presence of moderate to high correlations among the predictor variables is known as multicollinearity. In a regression model used to make forecasts, multicollinearity can (a) increase the variance for the estimates of the regression parameters (the b_i), causing the forecasts made by the model to be unstable or inconsistent, and/or (b) limit the accuracy of R^2 (Stevens, 1992).

To evaluate whether multicollinearity is a problem in candidate models, we need to compute a variance inflation factor (VIF) for each regression estimate (i.e., for each b_i).[8] In the absence of multicollinearity, each VIF is equal to 1. However, because some multicollinearity always will exist, this is an unrealistic benchmark for sales forecasting. VIFs increase as multicollinearity increases. As a rule of thumb, a VIF of 10 or greater indicates that an unacceptable level of multicollinearity exists among the predictor variables (Myers, 1990).

If the VIF indicates that there is too much correlation among the predictor variables, then remedies include the following:

- Deleting predictor variables with high VIFs
- Combining sets of correlated predictor variables into a single measure, that is, an index (Stevens, 1992)

As an example of the first remedy, suppose we found that among our model's predictor variables, x_1 has a VIF of 25, whereas all other VIFs are below 10. We could merely delete x_1 from the model. The second remedy requires that we ascertain which predictor variables are moderately to highly correlated.[9] An analysis of the VIFs, along with a determination of which predictor variables have correlations that are significant, will guide a decision of which predictor variables to replace with an index. An index is a predictor variable that is equal to the combination (e.g., the sum or the average) of a group of predictor variables that are highly intercorrelated (Stevens, 1992).

At this point, we have selected a group of predictor variables (variable selection), investigated which combination(s) of predictor variables to use in our regression model, and examined these models for the presence of model formulation errors and multicollinearity to yield a preliminary model(s) (model construction). The final step is validation of the preliminary model(s).

Model Validation

If a regression model used for forecasting is valid, then we should have some assurance that it will forecast demand using data other than those that were used to create the original model. For example, assume that a model has been created using 1996 data on household size and home loan interest rates to forecast demand for a line of residential lighting fixtures. When 1997 data on household size and interest rates become available, will the model be able to accurately forecast demand for that product line, or is the model accurate only when using the original data, that is, the data that were used to create the model?

Model validation can be assessed by computing the PRESS (*predicted residual sum of squares*) statistic for each model under consideration. PRESS is calculated by removing each period in the data and recomputing the regression estimates (b_i) for the model. Using these regression estimates, the squared residual for that period (the squared difference between the forecast dependent variable for that period, $\hat{y}_i^*$, and the actual value of the dependent variable in the data set, y_i) is calculated.[10]

$$\text{Squared PRESS Residual for Case}_i = (y_i - \hat{y}_i^*)^2. \qquad (4.7)$$

This is done successively for each period (i) in the data set ($i = 1 \ldots n$), and the squared residuals are added together to find the PRESS statistic.

$$\text{PRESS} = \sum_{i=1}^{n} (y_i - \hat{y}_i^*)^2 \qquad (4.8)$$

The PRESS statistic provides an estimate of how well the model fits when forecasts are obtained for data that were not used to compute the original regression estimates. There is no rule of thumb for the appropriate value of the PRESS statistic when evaluating only one model. The most valid way in which to apply this statistic is to compare PRESS statistics for more than one

TABLE 4.1 Three Regression Models

Model	R^2	C_P	PRESS
Model 1: $\hat{y} = 9.136 - 0.027x_1 - 0.269x_2 - 0.108x_3 + 0.505x_4$	.478	3.02	579.70
Model 2: $\hat{y} = 8.144 - 0.289x_2 - 0.079x_3 + 0.504x_4$	.472	2.14	571.74
Model 3: $\hat{y} = 6.575 - 0.252x_2 + 0.505x_4$	.467	0.94	567.48

model, choosing the model with the smallest PRESS statistic (Myers, 1990; Stevens, 1992).

To clarify this overall process, the next section provides an example of regression model construction and validation using both the all possible regression models and the stepwise approaches.

An Example

Suppose that we are trying to forecast the demand for residential lighting fixtures. Based on experience with this product, the factors that we believe will be significant in forecasting demand include average number of days of sunshine per year, housing starts for custom homes, the interest rates on home loans, and average household size.

Using data on the dependent variable (y = sales of residential lighting fixtures) and the predictor variables (x_1 = Sun, x_2 = Custom, x_3 = Interest, and x_4 = Size), all possible regression models are computed. Models are sorted by R^2, and the C_p is computed for each model. Although all possible combinations of Sun, Custom, Interest, and Size were tested, Table 4.1 contains only the three models that rated highly on both the R^2 and the C_p criteria. These three models have among the highest R^2 values of all the possible models, and $C_p \approx k$ for all three models (Model 1: $C_p = 3.02$, $k = 4$; Model 2: $C_p = 2.14$, $k = 3$; Model 3: $C_p = 0.94$, $k = 2$).

The next step is to evaluate the significance of the predictor variables in the three candidate models. Each set of predictor variables is entered into a regression analysis procedure. Table 4.2 contains the results of the significance testing on the three candidate models. Significance testing for models 1 and 2 in Table 4.2 indicates that neither x_1 (Sun) nor x_3 (Interest) contributes significantly to the prediction of y (demand for lighting fixtures); that is, the t value for each of these variables is less than 1.65. However, both predictor

TABLE 4.2 Models 1, 2, and 3

Variable	Regression Estimate (b_i)	t (significance)
Model 1		
Sun (x_1)	−.027	−1.07*
Custom (x_2)	−.269	−2.72
Interest (x_3)	−.108	−1.18*
Size (x_4)	.505	8.47
Model 2		
Custom (x_2)	−.289	−2.98
Interest (x_3)	−.079	−0.90*
Size (x_4)	.504	8.45
Model 3		
Custom (x_2)	−.252	−2.89
Size (x_4)	.505	8.48

*t value < 1.65; variable does not contribute significantly to prediction.

variables (x_2 [Custom] and x_4 [Size]) in Model 3 have t values greater than 1.65, indicating that both variables contribute significantly to predicting the demand for lighting fixtures. Thus, Model 3 will be further evaluated for systematic lack of fit and multicollinearity.

A residual plot for Model 3 produced in Figure 4.7 indicates no evidence of systematic lack of fit given that the data points are randomly distributed around the horizontal line passing through 0. The VIF values for the predictor variables Custom and Size appear in Table 4.3. Both VIFs are less than 10, indicating that multicollinearity is not substantially affecting model estimation for Model 3.

For the sake of comparison, PRESS statistics for Models 1, 2, and 3 were computed (Table 4.1). Although all three of the models had similar PRESS statistics, PRESS for Model 3, at 567.48, was the smallest of the three. In fact, the PRESS statistic for Model 3 was the smallest PRESS for any of the regression models tested. This comparatively small PRESS statistic for Model 3 indicates that it is the best of the models tested in terms of model validity, or most likely to forecast accurately with new data.

Based on the data analyses portrayed in this example, the best model to forecast demand for household lighting fixtures is Model 3:

Sales of Lighting Fixtures = 6.057 − (0.252 * Custom) + (0.505 * Size).

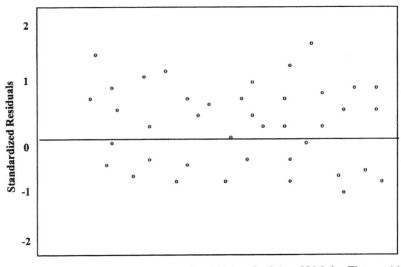

Predicted Values for Sales of Lighting Fixtures (y)

Figure 4.7. Residual Plot for Lighting Fixture Model

This, of course, does not mean that a better model might not be constructed with different predictor variables, but Model 3 is the best of the models that could be constructed with the four variables originally selected. If the resultant model from this process is not satisfactory (in terms of ongoing accuracy evaluation with mean absolute percent error [*MAPE*] or other measures of accuracy discussed in Chapter 2), data on additional variables can be gathered and new models constructed.

For purposes of illustration, the same data are used to develop a regression model using the stepwise approach. Using SPSS, the four predictor variables (x_1 = Sun, x_2 = Custom, x_3 = Interest, and x_4 = Size) are evaluated, stepwise, for their contribution to the prediction of the dependent variable (sales of residential lighting fixtures). The results of the stepwise analysis appear in Table 4.4. The model chosen by SPSS uses the predictor variables Custom (x_2) and Size (x_4)—the same two chosen in our previous example—to predict sales of residential lighting fixtures.

The C_p statistic for this model is calculated as 0.94 (see Table 4.4). Because the number of predictor variables in this model is equal to 2 ($k = 2$) and the model's $C_p \approx k$, this model is neither biased nor unstable. Further evaluation of the model chosen by the stepwise approach reveals no evidence of a systematic lack of fit because the data points are randomly distributed around the horizontal line passing through 0 in the residual plot (see Figure 4.7). In addition, the VIF values for the predictor variables Custom and Size (see Table 4.3) reveal that both VIFs are less than 10, indicating that significant multicollinearity is not present in the predictor variables of the model.

Finally, the PRESS statistic for the model chosen using the stepwise approach is calculated as 567.48 (see Table 4.4). As the preceding discussion of the PRESS statistic indicated, the PRESS statistic is best evaluated by comparing the PRESS statistics for multiple models. This ability to compare multiple models is an advantage of the all possible regression models approach. If the stepwise approach is followed for model construction, then the PRESS statistics should be recalculated as new data become available for the predictor and dependent variables. Increases in the PRESS statistic could indicate potential problems with model validity (i.e., generalizability).

The model generated using the stepwise approach follows:

Sales of Lighting Fixtures = 6.057 – (0.252 * Custom) + (0.505 * Size).

Although it will not always be the case, in this example, both the all possible regression models and the stepwise approaches yield the same model. As the discussion earlier in the chapter indicated, an advantage of the all possible regression models approach is the ability to view and examine a number of candidate models.

Conclusions

In this chapter, we discussed how to create and evaluate regression models used for forecasting demand. To facilitate discussion and understanding, the process of model creation and evaluation was divided into three steps: variable generation, model construction, and model validation. For each step, we provided criteria that are important to consider for regression models used in sales forecasting. Finally, example analyses illustrated both model creation and evaluation processes.

In concluding this chapter, two limitations and one warning about regression analysis should be mentioned. Although regression analysis is a powerful statistical approach that can be brought to bear on a forecasting problem, regression analysis requires a large amount of data to produce a reliable

TABLE 4.3 Variance Inflation Factors for Model 3

Variable	Variance Inflation Factor
Custom (x_2)	1.024
Size (x_4)	1.024

model. A good rule of thumb is that at least 5 observations should be available for every variable in a regression model. Because the dependent variable also counts as a variable, this means that for model construction with the variables as we had in our example (Sales of Lighting Fixtures, Custom, Size, Sun, and Interest), we should have at least 25 periods of data (5 variables times 5) before starting our analysis (i.e., before we leave the variable selection stage in Figure 4.3). This assumes that over the last 2 years, the relationships between the dependent and independent variables have remained stable. This often is a restrictive assumption for the use of regression analysis.

The second limitation is the fact that regression analysis does not consider seasonality as a cause of fluctuations in demand unless a seasonal predictor variable is entered in the variable selection stage. Because sales can vary from season to season, the effect of other predictor variables on sales may vary (thus violating our first limitation). For these reasons, it often is important to either include a seasonality variable in the selection process or "deseasonalize" the dependent variable before starting the entire process.

The warning that always should accompany any discussion of regression analysis is that regression analysis will tell us the *correlation* between the dependent variable and the predictor variables, but it *will not* tell us whether *causality* exists. In fact, regression analysis often is referred to incorrectly as *causal forecasting* or *causal analysis.* It is neither.

When two variables vary in a similar pattern over time, regression analysis will reveal that they are correlated—even when there is no true cause-and-effect relationship between them. The only way in which to tell whether there is true cause and effect is through the application of logic:

1. Is there correlation? If there is no correlation, then there cannot be causation.
2. Does the predictor variable always change before the dependent variable? If the answer to this is *no,* then the predictor variable is not *causing* the dependent variable.
3. Does it make logical sense that the dependent variable is caused by the predictor variable?

TABLE 4.4 Results of Stepwise Regression Approach

Variable	Regression Estimate (b_i)	t (significance)	Variance Inflation Factor	Model C_P	Model PRESS	Model R^2
Constant	6.575	5.31		0.94	567.48	0.467
Custom (x_2)	–.252	–2.86	1.024			
Size (x_4)	.505	8.47	1.024			

In fact, when the answer to the first question is *yes* and the answer to either the second or the third question is *no,* we have what is called *spurious correlation,* or a correlation between two variables that is accidental (they are correlated but not causally linked). It is important in the first stage of Figure 4.3 to select only variables that we believe have a cause-and-effect relationship with sales. Otherwise, we may end up constructing a regression model for forecasting that has a high R^2 value but is only a coincidence. When this accidental correlation changes in the future (and it eventually will change if there is no cause-and-effect relationship), our forecasting model will suddenly, and without warning, give us very inaccurate results.

With this warning and the limitations about data requirements and seasonality considerations kept in mind, regression analysis can be a very useful tool in our quest to forecast sales.

We have now examined the following:

1. Time-series analysis, which tends to adapt quickly to changing level, trend, and seasonality but does not consider external factors
2. Regression analysis, which considers external factors but requires a considerable amount of data to perform the analyses discussed in this chapter

What we have not considered to this point is how to incorporate experience into the forecasting process. Techniques that allow for experiential forecasting are called *qualitative techniques* and are the subject of the next chapter.

Notes

1. The PROC RSQUARE procedure in SAS (a trademark of SAS Institute, Inc.) can be used to generate all possible regression models, ranked according to R^2. Both SAS and SPSS (a trademark of SPSS, Inc.) compute R^2 and adjusted R^2.

2. Mallow's C_p is available in both SAS and SPSS.

3. SPSS refers to the t value as "T"; SAS refers to the t value as "T for H0."

4. Multicollinearity is the presence of intercorrelations among the predictor variables that make it difficult to determine the unique contribution that each predictor variable provides to the prediction of the dependent variable. Methods for determining the presence of multicollinearity among a set of predictor variables are discussed in the subsection titled "Further Evaluation of Candidate Models."

5. Stepwise selection techniques are available in SAS and SPSS.

6. Residual plots are available in SAS and SPSS.

7. SAS and SPSS allow higher order and/or linear regression model formulations to be specified.

8. VIFs are available in SAS and SPSS.

9. Intercorrelations for the predictor variables can be determined by examining the correlation matrix that is provided by regression analysis procedures.

10. PRESS (PREDICTED RESID SS) is available in SAS.

References

Cohen, J., & Cohen, P. (1983). *Applied multiple regression/correlation analysis for the behavioral sciences.* Hillsdale, NJ: Lawrence Erlbaum.

Myers, R. H. (1990). *Classical and modern regression with applications* (2nd ed.). Boston: PWS-Kent.

Ott, L. (1988). *An introduction to statistical methods and data analysis* (3rd ed.). Boston: PWS-Kent.

Pedhazur, E. J. (1982). *Multiple regression in behavioral research* (2nd ed.). New York: Holt, Rinehart & Winston.

Pedhazur, E. J., & Schmelkin, L. P. (1991). *Measurement, design, and analysis: An integrated approach.* Hillsdale, NJ: Lawrence Erlbaum.

Stevens, J. (1992). *Applied multivariate statistics for the social sciences* (2nd ed.). Hillsdale, NJ: Lawrence Erlbaum.

Weisberg, S. (1985). *Applied linear regression.* New York: John Wiley.

CHAPTER 5

Qualitative Sales Forecasting

During a visit with one manufacturer, we interviewed an analyst who was responsible for generating the sales forecasts used by logistics and production. As we began discussing the sales forecasting process used by his department, he explained that at the beginning of each month, he generated a quantitative forecast for the coming month for each product (stock keeping unit [SKU]) and then examined the forecast to see whether it needed to be adjusted. He explained that he made adjustments to each SKU forecast based on his knowledge of each item's behavior, information he obtained from marketing regarding upcoming promotions, and information he obtained from the employees responsible for handling orders from the company's distribution centers. In all, this single employee inspected and qualitatively adjusted between 200 and 300 SKUs each month! His insights into the business environment surrounding each product dramatically improved the forecasting accuracy for each but involved an incredible amount of information gathering on his part. Equally important, no one else in the organization seemed to realize the incredible resource to be found in this individual's knowledge—nor what would happen to forecasting accuracy (and production and logistics planning) if he left the company.

This employee that we interviewed had a wealth of knowledge about the products he was forecasting. He had developed effective cross-functional lines of communication within the organization, enabling him to integrate the knowledge and expertise of other functional areas into his forecasts. However, when you consider the time required along with the potential for bias inherent in generating forecasts for *between 200 and 300 stock keeping units (SKUs) each month,* you have to wonder whether there is not a better way in which to accomplish this task. The issue is not the fact that subjectivity or judgment is being used in this company's sales forecasting process. The issue is whether or not this judgment is being used efficiently and effectively.

Even when a company employs quantitative analysis techniques in its sales forecasting process, judgment always plays an important role. In fact, decisions as fundamental as how the forecasting process is managed are inherently subjective and judgmental. Because it is important to recognize the role and significance of subjective assessments in the management of the forecasting process, we devote the concluding chapter of this book (Chapter 10) to these managerial decisions.

Furthermore, although Chapters 3 and 4 contained detailed discussions of time-series and regression forecasting techniques, respectively, judgment is required when deciding which of these quantitative forecasting techniques is to be used. When using a quantitative forecasting technique, judgment also is exercised when deciding what data are to be processed during the quantitative analyses as well as whether any modifications should be made to the data before the analyses are performed (Hanke & Reitsch, 1995). Likewise, when making a decision about how to measure forecasting accuracy and what to do about forecast error (discussed in Chapter 2), judgment is essential.

However, the discussion in this chapter focuses specifically on the efficient and effective use of qualitative (also called *subjective* or *judgmental*) forecasting techniques as procedures that turn the opinions, knowledge, and intuition of experienced people (e.g., salespeople, corporate executives, outside experts) into formal forecasts. When qualitative forecasting techniques are used, these people become the information processors, replacing mathematical models that process the data when quantitative forecasting techniques are used (Makridakis, Wheelwright, & McGee, 1983).

Qualitative forecasting analyses can be used to formulate forecasts for new products for which there are no historical data, to devise or adjust mid- or long-range forecasts for corporate planning, to adjust quantitatively generated product line forecasts, or to adjust patterns (trends) generated by endogenous quantitative techniques (e.g., time series). When a forecaster uses an endogenous quantitative forecasting technique, there is an implicit assumption that there will be no systematic changes or departures from previously occurring patterns. If there is reason to believe that this assumption no longer is valid, then qualitative techniques provide the means to adjust the forecasts by tapping the experience and judgment of people knowledgeable about the product(s) being forecast and the environment affecting the forecast. In other words, one could say that qualitative forecasting emphasizes predicting the future rather than explaining the past (Makridakis & Wheelwright, 1989).

Prior to our discussion of specific qualitative techniques, we provide an overview of the advantages and problems inherent in qualitative forecasting analyses. Following this is a discussion of specific techniques and tools used to accomplish qualitative forecasting.

Qualitative Forecasting: Advantages and Problems

The discussion in this section examines the advantages to qualitative forecasting as well as its problems. This discussion is summarized in Table 5.1.

Advantages of Qualitative Forecasting Techniques

The principal, and very significant, advantage of qualitative forecasting techniques is their potential for predicting changes that can occur in sales patterns. Time-series quantitative techniques cannot predict changes in sales or demand patterns. Regression cannot predict changes in the relationships between sales and the predictor variables. Predicting the occurrence and nature of these changes can be accomplished by qualitative analyses based on the knowledge and experience of people internal or external to the company. This is valuable by itself or as additional information to be used to adjust the quantitative forecasts.

A second advantage of qualitative forecasting techniques is that they make use of the extremely rich data sources represented by the intuition and judgment of experienced executives, sales employees, channel members, and outside experts. The more experienced these members of the organization, the more prominently qualitative forecasting should be incorporated into the forecasting process. Quantitative forecasting techniques rarely make use of all the information contained within the databases used to generate the forecasts. Moreover, there are inherent limitations in the depth of information that can be conveyed by a quantitative data format.

TABLE 5.1 Qualitative Forecasting Technique Advantages and Problems

Advantages	*Problems*
Qualitative forecasting techniques have the ability to predict changes in sales patterns.	The ability to forecast accurately can be reduced when forecasters consider only readily available or recently perceived information.
Qualitative forecasting techniques allow decision makers to incorporate rich data sources consisting of their intuition, experience, and expert judgment.	The ability to forecast accurately can be reduced by the forecasters' inability to process large amounts of complex information.
	Accurate forecasts can be difficult to produce when forecasters are overconfident in their ability to forecast accurately.
	The ability to forecast accurately may be reduced significantly by political factors within organizations and between organizations.
	The ability to forecast accurately may be reduced because of forecasters' tendency to infer relationships or patterns in data when there are no patterns.
	The ability to forecast accurately can be affected by anchoring; that is, forecasters may be influenced by initial forecasts (e.g., those generated by quantitative methods) when making qualitative forecasts.
	Future ability to forecast accurately may be reduced when forecasters try to justify, rather than understand, forecasts that prove to be inaccurate.
	Qualitative forecasting techniques encourage inconsistencies in judgment due to moods and/or emotions as well as the repetitive decision making inherent in generating multiple individual product forecasts.
	Qualitative forecasting techniques are expensive and time intensive.

SOURCE: Adapted from Hogarth and Makridakis (1981).

Problems With Qualitative Forecasting Techniques

The problems inherent in qualitative forecasting stem from two sources: the tendency for bias to be introduced into the forecasts and the fact that qualitative forecasting is relatively expensive. Biased qualitative forecasts occur because of limitations on the forecasters' abilities to acquire and process complex information without being influenced by factors other than those pertinent to their decisions. Qualitative forecasting techniques are expensive because they require a lot of managerial and analyst time to complete.

The primary sources of qualitative forecast bias are the forecasters' limited ability to process complex information and their limited ability or lack of willingness to acquire information. It is difficult for people to integrate numerous, complex bits of information. People also have a tendency to make use of information that already is available to them or to which they have been exposed most recently. Consequently, qualitative forecasts frequently are generated without considering all relevant information or using only that information which is readily available or has been learned most recently. Providing relevant information and structuring complex information are important steps for reducing this source of bias in qualitatively generated forecasts.

Effective qualitative forecasting also can be difficult when forecasters are overconfident in their ability to produce accurate forecasts. Research has shown that confidence in the forecast and the accuracy of that forecast are not always related (Makridakis & Wheelwright, 1989). This result has disturbing implications for the application of qualitative forecasting techniques; just because a forecaster is confident in his or her forecast should not necessarily lend credence to the forecast unless the forecaster can produce evidence to support it. Requiring explanations or justifications for qualitatively generated or qualitatively adjusted forecasts can help to reduce overconfidence, as can requiring regular comparisons (i.e., accuracy measures) between actual demand and the forecasts.

In our research on forecasting, we have found that political elements within a company, as well as between companies, can significantly affect the ability of forecasters to produce accurate qualitative forecasts. Biased forecasts caused by political elements within organizations are due, in large part, to the tendency of participants in group decision-making situations to influence each other's thinking, a phenomenon known as *groupthink*. Research has shown that the assessments by groups frequently are biased because of a desire on the part of group members to support each other's positions, the influence of strong leaders within groups, and/or a superficial search for information relevant to decision making (Janis & Mann, 1982).

In many companies, there is considerable pressure to make sales forecasts agree with company business plans. This pressure frequently is manifested by the influence of a strong leader within a consensus forecasting committee. The influence of this leader, along with the tendency of the group to support each other's decisions and to proceed with only a token effort at making objective evaluations of additional information during the decision-making process, causes qualitative forecasts to be biased in the direction of revenue projections in the company's business plan.

Another political factor within organizations that affects forecasting accuracy concerns the sales forecasts generated by salespeople. When sales-people are required to generate forecasts, the tendency of many organizations to confuse forecasting with setting sales quotas introduces biases into the forecasts. Forecasts generated by salespeople may be biased downward be-cause they view the forecasting activity as an opportunity to make themselves appear effective by setting low sales quotas. Conversely, forecasts generated by salespeople may be biased upward because of their propensity toward optimism (brought on by considering only readily available or recent infor-mation and overconfidence in their ability to forecast). Either form of bias will adversely affect the accuracy of the resultant sales forecasts.

Finally, political factors between organizations frequently introduce bias into sales forecasts. These political pressures often occur between manufac-turers and independent distributors within a supply chain. Rather than provid-ing realistic forecasts of future product sales, distributors frequently view forecasting as an opportunity to engage in inventory management at the expense of the manufacturer. When distributors are allowed to provide input to the manufacturer's sales forecasts, they often will forecast high—following the logic that if demand is unexpectedly high, then the manufacturer will be carrying sufficient inventory (because of the higher forecasts) to cover the distributors' needs. Similar behavior can occur in response to trade promo-tions offered by manufacturers when distributors "stock up" on relatively inexpensive inventory, regardless of realistic sales projections. Finally, when a manufacturer introduces a new product and distributors are unwilling to take on significant inventory of the new product until they are sure of significant sales demand, distributors will provide unrealistically low forecasts.

When adjusting forecasts produced by quantitative techniques or when engaging in qualitative analyses of a limited number of data points, forecasters are prone to infer patterns in the data where no patterns really exist. These *false correlations* often result from a tendency to try to find patterns in complex situations, even where none exist. Tracking error that results from applying this supposed pattern is the best way to discover false correlations and discontinue their use.

A significant source of bias when forecasters are qualitatively adjusting quantitatively generated forecasts occurs as a result of a phenomenon known as *anchoring*. Research by Kahneman and Tversky (1973) suggests that starting values (or anchors) significantly affect subsequent predictions. In a forecasting context, quantitatively generated forecasts can act as anchors. The lower the value of the quantitative forecast, the more the forecast will be biased downward. The higher the value of the quantitative forecast, the more the forecast will be biased upward. Overcoming these biases requires forecasters to be aware of, and to guard against, the influence of the anchors by objectively considering all information available to them when qualitatively adjusting quantitatively generated forecasts.

When forecasters make predictions and those predictions prove to be wrong, the forecasters, being human, frequently try to explain or justify the predictions. This reaction often has the unfortunate effect of obscuring the reasons for mistaken predictions, thereby interfering with attempts to understand and learn from mistakes that were made. Instead of spending time trying to justify inaccurate forecasts, it is better to admit that mistakes were made and try to discover the reasons for the mistakes so that the inaccurate forecasts will not be repeated. Discovering the reasons why inaccurate forecasts occurred is easier if, at the time the forecasts are made, the rationales (i.e., the justifications or explanations for the forecasts) are recorded. Note that this is an activity that also was suggested in the preceding discussion on how to counteract overconfidence in qualitative forecasts.

Biased forecasts can be caused by inconsistencies in judgment that occur when large numbers of forecasts are produced or adjusted using qualitative techniques. The repetition inherent in these multiple forecasts encourages boredom, which leads to inconsistent and inaccurate forecasts. In addition, because forecasters are human, their moods and emotions can cause bias when multiple forecasts are generated using qualitative techniques (Makridakis & Wheelwright, 1989). The forecaster in the vignette at the beginning of this chapter risked inaccuracies because of the repetitive nature of his forecasting task. When large numbers of forecasts must be generated frequently (e.g., weekly or monthly forecasts for hundreds of SKUs), quantitative forecasting techniques are more appropriate. Instead of trying to qualitatively adjust for factors such as promotions and seasonality, they should be modeled quantitatively.

The final problem with qualitative forecasting techniques is that they are expensive. In general, they require large amounts of time on the part of the participants in the qualitative forecasting process, whether they are internal to the company (e.g., executives, forecasters, salespeople) or external to the company. The expensive, time-intensive nature of qualitative forecasting is another reason (in addition to the bias caused by inconsistencies in judgment that occur in repetitive decision making) that qualitative forecasting techniques are unsuitable for generating large numbers of forecasts such as forecasting products by SKU and by location (SKUL).

Summary: Qualitative Technique Advantages and Problems

Despite this rather long discussion of the problems associated with qualitative techniques, it should be kept in mind that qualitative techniques are a valuable resource for any forecaster. The value of experience and the ability to analyze complex situations as input to sales forecasts never should be discounted. Indeed, every sales forecast involves some degree of qualitative input. The discussion of the problems associated with qualitative techniques was presented here solely for the purpose of helping you make better qualitative forecasts by avoiding some of the common "traps" associated with these techniques. With these traps in mind, we can now move to a discussion of the qualitative techniques available.

Qualitative Techniques and Tools

In this section, we discuss several qualitative forecasting techniques using the judgment, knowledge, and intuition of experienced people to produce sales forecasts. The techniques discussed solicit expert evaluations via the jury of executive opinion, the Delphi method, and sales force composites. In addition, the information in this section includes a number of tools that enhance qualitative forecasting decisions by reducing the effects of the biases discussed in the preceding section that can affect the accuracy of qualitative forecasts. The tools discussed are market research (using both primary and secondary data) and decision analysis.

Expert Evaluation Techniques

Expert evaluations use the experience of people (e.g., executives, salespeople, outside experts), who are familiar with a product line or a group of products, to generate sales forecasts. The techniques in this section generally involve combining inputs from multiple sources (e.g., groups of executives, salespeople, outside experts). The advantage of soliciting contributions from more than one person, of course, is that it can offset biases introduced into a forecast when the forecast is produced by one person.

Jury of Executive Opinion

When executives from various corporate functions involved in forecasting sales (e.g., finance, marketing, sales, production, logistics) meet for the purpose of generating forecasts, it is termed a *jury of executive opinion*. The jury of executive opinion is one of the most familiar and frequently used of all forecasting techniques (Mentzer & Kahn, 1995). It is a relatively simple forecasting technique to implement and is quite valuable when changes in existing data patterns are anticipated or when there are no data available for quantitative forecasting analyses (e.g., new product forecasts). It also has the advantage of making use of the rich data represented by the intuition and judgment of experienced executives.

For example, a retailer with which we have worked makes extensive and very successful use of a jury of executive opinion for some of the long-term forecasts required for corporate planning. By using this technique, the company is able to tap the expertise of a number of its top-level managers who have had extensive experience in the industry.

Another example illustrating the use of a jury of executive opinion is a company whose personnel we interviewed in the benchmarking studies. In this company, a jury of executive opinion meets monthly to produce and update the product line-level quarterly sales forecasts. In addition to the jury's regular members, the group periodically solicits input from an economist employed by the company who functions as a consultant to the sales forecasting process.

In our research on sales forecasting, we have found that one of the most widespread uses of a jury of executive opinion is in a consensus forecasting process. In fact, this technique forms the backbone of a consensus process, consisting as it does of representatives from multiple functional areas (e.g., marketing, finance, sales, production, logistics). In many cases, quantitative sales forecasts are generated and the consensus forecasting committee meets to decide whether and how much to adjust the quantitative forecasts. These consensus forecasting committees frequently also are responsible for generating qualitative forecasts for new products. The effective use of the jury of executive opinion technique depends on the degree to which the organization is able to overcome the sources of bias inherent in individual and, in particular, group decision making. To the extent that these pressures constrain the decision-making process, biased forecasts will result.

The most frequent source of bias in a consensus forecasting context is political pressures within the company, usually in the form of influence exerted by the member of the jury whose department is the most powerful within the culture of the company (Hanke & Reitsch, 1995). Because of this influence, the contributions from other members of the jury carry relatively less weight in the final forecasts. In many companies, the most powerful member of the jury is from finance, and the influence of this member tends to constrain the forecasts so that they are biased in the direction of the revenue projections of the business plan. Qualitative forecasts that originate from these committees (e.g., new product forecasts) also can be influenced by these same pressures so that they are significantly biased in the direction of agreement with revenue projections.

In one manufacturer whose personnel we interviewed during Phase 3 of the benchmarking studies, the consensus forecasting committee meetings, although ostensibly for the purpose of arriving at a consensus forecast among marketing, finance, and operations, were in reality just a formality. The forecast had been qualitatively adjusted and arrived at by marketing and finance prior to the consensus forecasting meeting. Furthermore, because of significant influence by the finance member of the forecasting committee and a desire on the part of the rest of the committee to support the forecast presented by finance, the committee did not conduct an objective search for information to facilitate its decisions; rather, the committee simply accepted the sales forecast presented by finance.

To mitigate this source of bias, it is important for a company to understand the interaction between the business plan and the sales forecasts. Sales forecasting and business planning are separate but interdependent processes. Properly administered, sales forecasting can be used to facilitate business planning, but this outcome cannot occur if sales forecasts are forced to agree with independently generated revenue targets in the business plan. (For more information on the interaction between sales forecasting and business planning, see the discussion in the "Forecasting Versus Planning" section in Chapter 1 and in the "Approach" section in Chapter 8.)

Another means of decreasing the bias that group decision making introduces into the jury of executive opinion is to make selected, relevant background information available to the executives that comprise the jury. This information may consist of, for example, relevant economic data (e.g., leading or simultaneous indicators), information on industry trends, information on production or distribution constraints within the company, the results of market research such as focus groups, or information on forecast accuracy. Making this information accessible reduces the tendency of individuals in the group to depend entirely on their own available or recently experienced information sources and makes it less likely that the group decision-making process will proceed with only a token effort at objectively evaluating additional information that is important to the decision-making process.

An important caveat to the use of the jury of executive opinion is that the technique is not appropriate for short-term (i.e., daily, weekly, or monthly) forecasts of individual product items or product item-location combinations (i.e., SKUs or SKULs). A jury of executive opinion, by its very nature, requires valuable executive time; therefore, the most efficient use of this technique is to forecast monthly, quarterly, and/or yearly sales predictions for groups of products, that is, product lines. Using a jury of executive opinion for low-level, short-term forecasts encourages bias because of the repetitive nature of these forecasts and is a waste of costly executive time.

Companies using a jury of executive opinion in their forecasting process also should be aware of the tendency of this technique to disperse responsibility for forecasting accuracy. We have found that unless companies using a jury of executive opinion are relatively sophisticated in the management of their forecasting process, members of the jury are neither evaluated nor rewarded for forecasting accuracy. When no one has responsibility for forecast accuracy, inaccurate forecasts inevitably result. Companies that use a jury of executive opinion successfully do so, in part, because they both evaluate and reward members of their consensus forecasting committee for forecasting accuracy.

Another procedure that can be used to assign responsibility for accurate forecasts when using a jury of executive opinion is to require written justification for qualitative adjustments to quantitative forecasts. When this documentation is required, it not only has the effect of assigning responsibility for accurate forecasting but also makes it easier to perform post hoc analyses; that is, if forecasts prove to be inaccurate, then the documentation makes it easier to determine the reasons for the inaccuracies. One company with which we have worked has detailed notes taken at every jury meeting, thus documenting the logic behind each adjustment to the sales forecasts.

Delphi Method

When the Delphi method is used for forecasting, the input of experts, either internal or external to the company, is solicited and proceeds as follows:

1. Each member of the panel of experts chosen to participate writes an answer to the question being investigated (e.g., a forecast for product or industry sales and all the reasoning behind this forecast).
2. The answers of the panel are summarized and returned to the members of the panel, but without the identification of which expert came up with each forecast.
3. After reading the summary of replies, each member of the panel either maintains his or her forecast or reevaluates his or her initial forecast and submits the new forecast (and the reasoning behind changing the forecast) in writing.

The answers are summarized and returned to panel members as many times as necessary to narrow the range of forecast.

An appropriate use of the Delphi method is for the prediction of mid- to long-term company sales levels or long-term industry sales levels. When this technique is used within a company, it can be thought of as a type of "virtual" jury of executive opinion because the executives do not meet face to face. The purpose of this distance is to allow each member to use his or her reasoning to develop a forecast without the influence of strong personalities or the fact that the "boss" has a pet forecast.

The Delphi method also reduces the effects of "groupthink" on the decision-making process. Because the participants do not meet face to face, the bias that occurs because of a desire on the part of group members to support each other's positions or because of the influence of a strong leader within the group is minimized. Removing this source of bias enables conflicting ideas to survive long enough to be examined, thus allowing a range of scenarios to emerge from the process, an outcome that is more legitimate, particularly when long-term sales forecasts are being made.

Problems with this method of qualitative forecasting focus on its tendency to be unreliable; that is, the outcomes can be highly dependent on the composition and expertise of panel members. To some extent, this source of bias is the result of group members not being willing or able to seek out information other than what is readily available or recently perceived. Supplying panel members with relevant information (e.g., economic or industry indicators) can reduce this source of bias.

Sales Force Composite

The sales force composite is a qualitative forecasting method that uses the knowledge and experience of a company's salespeople, its sales management, and/or channel members to produce sales forecasts. The grassroots approach to a sales force composite accumulates sales forecasts for the regions, products, and/or customers of individual salespeople. The sales management approach seeks sales forecasts from sales executives and is essentially a jury of executive opinion, albeit consisting of a narrower range of executives (i.e., only sales executives or only sales and marketing executives). The distributor approach to the sales force composite solicits the sales predictions of independent distributors of a company's products.

An important advantage of the sales force composite technique is that it has the potential for incorporating the expertise of people who are closest to the customers. In addition, the technique places forecasting responsibility on those who have both the ability to directly affect product sales and the potential to experience the impact (e.g., in the form of their customers' displeasure) of forecasting errors.

Biased sales force composite forecasts occur when salespeople or independent distributors use only information that is readily available or recently perceived and when political pressures within and between organizations are prevalent. Because they may not be aware of, or have sufficient perspective on, economic conditions or the accuracy of previous forecasts, individual salespeople or independent distributors may produce biased (e.g., overly optimistic) forecasts. To counteract this bias, information on leading and/or simultaneous economic indicators, industry trends, and the accuracy of previous forecasts should be provided to salespeople or independent distributors to assist them in their forecasting efforts.

Another way in which to counteract biased sales force composite forecasts is to compare these forecasts to forecasts generated by a traditional jury of executive opinion (i.e., with broader base corporate representation and perspective) and/or to quantitatively generated forecasts. Finally, requiring forecast rationales from salespeople or independent distributors will encourage them to make full use of information that could be relevant to their forecasting efforts.

Another consideration when using either the grassroots or the distributor approach is the time required to obtain these forecasts. By the time the individual forecasts are obtained and integrated with other information (e.g., corporate assessments of the plausibility of individual salespersons' forecasts or quantitatively generated forecasts), a substantial amount of time may elapse.

Political pressures within organizations affect sales force composite forecasts because of a lack of understanding of the difference between sales forecasting and setting sales quotas. A sales forecast should be a realistic prediction of product sales for a certain interval of time given a set of assumptions regarding the environment. A sales quota is a motivational tool that assigns a portion of required revenues to each sales region and salesperson. Sales quotas and sales forecasts developed by the sales function should be developed with these differences in mind.

In addition to the problem of confusing sales forecasts and sales quotas, we frequently have observed that in companies requiring their sales staff to generate forecasts, little or no forecasting training is provided to the sales staff. This lack of training in forecasting only compounds the problem of biased forecasts generated by salespeople. Not only do salespeople not understand the difference between sales quotas and sales forecasts, but even if they did, lack of training in how to forecast guarantees an uninformed approach.

Political pressures between organizations in the form of inventory game-playing between manufacturers and distributors can bias sales force composites solicited from independent distributors. When distributors view the process of generating sales forecasts for the manufacturer as an opportunity—not to accurately forecast future sales but rather to adjust inventory (increase distributor inventory in response to trade promotions, increase manufacturer inventory as a distributor "safety stock," or avoid building "pipeline" inventory for new products)—these actions can make a mockery of the sales forecasting process. Manufacturers possessing a certain level of sophistication in their sales forecasting process realize that conventional distribution channels (i.e., those consisting of independent organizations) are, in general, characterized by manifestations of channel power and conflict (Gaski, 1984; Keith, Jackson, & Crosby, 1990), such as inventory game-playing, and take this into account by qualitatively adjusting the forecasts they receive from channel members.

To reduce the unreliability of distributor-generated sales forecasts, manufacturers should recognize the effects of trade promotions on this process. We have found that trade promotions can play havoc with the sales forecasting process, creating promotion-driven seasonality in historical sales data when distributors increase their inventories in response to periodic price promotions from manufacturers rather than to anticipated increases in consumer demand.

One possibility for reducing the forecasting error that is caused by trade promotions is to include the effects of these promotions within quantitative forecasting models. Using another approach, many consumer packaged goods manufacturers have begun to embrace the concept of everyday low prices, which eliminates trade promotions along with the problems these promotions cause for the sales forecasting process.

A related approach to managing the reliability of distributor-generated sales forecasts are the vendor-managed inventory relationships many manufacturers and distributors are developing. In these relationships, manufacturers and distributors alter the nature of their relationship from the conflict-ridden, competitive relationship characteristic of a conventional channel to what essentially are strategic alliances (Stern, El-Ansary, & Coughlin, 1996). Generally, the cooperation and collaboration that characterize these altered channel structures extend to the forecasting process, thereby reducing the political pressures that introduce bias into the forecasts.

Distributors deliberately under forecasting demand because they do not want to assume liability for new product inventories is, to a large extent, simply another manifestation of the competitive nature of conventional channel relationships. This situation can be mitigated to some extent by improved product research and development on the part of the manufacturer. In one manufacturer whose personnel we have interviewed, new product ideas come exclusively from upper management, and there is little or no market research undertaken before introducing the products. Skepticism on the part of independent distributors regarding new product introductions causes distributors to deliberately underforecast sales for this manufacturer's new products until sales convince them that the product concepts are sound. Contrast this to a similar manufacturer that conducts extensive new product research and shares the results with its distributors. The result is more confidence in the channel in new products and more informed forecasts of their demand.

Market Research Tools for Qualitative Forecasting

The information disclosed by market research efforts serves to reduce the bias in qualitative forecasts that results from forecasters using only readily available or recently perceived information in their decision making. For example, assume that a jury of executive opinion is attempting to formulate a long-range forecast for corporate planning, that is, capacity and budgeting decisions. One possibility is to simply extend or extrapolate the sales trends for the company's product lines, which were derived using quantitative techniques such as time-series analyses. Remember from Chapter 3 that sales trends are continuing patterns of sales increases or decreases and that those patterns can take the form of either straight lines or curves.

Simply extending a sales trend is fine so long as we are sure that the pattern will not change. But what if there are changes? How can we forecast these? Remember that an advantage of qualitative forecasting techniques is their ability to forecast changes in existing patterns. Using these techniques, trend extensions may be made with the benefit of input from individuals or groups of people with the knowledge and expertise to correctly modify existing trends. Providing additional information obtained through marketing research enhances these decisions.

Information obtained from market research can be provided to a jury of executive opinion, to members of a panel participating in the Delphi method, or to salespeople, sales managers, or independent distributors participating in a sales composite technique, that is, to anyone involved in qualitative forecasting. Market research can be conducted using primary data, secondary data, or a combination of primary and secondary data. Primary data are collected by a company for a specific purpose (e.g., focus groups conducted specifically to obtain information on the demand for a new product). Secondary data have been previously collected, either by the company using the data or by some other source (e.g., syndicated volume tracking data collected by A. C. Nielsen) (Malhotra, 1996).

Market Research Using Primary Data

If a company has sufficient resources to undertake market research, then it can conduct surveys to obtain primary data. These data can provide information on anticipated product demand or anticipated economic activity to assist in qualitative mid-range (e.g., monthly, quarterly) or long-range (e.g., 1- to 5-year) product or industry sales forecasts or in qualitative adjustments to short-range product forecasts. For example, a company could survey (using face-to-face interviews, telephone surveys, or mail survey methodology) a sample of its business/institutional customers to obtain information on anticipated purchases of new or existing products. A manufacturer could use this methodology to systematically secure sales forecasts from independent distributors. A company could survey a sample of households or consumers to obtain information on purchase intentions for new or existing products. Still another example of using surveys involves a company surveying a sample of economic experts for forecasts of national economic activity or economic activity within an industry.

Another means for obtaining primary data that contribute to the forecasting process is to conduct focus groups. Focus groups are small groups of people (e.g., 7-10) gathered together to exchange ideas on a specific topic. This methodology requires a moderator to conduct the focus groups and is relatively time-consuming (Krueger, 1994). However, focus groups can be an effective method of gathering information to aid in qualitative forecasts, particularly for new products. Focus groups can be used to solicit new product ideas and to obtain feedback on products that are in the development process. One manufacturer with which we have worked uses focus groups very effectively as an adjunct to its new product forecasting process. The focus groups consist of potential users of new products that are under consideration.

Market Research Using Secondary Data

An alternative to a company gathering specific data for the purpose of enhancing qualitative forecasting decisions is the use of secondary data, that is, data that have been gathered previously, either within a company or by sources external to the company. For example, instead of conducting its own surveys when attempting to forecast changes in sales trends, a company can obtain information from surveys conducted by external sources, some of which are detailed in the following:

- A survey of household/consumer attitudes and anticipated purchases is conducted regularly by the Survey Research Center at the University of Michigan.
- Surveys on expected investments are conducted by McGraw-Hill (results appear in the November issue of *Business Week*) and by the Office of Business Economics of the Securities and Exchange Commission (results are available in March).
- Surveys on anticipated inventory levels are conducted by the Office of Business Economics of the Securities and Exchange Commission (Granger, 1980).

Another source of secondary data is tracking data in the form of leading and/or simultaneous (coincident) indicators. Economic indicators for the United States are available monthly in the *Business Conditions Digest,* published by the U.S. Department of Commerce (Granger, 1980). When trying to forecast changes or turning points in a company's product sales, knowledge of the behavior of business cycles in the aggregate economy is a valuable input. Of course, the rationale underlying leading indicators, for example, is that some sectors of the economy will expand ahead of others, thus signaling changes in the overall level of economic activity (Granger, 1980). Consequently, it is important that each company possess and maintain a sufficient level of intelligence and expertise with respect to its own industry. This will enable the company to recognize which indicators are leading and which indicators are coincident for its industry, thereby providing information pertinent to the company's forecasting decisions.

During the benchmarking studies, we observed that a characteristic of companies with highly sophisticated forecasting processes was their ability to conduct ongoing analyses of their businesses and industries. This ability of a company to successfully analyze its business resulted from selecting employees who possessed (or could acquire) both expertise in analysis tools and knowledge about the company and the industry. In addition, upper management was willing to support the business analysis process with systems (e.g., hardware, software) and continuous training. An ongoing program of business analysis is the only way in which to understand not only which economic indicators are pertinent to a company but also, for example, the effects of trade and consumer promotions as well as price elasticity of demand for a company's products (including the effects of competitors' price changes).

Keeping in mind that it is up to you to decide which indicators are leading for your particular industry, common leading economic indicators include the following:

- Average work week (production and manufacturing workers)
- New manufacturing orders
- Durable goods orders
- Construction contracts
- Plant and equipment purchases
- Capital appropriations
- Business population
- After-tax corporate profits
- Stock price indexes
- Level of, and changes in, business inventories
- Consumer spending
- Growth in durable goods industries
- Growth in capital equipment industries
- Level of, and changes in, money supplies (e.g., M1, M2)
- Bond prices

The rationale underlying simultaneous or coincident indicators is that these statistics will roughly correspond to changes in aggregate economic trends, essentially serving to confirm that a change in trend, anticipated on the basis of leading indicators, is actually occurring. As with leading indicators, the ability of these statistics to contribute to qualitative forecasting decisions depends on how well a company understands which simultaneous indicators are significant for the company and its industry. Some examples of simultaneous indicators are as follows:

- Unemployment rate
- Index of "help wanted" advertising in newspapers
- Index of industrial production
- Gross domestic product
- Personal income
- Retail sales
- Index of wholesale prices

The secondary data sources discussed in this section are appropriate to enhance long-term forecasting (e.g., 1-5 years). There are, however, a number of syndicated services that regularly make available secondary data in the form of consumer point-of-sale data (i.e., volume tracking data) for a sub-scription fee. The information provided by these services can serve as an appropriate input to mid-range forecasts (e.g., monthly, quarterly). Sources of syndicated volume tracking data include A. C. Nielsen (National Scan Track), the Newspaper Advertising Bureau, and Tele-Research, Inc. (Malhotra, 1996). Several of the consumer package goods manufacturers with which we have worked use these syndicated data sources and information from independent distributors to estimate market share and existing product inventories, respec-tively. This information is valuable in producing qualitative forecasts of product line demand for the coming month or quarter.

Decision Analysis Tools for Qualitative Forecasting

The purpose of using the tools of decision analysis is to structure the qualitative forecasting decision process in such a way that participants are required to examine and state the assumptions used in their decisions. The discipline and structure imposed by these decision tools minimize bias in qualitative forecasting by (a) diminishing overconfidence in forecasters' abil-ity to forecast accurately, (b) forcing forecasters to seek out and consider information that is relevant to the forecasting decisions, and (c) enhancing forecasters' ability to process large amounts of complex information. The tools discussed in this section include decision tree diagrams and simulation.

Decision Tree Diagrams

The advantage of decision tree diagrams is that they enable participants to visualize the context of a complex decision, thereby reducing biases that occur because of limitations on forecasters' abilities to process complex information. Constructing the diagrams forces decision makers to consider all alternatives and to assign probabilities to each alternative based on their experience and knowledge of their company and industry. When combined with a statistical concept known as Bayesian analysis, the estimates of prob-abilities for future events in decision tree diagrams can be revised based on experience, judgment, and/or additional information such as that gained from market research (Granger, 1980).

The tree diagram in Figure 5.1 illustrates these concepts. This tree diagram helps analysts focus their forecast of sales of a new product. Suppose that for national sales of a new product, analysts can only forecast (without any additional information) a 50%-50% probability of high sales versus low sales. However, suppose that, based on past experience with other new products, forecasters know that when the results of market research (e.g., surveys of prospective customers) have forecast success for a product, 80% of the time high sales actually do occur. On the other hand, when a new product has been introduced in the past and market research forecast product failure, 85% of the time low sales actually do occur.

Using Bayesian analysis, the probabilities of both high and low product sales for national introduction of the new product can be revised from their former (and uninformative) 50%-50% probabilities. As Figure 5.1 indicates, the probability of market research indicating product success, Pr(Success), is the sum of 40.0% (the probability of market research forecasting product success when national sales will, in fact, be high) and 7.5% (the probability of market research forecasting product success when national sales will, in fact, be low), or 47.5%. On the other hand, the probability of market research indicating product failure, Pr(Failure), is the sum of 10.0% (the probability of market research forecasting product failure when national sales will, in fact, be high) and 42.5% (the probability of market research forecasting product failure when national sales will, in fact, be low), or 52.5%. From these forecasts, the probabilities of both high and low national sales can be revised as indicated in the following (adapted from Hanke & Reitsch, 1995):

- The probability of high national sales when market research forecasts success is 84%, that is,

$$Pr(High\ Sales/Success) = 40.0\% \ / \ 47.5\% = 84.0\%.$$

- The probability of low national sales when market research forecasts failure is 81%, that is,

$$Pr(Low\ Sales/Failure) = 42.5\% \ / \ 52.5\% = 81.0\%.$$

Thus, through this decision analysis, we have improved our ability to forecast success in our new product introductions if we heed the input from market research.

Simulations

Another decision analysis tool that can be used in the qualitative forecasting decision process is simulation. Like decision tree diagrams, simulation requires forecasters to structure their decision making by examining and stating their assumptions. Essentially, simulation demands that the system under investigation be defined, enabling that system to be manipulated so that

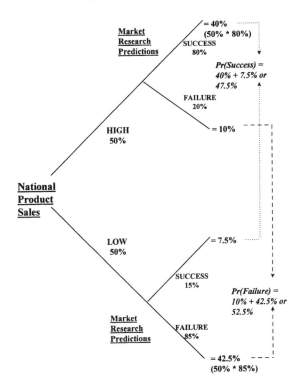

Figure 5.1. Decision Tree Diagram
SOURCE: Adapted From Hanke & Reitsch (1995)

"what if" analyses can be performed to explore alternatives (Pritsker, 1986). For example, forecasters predicting sales for a new product could use simulation to explore alternative outcomes based on the probabilities of various economic conditions occurring. Simulation software currently is available that greatly facilitates the use of this decision tool, requiring, for example, that the user merely create a graphical diagram of system components (similar to what is done for a decision tree diagram) (Pritsker, Sigal, & Hammesfahr, 1989).

However, simulations do not necessarily need to involve the computer or complex software. One consumer products company simulates the introduction of new products by giving them away at a test mall. Subjects are given a free sample of the product, asked to try it, and told they will be sent a short questionnaire to complete. Several days later, each subject receives the questionnaire asking what he or she thought of the product. Each subject also receives a form to order more of the new product. Various prices are tried with different subjects to see how likely customers are to order more of the product. In this way, the company can simulate new customers' price sensitivity and, thus, forecast new product sales at various introductory price levels.

Summary

This chapter has focused on the use of qualitative forecasting techniques that turn the opinions of experienced people into formal forecasts. The information presented included an overview of the advantages inherent in qualitative forecasting analyses, with the discussion of problems focusing on the sources of bias that cause inaccuracies in qualitative forecasts. Qualitative forecasting techniques that were discussed as methods for tapping the knowledge and intuition of experts included the jury of executive opinion, the Delphi method, and the sales force composite. In addition, we presented a number of tools that are important adjuncts to the qualitative forecasting process, primarily because of their ability to enhance qualitative forecasting decisions through the reduction of the effects of the biases that can affect the accuracy of qualitative forecasts.

The next chapter discusses the systems (hardware and software) that surround the forecasting process we use to efficiently and effectively conduct the business of developing and using sales forecasts.

References

Gaski, J. F. (1984, Summer). The theory of power and conflict in channels of distribution. *Journal of Marketing, 48*, 23-41.

Granger, C. W. J. (1980). *Forecasting in business and economics.* New York: Academic Press.

Hanke, J. E., & Reitsch, A. G. (1995). *Business forecasting* (5th ed.). Englewood Cliffs, NJ: Prentice Hall.

Hogarth, R., & Makridakis, S. (1981). Beyond discrete biases: Functional and dysfunctional aspects of judgmental heuristics. *Psychological Bulletin, 90,* 115-137.

Janis, I. L., & Mann, I. (1982). *Decision making: A psychological analysis of conflict, choice, and commitment* (2nd ed.). New York: Free Press.

Kahneman, D., & Tversky, A. (1973). On the psychology of prediction. *Psychological Review, 80,* 237-251.

Keith, J. E., Jackson, D. W., & Crosby, L. A. (1990, July). Effects of alternative types of influence strategies under different channel dependence structures. *Journal of Marketing, 54,* 30-41.

Krueger, R. A. (1994). *Focus groups: A practical guide for applied research* (2nd ed.). Thousand Oaks, CA: Sage.

Makridakis, S., & Wheelwright, S. C. (1989). *Forecasting methods for management* (5th ed.). New York: John Wiley.

Makridakis, S., Wheelwright, S. C., & McGee, V. E. (1983). *Forecasting: Methods and applications* (2nd ed.). New York: John Wiley.

Malhotra, N. K. (1996). *Marketing research: An applied orientation* (2nd ed.). Upper Saddle River, NJ: Prentice Hall.

Mentzer, J. T., & Kahn, K. B. (1995). Forecasting technique familiarity, satisfaction, usage, and application. *Journal of Forecasting, 14,* 465-476.

Pritsker, A. A. B. (1986). *Introduction to simulation and SLAM II* (3rd ed.). New York: John Wiley.

Pritsker, A. A. B., Sigal, C. E., & Hammesfahr, R. D. J. (1989). *SLAM II: Network models for decision support.* Englewood Cliffs, NJ: Prentice Hall.

Stern, L. W., El-Ansary, A. I., & Coughlan, A. T. (1996). *Marketing channels* (5th ed.). Upper Saddle River, NJ: Prentice Hall.

CHAPTER 6

Sales Forecasting Systems

*W*e were amazed at the number of companies in
*Phase 2 of the benchmarking studies that have
little or no systems connectivity. The sales forecasters
often do not have access to the management information
systems; when they need data for forecasting, they have to
type them into their computers. Furthermore, users of the
forecasts do not have direct access to the sales
forecasting systems. When a user needs the forecast, the
sales forecaster prints out the results and someone
carries the printout to the user's office and types the
results into the user's planning system. Such manual data
transfers are time-consuming, frustrating, and prone to
input errors. In addition, the users of the forecasts cannot
provide electronic input to the sales forecasts.*

*However, not all companies suffer from such lack of
systems connectivity.*

*"I was working on a spreadsheet for one of our
product forecasts," said a sales forecasting analyst for a
large manufacturer of automotive parts. "As I worked, a
message came across the bottom of the screen which said,
'I used to be responsible for forecasting the same
product, and I have seen this situation before.' The sender
went on to suggest ways I could adjust the system
forecast to improve its accuracy."*

> *When we asked her if she followed the sender's advice, she said, "Well, of course! The message was from the CEO!"*

Although not everyone gets such "helpful hints" from the CEO as did the sales forecaster in this example, it is just this type of systems connectivity that is a necessary component of forecasting systems. Forecasting systems are not just the personal computer on which the forecasting software package resides. Rather, *sales forecasting systems are all the computer and communication systems used by the developers and users of the sales forecasts*; they are the integrating template that overlays all the processes, procedures, and reporting associated with sales forecasting.

How these computer and communications systems should be designed is the topic of this chapter. In discussing this topic, we are guided by the *seven principles of sales forecasting systems* that we have developed from working with a number of companies in defining, developing, and refining sales forecasting systems. These seven principles are as follows:

1. The sales forecasting system should serve as a communication vehicle between users and developers of the forecasts.
2. The tool should fit the problem, not the other way around.
3. Complex forecasting systems do not have to look that way to the user.
4. Think in terms of a "suite" of time-series techniques, not just one technique.
5. Think in terms of qualitative techniques, time-series techniques, *and* (not *or*) regression analysis.
6. Let the system tell you which techniques to use.
7. You tell the system which forecasts are important.

We discuss each of these principles individually. This is followed by a description of a system, which personifies these principles and is used by a number of companies, to illustrate how these principles can be put into practice.

The Sales Forecasting System as a Communication Vehicle

As we mentioned at the opening of this chapter, we were surprised in Phase 2 of the benchmarking studies (discussed in Chapter 7) with the number of companies that reported "system disconnects" and "islands of analysis" in their sales forecasting processes. *System disconnects* exist when the information needed to develop sales forecasts is not electronically available to the developers of the sales forecasts. When market research information, inventory levels, confirmed orders, electronic data interchange input from suppliers and customers, and sometimes even historical demand information are not available to the forecasters, they simply do not have the information necessary to do their jobs. No one can forecast in the absence of information. Conversely, the more information that is available, the better the forecasts that can be developed. When the information is available but not in an electronic form, a considerable amount of error will creep into the forecasting process as a result of mistakes in manual data entry. Thus, system disconnects can be cured by providing the forecasters with electronic access to the systems that contain the information necessary to develop informed sales forecasts.

The second systems communication problem is *islands of analysis,* which exist when the *users* of the sales forecasts do not have electronic access to the sales forecasting systems. As we discussed in Chapter 1, managers in all the functional areas of a business (marketing, sales, finance, production, and logistics) need sales forecasts. When these managers cannot obtain electronic access to the sales forecasts, at the very least, the same types of manual data entry mistakes occur when these functional managers enter the forecasts into their systems. At the worst, the functional managers become frustrated with the inability to interact with the forecasting process and to provide their input to the forecasts while they are being developed. This frustration often results in each functional area independently developing its own forecasts for its own use. These islands of analysis result in duplication of effort, each function forecasting without access to all the information it needs and no function having input from the other functions.

The cure for both system disconnects and islands of analysis is a client-server systems architecture, both internal and external. Internally, a client-server systems architecture means that all the systems used by the functional areas, sales forecasting, and the management information system (MIS) area are tied together to a central "server" system that has access to the corporate "data warehouse." The data warehouse means that all information gathered by MIS is stored in a central location so that all information relevant to sales forecasting can be easily and electronically accessed. The central server system means that all functional systems (including the sales forecasting system) can be accessed by all other functional systems through this central server.

Such an internal client-server system means that anyone involved in *developing* the sales forecasts can electronically access whatever information is needed, whether this information is sales history, order history, market research information for regression analysis, financial plans, production schedules or capacity, or inventory levels. Furthermore, this means that anyone involved in *using* the sales forecasts can electronically provide input to the developers of the sales forecasts and conduct his or her own analyses and planning based on the existing sales forecasts.

External client-server architecture, recently called collaborative forecasting and replenishment (CFAR) (Verity, 1996), means that the corporate system has access to the corporate systems of as many customers and suppliers as is possible. The reason for access to customers is to provide more accurate and timely information on the demand companies are receiving from their customers and the inventory they are presently carrying to meet that demand. With this information, more accurate forecasts can be derived by each major customer, thus reducing overall forecasting error. The reason for access to suppliers is to provide more accurate information on the availability of materials for the production system and to improve the forecasting accuracy of the suppliers (an improvement that eventually should lower their costs and prices).

Figure 6.1 illustrates this internal and external client-server architecture. To the degree that this complete architecture can be achieved, communication between the functional areas and sales forecasting will be improved, manual data entries will be minimized, islands of analysis will be eliminated, and sales forecasting will become a much more informed and accurate process.

The Tool Should Fit the Problem

Principle 2 relates to a basic systems principle that business systems exist to serve the business, not the other way around. Unfortunately, the philosophy of many software vendors is essentially, "If you can just make your company run the way our system operates, then we can solve all your problems."

It ought to be the other way around; the sales forecasting system (or any business system, for that matter) should be customized to meet the forecasting needs of the company. If the company wants to forecast weekly with monthly, quarterly, and yearly roll-ups, then the system should be customized to provide forecasts for these intervals and horizons. If the company wants to forecast at the stock keeping unit by location (SKUL), the stock keeping unit (SKU), the product line, and the corporate levels with adjustments at any level automatically reconciled at all other levels, then the system should accommodate this. If the company wants analysts and managers to be able to make

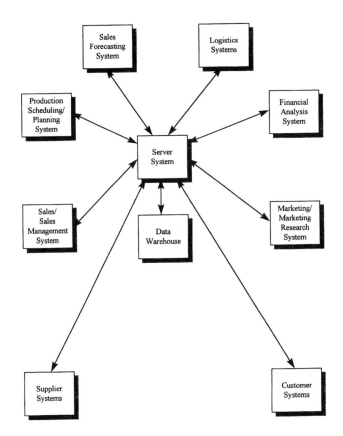

Figure 6.1. Sales Forecasting Systems Client-Server Architecture

qualitative adjustments to the forecasts and capture the effect of each on forecasting accuracy, then this also should be possible. Too often, requests such as these are met with the response, "But the system does not work that way."

A sales forecasting system for a sales forecaster is much like the tool box for a mechanic; the tool box exists to provide the tools for the mechanic to do his or her job. If the mechanic needs a screwdriver, then the tool box should not have only hammers. In the same sense, it is up to the sales forecasting function in a company to define how it wants to forecast sales and the analytic and reporting tools needed to do this job. It is up to the sales forecasting system to provide these tools. As we go through the rest of the seven principles and through the example system, the potential of these tools should become clearer.

Complex Systems Do Not Have to Look That Way

As we observed in Chapters 2 through 5, the job of sales forecasting can get a bit complex. Involved procedures, logic, and calculations may be necessary to arrive at the final forecast. In addition, implementing these seven principles can involve incredibly complex systems solutions—solutions that access information from multiple sources and then perform hundreds of thousands of calculations. However, none of this complexity needs to be apparent to the sales forecaster. The job of the sales forecaster is to understand the uses and limitations of the two quantitative groups of sales forecasting techniques (time series and regression) and to understand how each is used in the sales forecasting system to arrive at the system-generated forecast. From this understanding, sales forecasters should bring their own experience to bear to qualitatively improve the quantitatively generated system forecast.

None of this requires an in-depth understanding of the actual systems functions or the mathematical calculations that must be conducted to bring the quantitative forecast to them. The systems functions are the responsibility of MIS. The mathematical calculations are the responsibility of the developers of the actual sales forecasting system. What the sales forecaster should see is the quantitative forecasts, laid out in a format that is easy to understand and lends itself well to the analysis the sales forecaster may want to do while making qualitative adjustments. We have found that the best environment in which to accomplish this is a spreadsheet environment. As the example system described later will illustrate, the complex systems functions and mathematical calculations all can be performed without direct input from the sales forecaster. All the sales forecaster needs to do is access a spreadsheet and follow some straightforward instructions to finalize the sales forecasts. This also is the case with the demonstration software provided with this book (and described in Chapter 9) and should be the case for any sales forecasting software.

A "Suite" of Time-Series Techniques

Time-series-based forecasting systems traditionally have been centered around one time-series technique. The state of computer technology historically only allowed a computer system to have one of the time-series techniques discussed in Chapter 3. As a result, companies had to go through considerable analysis prior to selection or development of their sales forecasting systems to determine which time-series techniques worked best for the largest number of their products. Alternatively, companies simply purchased software packages and hoped that the one time-series technique included would work for their products.

Modern computer technology has eliminated the need for such a narrow focus on one time-series technique. With the availability of systems such as the one discussed later in this chapter (as well as the demonstration version included with this book and discussed in Chapter 9), there is no reason why a company should use a naive, one time-series technique system today.

Rather, modern sales forecasting systems include a "suite" of time-series techniques; that is, all the techniques discussed in Chapter 3 are available in the systems. Any and all of these techniques can be brought to bear in forecasting each individual product. For example, exponential smoothing with an α of .14 might be best for the first product forecast, the same technique with a different α might be best for the next product forecast, exponential smoothing with trend and seasonality might be best for the next product, and so on until the best technique is selected for each product to be forecast.

As we discuss in a later section, this selection of which technique for each product can be automatic or can be conducted by the forecaster. The system included with this book and discussed in Chapter 9, in fact, gives you both of these options. The ability to select the technique for each item to be forecast usually is not a necessary characteristic of large systems (such as the one discussed later in this chapter) that are designed to forecast thousands of products in any given period. Regardless of whether the system selects the technique or you select one, however, the point of principle 4 is that a suite of time-series techniques must first be available in the system. There is no excuse today for using a sales forecasting system that does not offer this feature.

Qualitative, Time-Series, *and* (not *or*) Regression

In this book, we have talked about qualitative techniques, time-series techniques, and regression analysis separately—each in its own separate chapter, in fact. Unfortunately, these techniques also are treated as separate in many sales forecasting systems; that is, if you use one, then you do not need to use the others. This leads to systems that "take a time-series approach" or "are regression based," both of which often make it difficult or impossible to make qualitative adjustments to the quantitative forecasts.

In fact, time-series techniques, qualitative techniques, and regression analysis each have their own unique advantages and disadvantages with respect to sales forecasting (as we discussed in Chapters 3 through 5). However, these advantages and disadvantages are largely complementary. Time-series techniques are designed to identify and forecast trends and seasonal patterns in data and to adjust quickly when the trends or seasonal patterns shift. The disadvantage to times-series techniques is that they do not consider external factors.

Regression analysis does a poor job of identifying trends and seasonality and does an even poorer job of adjusting to changes in either. (Remember that regression analysis requires a considerable amount of data, so it do not adjust "quickly" to anything.) What it does do well is consider external factors and their impact on the forecast; that is, after all, what it is designed to do.

What neither time-series techniques nor regression analysis do well is deal with changes in the business environment that have never happened before or that have happened before but for which we have no data in the system that describe what happened (i.e., we have no previous data to analyze). This is exactly what experienced forecast analysts and managers do well—take various "feelings," "impressions," and "interactions" from themselves, others in the company, suppliers, and customers and translate those into a qualitative adjustment to the quantitative forecast. This translation often is based on a keen analysis of the business environment but involves no quantifiable data. What forecast analysts and managers do not do well is look at masses of data and precisely identify trends, seasonal patterns, or relationships with external factors.

Thus, each of the three approaches to sales forecasting does something well that the other two do poorly. For this reason, we have found that the most effective sales forecasting systems start with a time-series forecast (using the suite approach just discussed) to develop an initial forecast, use regression analysis of external factors to improve this initial forecast, and then make it easy for the sales forecasters to analyze the resultant forecasts and make qualitative changes based on information they have that was not considered by the time-series or the regression analysis.

A brief example might help. Suppose that we are forecasting a product that has a definite trend and for which we run a trade promotion every May. However, suppose that we also run consumer price promotions at various times during the year for this product. Time series will very effectively identify and forecast the trend and the effect on demand of the May trade promotion (this promotion that happens at the same time every year will show up in time-series analysis as a seasonal pattern). What time series will not figure out is the impact on the forecast of consumer price promotions because they do not happen at regular times each year. Time series will treat this pattern as "noise."

It is precisely this pattern that regression analysis will identify (by finding a correlation between the event of consumer price promotions and the jump in demand). Thus, we have a quantitative forecast that is better than either time series or regression could have obtained alone.

If we make this information available to the sales forecaster—identifying the trend, the seasonal trade promotions, and the consumer price promotion effects so that the sales forecaster can understand them—then we can build on this forecast. For example, suppose that the sales forecaster knows that a special order will be coming from a key customer that will increase demand next month by 50% but will decrease demand for the subsequent 3 months by 15%. Knowing how the system identified the historical trend, trade promotion, and consumer price promotion effects on demand, the sales forecaster can use his knowledge that is not available to the system to make a qualitative adjustment. Thus, the accuracy of the resultant forecast is further improved.

Let the System Tell You Which Techniques to Use

Back in the 1980s, we developed a *sales forecasting expert system.* This system allowed the user to answer a series of questions about his or her company, the number of products the user forecast, whether trend and seasonality existed, the availability of external information, the sophistication of the company's personnel and computer systems, and a host of other questions. Based on their answers to all of these questions, the expert system made specific recommendations as to which forecasting technique should be used for each product in the company.

After more than 300 companies had used this expert system and provided us with feedback on its usefulness, we realized that the one thing the system did not need was the person sitting at the computer answering the questions. If we could design a sales forecasting system that had the access to corporate information that is depicted in Figure 6.1, then the system could automatically select the best forecasting technique for each situation—all without input from the user. This resulted in the development of a number of sales forecasting systems that follow this principle. The one discussed later in the chapter, and its demonstration version in Chapter 9, is an example of this process.

The embodiment of Principle 6 simply means that a system that has access to demand history for all the products to be forecast can take each product one at a time, try a number of different time-series techniques on that one product, and select the technique that provides the best forecast for that one product. The system can then go on to the second product and repeat the process until all products to be forecast have been analyzed. The result is the selection of the most accurate time-series technique to use for each product to be forecast.

The system also should have access to data on all the variables that might affect demand for any of the products (see the discussion of variable selection in Chapter 4). With this access, the system can automatically follow the process outlined in Figure 4.3 in Chapter 4 to find the variables that do the best job of improving each time-series forecast for each product. (The variables used may be different for each product.)

The result is that the sales forecaster sees a quantitative forecast—with the trend, seasonality, and regression effects identified—without going through the tedious process of trying different time-series techniques and regression variables for each product. The user trusts the system to do this analysis, using the criterion of increased accuracy for time-series technique selection and the criteria presented in Figure 4.3 for regression analysis. The user can then concentrate on what he or she does best, qualitatively improving the system forecast.

Tell the System Which Forecasts Are Important

The previous section pointed out that modern sales forecasting systems can do much of the analysis for you concerning which techniques to use. However, you still need to tell the systems which forecasts are important and which are not. In many cases, sales forecasting systems in large companies make thousands (or hundreds of thousands) of forecasts per month. Of these thousands of forecasts, which should be analyzed qualitatively and which are "good enough" and do not require valuable and limited sales forecaster time?

Effective sales forecasting systems assist the sales forecaster in answering this question with a *management by exception* approach. In Chapter 8, we will identify a number of criteria by which sales forecasting managers can decide which products need more accurate forecasts and which can tolerate less accuracy. The management by exception approach to sales forecasting systems dictates that, for each product to be forecast, management agrees on what constitutes an acceptable level of mean absolute percent error (*MAPE*). Any products for which the system achieves a *MAPE* lower than the acceptable level do not show up on the *exception report,* which lists all the products for which the system is not automatically achieving acceptable *MAPE*'s and, thus, need to be qualitatively analyzed by the sales forecasters. Any product for which the *MAPE* achieved with time-series techniques and regression analysis is greater than the acceptable level show up on the exception report.

This does not mean that the sales forecaster cannot also analyze other products that are not on the exception report. It simply means that the majority of the attention of the sales forecaster is focused on the products that need it most—those for which the system is not already achieving acceptable levels of accuracy.

Summary: Sales Forecasting Systems Principles

We have presented seven principles that should be embodied in any sales forecasting system today. Given the considerable savings resulting from lower supply chain costs, higher customer service levels, improved coordination between business planning functions, and improved coordination with suppliers and customers, the cost of implementing these principles is well worth the effort.

To demonstrate how these principles can be implemented, an example of a sales forecasting system that embodies all seven of these principles is presented. Again, to demonstrate the benefits from such a system, one company using this system reported a monthly improvement in sales not lost due to stockouts of $6 million—a direct result of improved forecasting accuracy (Mentzer & Schroeter, 1993).

MULTICASTER: An Example System

A description of the large-scale production version of the MULTICASTER Forecasting System (MFS)[1] is included in this chapter for two reasons. First, MFS incorporates the seven principles just discussed and, as such, provides a good example of how each can be implemented in a sales forecasting system. Second, the production version of MFS was the model from which the book version of MULTICASTER, included with this book and described in Chapter 9, was derived.

MFS provides a communications vehicle for the sales forecasting function by interacting with the MIS to obtain data on past demand, forecasts, and exogenous events and by providing access to the forecasting results for the sales forecasters and the users of the forecast.

MFS can be customized to the forecasting environment of any organization. It has been used to forecast weekly, monthly, quarterly, and yearly. It has been used to forecast SKULs, SKUs, product lines, divisional sales, and corporate sales. It has been used to forecast in units, dollars, weight, and volume for products and services and in number of loads for transportation vehicles. It has been used by manufacturers, wholesalers, retailers, government agencies, and transportation companies. It has been used in consumer and industrial product and service industries. This litany of uses is provided only to demonstrate the ability of a sales forecasting system to be customized for a wide variety of situations in which to accomplish Principle 2, that is, making the tool fit the problem instead of the other way around.

Although, as we will see in a moment, MFS provides a sophisticated forecasting environment, all the user sees is a spreadsheet. Thus, the complex system does not look that way to the user.

MFS uses a suite of 19 time-series techniques and selects the one technique that provides the lowest *MAPE* for each product to be forecast. This is followed by the use of regression analysis to forecast that part of the demand pattern that time series could not. The results of the time series and the regression forecasting are then placed in the spreadsheet for the user to analyze, thus combining qualitative, time-series, and regression forecasting techniques and letting the system select which techniques to use.

Finally, an exception report is available to direct the attention of the sales forecasters to those forecasts that most need qualitative adjustment.

MFS is designed to forecast down to a level of detail equal to each SKU at each distribution location (SKUL), but forecasts can be made and reconciled at any level above this. At the beginning of each forecasting period, a data file that contains all changes to the product list and the prior month's demand history is loaded into MFS. This process triggers MFS to reforecast all products that have additional demand data, and creates a spreadsheet for each product, allowing the sales forecasters to see the latest demand history and forecasts available. Once the sales forecasters have finished examining and qualitatively adjusting the spreadsheets, the final forecasts are released to the user systems. However, during this qualitative forecasting stage, the ability exists for the user to view the spreadsheets and, electronically, make suggestions for adjustments. In this way, the system facilitates involvement of all the functions in Figure 6.1 in the sales forecasting process.

Thus, MFS is designed to be a system that interacts with the other information systems illustrated in Figure 6.1, provides relevant analysis of historical data using a suite of time-series techniques and regression analysis, and communicates the analysis to the sales forecaster and users of the forecasts in a convenient analytical environment, that is, a spreadsheet. To further understand this system, it is helpful to discuss the MFS forecasting techniques, spreadsheets, and systems.

MFS Techniques

MFS uses any of up to 19 time-series forecasting techniques to determine baseline (level), trend, and any seasonal patterns in the data for each product forecast. Table 6.1 provides a descriptive list of these techniques. The first 3 are naive techniques, and the next 4 are variations of a moving average. The remaining 12 are exponential smoothing techniques. Techniques 8 through 10 are variations of exponential smoothing (Brown & Meyer, 1961). Techniques 11 through 13 are adaptive smoothing (Trigg & Leach, 1967). Techniques 14 through 19 are variations of extended exponential smoothing (Mentzer, 1988; Winters, 1960). Notice that this list includes all the techniques discussed in Chapter 3.

The technique that produces the lowest error in forecasting the existing data for each product is selected each period by MFS to produce the time-series forecast for that product. Each product has its own unique spreadsheet in which the forecast baseline, trend, and seasonality are recorded separately. Although the MFS techniques calculate baseline, trend, and seasonality multiplicatively (as was discussed under fixed-model time-series techniques in Chapter 3), the components are recorded in the spreadsheet as separate components to be added together for the purpose of displaying each time-series component for the sales forecaster.

For example, suppose that Technique 14 is selected by MFS and that the time-series components are calculated by the technique to be as follows:

Baseline = 1,000
Trend = 150
Seasonality = 1.15

The formula from Chapter 3 for the final forecast in Technique 14 is as follows:

Forecast = (Baseline + Trend) * Seasonality.

Thus, the forecast would be [(1,000 + 150) * 1.15], or 1,323. However, this information would be presented in the first three lines of the spreadsheet as follows:

TABLE 6.1 Multiple Forecasting System Time-Series Techniques

Technique	Description
1	$\text{Actual}_t = \text{Forecast}_{t+1}$
2	$\text{Actual}_t + (\text{Actual}_t - \text{Actual}_{t-1}) = \text{Forecast}_{t+1}$
3	$\text{Actual}_{t-11} = \text{Forecast}_{t+1}$
4	Moving average (user specifies number of months in average)
5	Moving average with multiplicative seasonality (user specifies number of months in average)
6	Weighted moving average (user specifies number of months in average and weights)
7	Weighted moving average with multiplicative seasonality (user specifies number of months in average and weights)

Techniques 8 through 19 are exponential smoothing

Technique	Alpha	Beta	Gamma
8	F	N	N
9	F	N	F
10	F	F	N
11	A	N	N
12	A	N	F
13	A	F	N
14	F	F	F
15	A	A	A
16	A	F	F
17	H	H	H
18	H	F	F
19	H	N	N

NOTE: F = fixed; N = not included; A = adaptive; H = heuristic. Technique descriptions: 8 = exponential smoothing; 9 = exponential smoothing with seasonality; 10 = exponential smoothing with trend; 11 = adaptive smoothing; 12 = adaptive smoothing with seasonality; 13 = adaptive smoothing with trend; 14 = Winter's technique; 15 = adaptive extended exponential smoothing with calculated smoothing constants; 16 = adaptive extended exponential smoothing; 17 = adaptive extended exponential smoothing with heuristic selection of smoothing constants; 18 = adaptive extended exponential smoothing with fixed beta, gamma, and alpha heuristically selected; 19 = exponential smoothing with alpha heuristically selected.

Baseline = 1,000
Trend = 150
Seasonality = 173

This still equals 1,323. For techniques that do not consider trend or seasonality, those lines in the spreadsheet are simply left blank.

The part of the data not explained by the time-series forecast (the residual or, in time-series terminology, the noise) is further subjected to multiple regression analysis. Data on up to 500 potential exogenous variables are stored in the regression module of MFS, and each variable is compared to the residual for each product. Up to 10 of these variables that are significantly related to the residual of each product are selected by the regression module to forecast the residual portion of the demand for that product using the stepwise approach discussed in Chapter 4. Once this analysis is completed, the regression-based forecast of the residuals also is recorded in the spreadsheet for that particular product. The baseline, trend, seasonality, and regression forecasts of the residual are then added together in the spreadsheet to present the MFS forecast. Thus, time-series and regression forecasting are combined automatically to provide the advantages of each technique to each individual forecast.

The sales forecaster is now in a position to view each spreadsheet and analyze the MFS forecast and its four components (time-series baseline, trend, and seasonality as well as the regression forecast of the residual). Based on previous experience with the company and its business environment, with MFS and knowledge of future events, the sales forecaster has the ability to adjust the MFS forecast to arrive at the final forecast.

MFS Spreadsheet

To achieve Principle 3 of sales forecasting systems, it is important to create an environment in which the sales forecaster can easily make changes in the system forecasts based on his or her unique knowledge and experience. In MFS, this is accomplished by creating a spreadsheet for each item to be forecast. The spreadsheet can be customized to the needs of the organization, and Figure 6.2 provides an example of such a spreadsheet. The columns in the spreadsheet represent the forecast periods (months in this example). Each spreadsheet can display up to 250 periods. Part of these periods display historical demand data, and the remaining periods display forecasts into the future.

The rows in Figure 6.2 represent various information useful to the sales forecaster. Rows 1, 2, and 3 are the Base Line, Trend, and Seasonality components determined by the MFS time-series forecast. The Predictor Effect row (Row 4) is the summed effects that all regression (predictor) variables (shown later in the spreadsheets) have had on the remaining demand history after the time-series forecast was removed (the residual or noise). All four of these rows are summed into the MFS Forecast (Row 5). This is the forecast value that will be sent to the user systems each period if no user adjustments take place.

The next area of the spreadsheet (Figure 6.2) shows rows that either the sales forecaster or the sales forecast manager can use to adjust or override the model forecast. The Sales Forecaster Adjustment row (Row 6) is a relative number that is added to (or subtracted from) the model forecast. This is the typical row in which forecasters enter adjustments to the model forecast. Row 7, Management Adjustment, allows the sales forecasting manager to enter a relative number that adds to (or subtracts from) the combined model and forecaster rows. The distinction between forecaster and management rows is important because MFS keeps track of the forecast error of sales forecaster adjustments separate from the forecast error of sales forecasting management adjustments. These performance tracking rows are shown at the bottom of each spreadsheet. This also is why MFS does not allow someone logged on as a sales forecaster to make changes in the Management Adjustment row and vice versa. Row 8 shows the model forecast with the total of forecaster and management adjustments included.

Finally, in this example, there is a sales Forecast Override row (Row 9 in Figure 6.2). Any value in this row is treated as an absolute forecast setting; that is, if a value is present in this row, then it will be sent to the user systems as the final monthly forecast, regardless of the MFS forecast or any forecaster or management adjustments. The final value that will be sent to the user systems is shown in the Final Forecast row (Row 10). This value is summed quarterly and annually and is placed in the Quarterly Forecast and Annual Forecast rows (Rows 11 and 12, respectively). The Actual Demand row (Row 13) shows the demand values that actually occurred up to the current month. This also is summed quarterly and annually (Rows 14 and 15, respectively).

There are several gauges of the performance of the MFS model, the sales forecaster adjustment, and the management adjustment. These measures give the forecaster a feeling for how much reliance can be placed on the MFS model, whether the model is improving over time, and how the forecaster should be adjusting the model to improve accuracy.

Three measures of accuracy (all discussed in Chapter 2) are used: percentage error (*PE*), *MAPE,* and year-to-date *MAPE* (*YTD MAPE*). The *PE, MAPE,* and *YTD MAPE* for MFS are shown in Rows 16, 17, and 18; for the sales forecaster are shown in Rows 19, 20, and 21; and for management are shown in Rows 22, 23, and 24, respectively.

Row Number		May-97	Jun-97	Jul-97
1	Base Line	200	299	304
2	Trend	5	15	17
3	Seasonality	57	76	−22
4	Predictor Effect	83	103	89
5	MFS Forecast	345	493	388
6	Sales Forecaster Adjustment	35		
7	Management Adjustment	−24		
8	Adjusted Forecast	356	493	388
9	Forecast Override		500	
10	Final Forecast	412	500	388
11	Quarterly Forecast		1,055	
12	Annual Forecast	3,941	4,010	4,077
13	Actual Demand	365	534	
14	Quarterly Demand		1,078	
15	Annual Demand	3,272	3,332	
	MFS:			
16	Percent Error	−5.5%	−7.7%	
17	MAPE	12.0%	11.6%	
18	YTD MAPE	5.6%	5.5%	
	Sales Forecaster:			
19	Percent Error	4.1%	−7.7%	
20	MAPE	11.7%	11.8%	
21	YTD MAPE	4.9%	5.0%	

Figure 6.2. MFS Spreadsheet

Row Number		May-97	Jun-97	Jul-97
	Management:			
22	Percent Error	–2.5%	–7.7%	
23	MAPE	10.3%	10.3%	
24	YTD MAPE	4.5%	4.5%	
25	Price	21	21	22
26	Effect	33	33	27
27	Promotional Expenditures ($000)	1	2	1.4
28	Effect	50	70	62

Figure 6.2. Continued

The next rows in the spreadsheet (Rows 25-28 in Figure 6.2) are occupied by up to 10 regression variables and their associated predictor effects. These are the data that are used by the regression analysis to forecast the time-series residual. The summed effect across all predictor variables is placed in the predictor effect row near the top of the spreadsheet (Row 4).

Because each SKUL has a fully functional spreadsheet within a Windows environment, all the features that an experienced user would expect to find in a spreadsheet are available. However, several additional features are provided that are important to forecasting.

The notepad. This is a simple word processor used to keep notes on why sales forecast adjustments or changes have been made to a particular spreadsheet. Each spreadsheet has a unique notepad attached that can contain up to 30 pages of text. This feature augments the qualitative forecasting process.

Conversions. A conversion button is available that can convert a spreadsheet with forecasts in units (something production typically wants) to dollars (something often needed by marketing, sales, and finance), to cubic volume (something often needed by distribution center managers), or to weight (something often needed by transportation planning).

Because these different areas may need the forecast at different forecast levels, the spreadsheet can be aggregated up or broken down to any level in the "forecasting hierarchy" that is defined by the company. For example, a forecasting hierarchy may go from SKUL to SKU, to product, to product line, to division, to corporate. MFS allows the sales forecaster to analyze and make changes at any of these levels with the changes reconciled with the other levels.

Graphs. A number of graphs are available to assist the sales forecaster in qualitatively forecasting and in analyzing forecasting performance. These include graphic comparisons of (1) sales forecasters' forecasts versus actual demand, (2) MFS forecasts versus actual demand, (3) management-adjusted forecasts versus actual demand, (4) sales forecasters' forecasts versus MFS forecasts, (5) sales forecasters' forecasts versus management-adjusted forecasts, (6) actual demand, (7) sales forecasters' forecasts versus MFS forecasts versus actual demand, (8) *PE,* (9) *MAPE,* and (10) *YTD MAPE.*

To make the process of adjusting forecasts easier, Graph 7 (the sales forecasters' forecasts versus MFS forecasts versus actual demand graph) allows the forecaster to "click and pull" the forecast. In other words, rather than having to enter forecast adjustments in each future period of the spreadsheet, the forecaster can use the cursor with this graph to reshape (draw) the forecast into a line that the forecaster believes is more accurate. When this process is completed, MFS calculates the actual values from the new line and enters them in the forecast override row of the spreadsheet. In this manner, the forecaster can enter adjustments directly into the spreadsheet or enter values that visually seem more accurate.

New product forecasting. MFS allows for "looks like" forecasting of new products. This feature allows the user to specify for a new product that the demand for the first year will look like that for another product, an aggregate of several products, or a line drawn on the screen by the user. MFS will use this "looks like" forecast until one of the time-series techniques has sufficient data to produce more accurate forecasts.

Reports. MFS can be customized to present any number of reports on forecasting performance. For purposes of illustration, one company using MFS has five reports customized to its needs. The *general purpose report* can be customized at the user's discretion and is used primarily for preparing presentations and measuring system activity. The *regression variable assignment report* details which regression variables were selected for a specific product. The *sales forecaster usage report* documents which spreadsheets were accessed by forecasters in any given period; it is a measure of sales forecaster analysis activity. The *new part number models report* describes new products that have been introduced recently and the forecasting approaches presently used to forecast them. The *MAPE counter report* lists products in descending order by the *MAPE*'s that have been achieved.

MFS Systems

Figure 6.3 illustrates the interaction of corporate systems with MFS necessary to achieve Principle 1. For each forecast period, historical information is downloaded from the corporate MIS to the personal computer on which MFS is operating. MFS automatically makes the time-series and regression forecasts and updates the spreadsheets for each forecast item (thus accomplishing Principles 3, 4, 5, and 6). Forecasters can then access each spreadsheet and make adjustments to the MFS forecasts or simply not access a spreadsheet and accept the MFS automatic forecast. Reports and graphs can be viewed and printed, and management can adjust any forecasts deemed appropriate.

When this process is completed, the final forecast is uploaded to the corporate MIS for distribution to all the systems illustrated in Figure 6.1. Throughout the forecasting process, users of the sales forecasts (and suppliers and customers, if the company wishes) also can access the sales forecasting system and provide input to the development of the forecasts.

As an aspect of Principle 2, the MFS system can consist of a single personal computer performing all forecasts or a network of computers connected by a local area network with each computer having certain forecast items assigned to it. In total, this forecasting system allows for historical data storage in the data warehouse and within MFS, allows personal computers to be used for what they do best (analysis), and provides a coordinated forecasting system with specific data maintenance, forecasting, and reporting assignments well defined within the organization.

Sales Forecasting Systems: Summary

In this chapter, we have presented seven principles that should be followed by any organization in its sales forecasting system. To the degree that a company can implement all of these principles, the sales forecasting system will become a valuable tool to the sales forecaster rather than a hindrance. Although many systems exist that, to various degrees, accomplish these principles, one par-

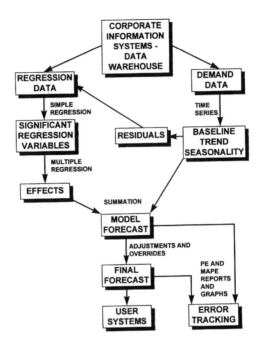

Figure 6.3. MFS Systems Flow
NOTE: MFS = MULTICASTER Forecasting System; PE = percentage error; MAPE = mean absolute
percent error.

ticular system was presented here as an example of how all seven principles
can be accomplished.

These seven principles (and much of the rest of what is included in this
book, for that matter) were developed through our extensive work with
companies in the area of sales forecasting management and the information
we have gathered through the three phases of the benchmarking studies. To
share more fully all the insights we gained from these studies, the next two
chapters are devoted to discussing Phases 1 and 2 (Chapter 7) and Phase 3
(Chapter 8) of the benchmarking studies.

Note

1. Developed by John T. Mentzer in conjunction with JTM and Associates, Inc.

References

Brown, R. G., & Meyer, R. F. (1961). The fundamental theorem of exponential smoothing. *Operations Research, 9,* 673-685.

Mentzer, J. T. (1988, Fall). Forecasting with adaptive extended exponential smoothing. *Journal of the Academy of Marketing Science, 16,* 62-70.

Mentzer, J. T., & Schroeter, J. (1993, Fall). Multiple forecasting system at Brake Parts, Inc. *Journal of Business Forecasting, 12,* 5-9.

Trigg, D. W., & Leach, A. G. (1967). Exponential smoothing with an adaptive response rate. *Operational Research Quarterly, 18,* 53-59.

Verity, J. W. (1996, October 21). Clearing the cobwebs from the stockroom. *Business Week,* p. 140.

Winters, P. R. (1960). Forecasting sales by exponentially weighted moving averages. *Management Science, 6,* 324-342.

CHAPTER 7

Benchmarking Studies:
The Surveys

*T*he impetus for the benchmarking studies was borne
primarily out of frustration. In the 1970s and early
1980s, it seemed that every time we worked with a
company, the question got asked, "What are other
companies doing?" This question usually was aimed at
what techniques were being used or what level of
accuracy was being achieved, but we always had to
answer with what the dozen or so companies with which
we worked at that time were doing. Of course, the
response was always, "That's fine, but what are other
companies [besides these few] doing?"

After being asked this repeatedly, we decided to find
out; thus, the benchmarking studies were born, although
we did not call them benchmarking studies back then
because the term had not yet been invented (we were
doing benchmarking before we knew what to call it).
What is now called Phase 1 of the benchmarking studies,
conducted in the early 1980s, was a mail survey
completed by 157 companies that primarily dealt with
what techniques companies were using, the accuracy they
were achieving, and their satisfaction with the techniques.

Ten years later, Dwight Thomas at AT&T approached
us and asked us to repeat the Phase 1 study to see how

things had changed. We agreed but told Thomas that our thinking about sales forecasting management had changed as well; we wanted to look not only at techniques but also at forecasting systems and management and the effect of all three on accuracy and satisfaction. This mail survey of 208 companies became Phase 2 of the benchmarking studies.

It is the results of these first two phases that are addressed in this chapter. Phase 3, the in-depth analyses of 20 companies, will be discussed in Chapter 8.

Incidentally, Phase 4 is what has come to be called sales forecast audits, in which we work with individual companies to assess their performance in sales forecasting management against the Phase 3 benchmark companies. Because this phase still is in progress, the results cannot be presented until a later edition of this book. (Our marketing side could not resist putting in a "teaser" for a later edition.)

This chapter discusses the results of Phases 1 and 2 of the benchmarking studies. We begin this discussion by reviewing other studies besides Phases 1 and 2 that also have assessed the state of the art of sales forecasting. Because part of Phase 2 was a replication of Phase 1 10 years later, we follow this description of the literature with a comparison of the results from Phases 1 and 2. Because much of what we learned in Phase 2 was new, we then provide the new findings, in particular, an examination of a question many executives have asked us: "What is the difference between forecasting for consumer markets and forecasting for industrial markets?"

Studies Prior to Phase 1

Phase 1 built on previous studies (Conference Board, 1970, 1971; Dalrymple, 1975; Pan, Nichols, & Joy, 1977; Reichard, 1966; "Sales Forecasting," 1967; Wheelwright & Clarke, 1976) (see Table 7.1) to examine the relationship between sales forecasting and the issues of technique familiarity, satisfaction, usage, and application. These four Phase 1 issues were characterized as follows:

TABLE 7.1 Surveys on Sales Forecasting Practices Prior to Phase 1

	Reichard	Sales Management	National Conference Board	National Conference Board	Dalrymple	Wheelright and Clarke	Pan, Nichols, and Joy
Year of publication	1966	1967	1970	1971	1975	1976	1977
Year of survey	Not reported	Not reported	Not reported	Not reported	1975	1975	1974
Sample size (number of firms responding)	126	182	161	93	175	127	139
Population	Leading business firms	Not reported	Conference Board's marketing executives panel	Primarily companies with fewer than 2,000 employees in United States and Canada	Midwestern businesspeople	Fortune 500 firms	Fortune 500 firms
Response rate (percentage)	42	Not reported	Not reported	Not reported	35	25	55
Representativeness of sample	Not claimed to be representative	Not reported	Not reported	Not reported	Claimed to be representative	Not claimed to be representative	Some data given to indicate representative
Type of instrument used	Mail questionnaire	Not reported	Mail questionnaire	Mail questionnaire	Mail questionnaire	Mail questionnaire	Mail questionnaire

1. Familiarity: how familiar executives are with various forecasting techniques and what avenues are used to learn about new methods and applications
2. Satisfaction: how satisfied managers are with using different forecasting techniques
3. Usage: which forecasting techniques are most commonly used for different time horizons and forecast levels
4. Application: the decision making to which forecasts are applied, the criteria used to evaluate forecasts, and the rate of adoption of new techniques

As shown in Table 7.2, the results of Phase 1 (Mentzer & Cox, 1984a, 1984b) received general support from subsequent studies by Fildes and Lusk (1984), Sparkes and McHugh (1984), Dalrymple (1987), Wilson and Daubek (1989), and Drury (1990). However, Fildes and Lusk (1984) reported greater practitioner familiarity with Box-Jenkins (open-model time-series [OMTS]) analysis, whereas Dalrymple (1987) and Wilson and Daubek (1989) found increased application of computer-based forecasting.

Between Phases 1 and 2, additional issues associated with sales forecasting were investigated. As shown in Table 7.3, such issues included the evaluation of forecasting performance across business functions (Lowenhar, 1984), the influence of forecasters (Sparkes & McHugh, 1984), software support (Davidson, 1987), academic/experience background (Davidson, 1987), forecaster salary (Davidson, 1987), number of products forecast (Davidson, 1987), needs in forecasting research (Armstrong, 1988), forecasting research interests (Armstrong, 1988), sources of forecast error (Drury, 1990), and forecast improvements needed (Drury, 1990). Interestingly, all subsequent studies continued to overlook the issue of satisfaction, which Phase 1 noted as overlooked prior to 1984. The importance of examining satisfaction is that it "should give an idea of which techniques have been most successful in real world applications" (Mentzer & Cox, 1984a, p. 27; see also Mentzer & Cox, 1984b). Consequently, the replication of Phase 1 was part of the goal of Phase 2 (Kahn & Mentzer, 1994, 1995; Mentzer & Kahn, 1995, 1997). Such a replication effort was valuable for providing better evidence to substantiate the Phase 1 findings and indicate changes in forecasting management over the ensuing decade.

Phase 2 Methodology

A mail survey comprising an eight-page questionnaire, cover letter, and a list of forecasting technique definitions was sent to a random sample of forecasting executives in 478 companies. The questionnaire included measures of

(Text continues on page 159)

TABLE 7.2 Comparison of Phase 1 to Other Surveys on Sales Forecasting Practices

	Phase 1	Fildes and Lusk (1984)	Sparkes and McHugh (1984)	Dalrymple (1987)	Wilson and Daubeck (1989)	Drury (1990)
Population	U.S. forecasting managers	U.S. and U.K. forecasting academics and practitioners	British cost and management accountants	Marketing and forecasting managers	American Marketing Association members	Officers of Canadian companies
Respondents and response rate (percentages in parentheses)	160 (32)	N/A (31)	76 (25)	134 (16)	168 (11)	234 (23)
Methodology	Mail survey	Mail survey	Mail survey	Mail survey	Mail survey	Mail survey
Familiarity	Majority of respondents familiar with all techniques except Box-Jenkins, life cycle analysis, and classical decomposition Techniques learned from (a) conferences, (b) textbooks, and (c) trade journals	Box-Jenkins models well known to respondents U.S. and U.K. responses similar except for Bayesian methods, with which U.K. respondents more familiar	General lack of awareness of Box-Jenkins time series, Delphi method, and cross-impact analysis Bias toward more subjective techniques	Most popular forecasting techniques were sales force composite and jury of executive opinion Most popular extrapolation forecasting method was naive approach Industrial firms have a strong preference for sales force composite methods	Survey and opinion polling judged as the most important method, followed by jury of executive opinion	

Satisfaction	Majority satisfied with regression, exponential smoothing, moving average, trend line analysis, classical decomposition, simulation, jury of executive opinion Majority dissatisfied with Box-Jenkins time series			Management judgment, or a variant thereof, remains highly used (86% of respondents) U.K. firms appear to use more forecasting techniques than do companies in the United States or Canada
Usage	Majority use subjective techniques for short-range forecasts (less than 3 months) Jury of executive opinion favored across all time horizons and corporate levels of forecasts	The more sophisticated the techniques, the lower the level of usage Executive opinion was most widely used by those familiar with it Moving averages rival executive assessments for short-term forecasts No trends found across time horizons	Naive method most popular method for short-range forecasts Identified differences between this study and Mentzer and Cox (1984a, 1984b)	

(continued)

TABLE 7.2 Continued

	Phase 1	Fildes and Lusk (1984)	Sparkes and McHugh (1984)	Dalrymple (1987)	Wilson and Daubeck (1989)	Drury (1990)
Application: accuracy	Accuracy generally decreased as forecast level moved down to individual product forecasts Accuracy decreased significantly as time horizon increased Average accuracy across forecast levels and forecast periods was 85%	Box-Jenkins ranked as most accurate for short lead times, whereas trend analysis ranked first for longer lead times Exponential smoothing considered more accurate than adaptive smoothing Familiar techniques judged more accurate	Executive assessments judged as having an acceptable level of accuracy	Typical 1-month forecast error was 9.5% with a variance of 7.7% Typical 1-year forecast error was 9.9% with a variance of 7.9% Computers, firm size, and use of seasonal adjustments all appeared to reduce forecast error	Multiple regression judged as most accurate, followed by survey and opinion polling Naive models judged as least accurate Strong association between importance and accuracy	
Evaluative criteria	Ease of use top criteria		Ease of use most mentioned			
Management considerations	Production planning and budgeting top application areas			38% of respondents always or frequently combined forecasts	62% of respondents always or usually combined forecasts	
Technology diffusion	Some use of computer modeling			64% of respondents always or frequently used computers	87% of respondents used computers to forecast	

familiarity, satisfaction, usage, and application of forecasting techniques, paralleling those used in Phase 1. In addition, questions about forecasting systems and management were included. The cover letter directed the questionnaire to the manager responsible for the sales forecasting function, asking for his or her participation in the study. Prior to the initial mailing, a pretest was undertaken with forecasting managers from nine companies to check the appearance and comprehensibility of the questionnaire, cover letter, and technique definitions.

Two survey waves provided 208 completed questionnaires for a 43% response rate. This response rate was deemed acceptable in comparison to response rates of the previous studies (see Tables 7.1 and 7.2). A review of business cards enclosed with survey responses confirmed that surveys were completed by forecasting managers.

Analysis revealed no demographic differences between each wave of respondents. The majority of responding firms were consumer products manufacturers. Like Phase 1, there was a slight bias toward larger companies, but the range of corporate demographics indicated a representative sample. On average, responding firms had sales of $1.375 billion (range of $1 million to more than $10 billion), assets of $1.984 billion (range of $1 million to more than $10 billion), and employment of 12,032 individuals (range of less than 100 to 100,000 employees). Geographically, 91% of the responding firms were U.S. firms, with 28% of these coming from the Great Lakes region, 24% from the mideast region, and 20% from the southeast region.

Findings Comparing
Phase 2 to Phase 1

To compare findings of Phase 2 to those of Phase 1, *t* tests on proportions were used. Cases in which statistical differences were identified ($p \leq .05$) suggested possible changes in sales forecasting practices over the ensuing years between Phases 1 and 2.

Familiarity

Similar to Phase 1, moving average, exponential smoothing, straight line projections, and regression remained very familiar techniques (Table 7.4). To reflect emerging forecasting technique trends, two additions to the Phase 1 list of techniques were expert systems and neural networks. However, a majority of respondents in Phase 2 were unfamiliar with neural networks.

(Text continues on page 162)

TABLE 7.3 Other Findings From Past Surveys on Sales Forecasting Practices

	Lowenhar (1984)	*Sparkes and McHugh (1984)*	*Davidson (1987)*	*Armstrong (1988)*	*Drury (1990)*
Population	Sales forecast users and preparers	British cost and management accountants	Sales forecasters of U.S. and Canadian manufacturing firms	Members of the International Institute of Forecasters	Officers of Canadian companies
Respondents and response rate (percentage in parentheses)	32	76 (25)	N/A	113	234 (23)
Methodology	Mail survey	Mail survey	Mail survey	Mail survey	Mail survey

Findings			
Evaluations of forecasting performance across business functions: Departments rated themselves better on accuracy criteria than did other departments rating them	Influence of forecasters: 75% of companies using executive assessment considered their influence to be extensive	Software support: 90% of respondents regularly relied on software for forecasting Academic and experience background: A college degree was found to be most important for sales forecasting Forecaster's salary: Average salary was $33,875, ranging from $17,000 to $60,000 Number of products forecast: Where a bottom-up approach was used, the forecaster was responsible for an average of 1,122 products (range was 100 to 5,000) Where a top-down approach was used, the forecaster was responsible for 40 products on average (range was 1 to 80)	Needs in forecasting research: Wide variety of responses; however, implementation of forecasts was mentioned most frequently Research interests: Strong interest in applications, not only by practitioners but also by academics	Sources of forecast error: Unexpected events was the top reason for forecast error Forecast improvements needed: A top need is for systems and procedures to analyze forecast error

TABLE 7.4 Familiarity

Technique	Sample Size		Percentage Familiar		Percentage Somewhat Familiar		Percentage Not Familiar	
	Phase 1	Phase 2	Phase 1	Phase 2	Phase 1	Phase 2	Phase 1	Phase 2
Qualitative								
Jury of executive opinion	158	204	81*	66*	6*	16*	13	18
Sales force composite	159	203	79	71	5*	14*	16	15
Customer expectations	158	205	73	64	7*	19*	20	17
Quantitative								
Moving average	158	201	85*	92*	7	6	8*	2*
Straight line projection	157	204	82	85	11	11	7	4
Exponential smoothing	157	201	73*	90*	12	6	15*	4*
Regression	157	206	72	78	8	10	20*	12*
Trend line analysis	75	205	67	73	16	16	17	11
Simulation	156	205	55	50	22	26	23	24
Life cycle analysis	153	205	48	50	11*	22*	41*	28*
Decomposition	151	205	42	43	9*	20*	49*	37*
Box-Jenkins (open-model time series)	156	205	26*	38*	9*	23*	65*	39*
Expert systems		204		33		29		38
Neural networks		20		19		23		58

*Statistically different at $p \leq .05$.

The differences in familiarity across the two phases concerned the techniques of jury of executive opinion, sales force composite, customer expectations, moving average, exponential smoothing, regression, life cycle analysis, decomposition, and Box-Jenkins analysis. Surprisingly, respondents in Phase 2 were less familiar with jury of executive opinion than were respondents in Phase 1. However, respondents in Phase 2 were more familiar with exponential smoothing and somewhat more familiar with the techniques of moving average, regression, life cycle analysis, classical decomposition, and, in particular, Box-Jenkins analysis. These findings support the findings of Fildes and Lusk (1984) and suggest that firms have a better understanding of quantitative forecasting techniques than of qualitative techniques.

A second issue of familiarity considered where respondents learned about sales forecasting techniques. As shown in Table 7.5, it appears that forecasters

TABLE 7.5 Where to Learn About Forecasting

		Percentage Important	
Source	Sample Size in Phase 2	Phase 1	Phase 2
Conferences	204	68	59
Books	204	56	65
Trade journals	203	49	59
Consultants	204	38	46
Colleagues	204		65
College courses	204		45
Public seminars	204		35
Company seminar	205		23

rely on the same sources for learning about sales forecasting techniques. However, Phase 2 respondents identified several new sources to learn about sales forecasting techniques. Among these, the majority of respondents identified colleagues as an important source.

Satisfaction

As in Phase 1, only Phase 2 respondents who were familiar with each technique were included in the satisfaction analysis for that technique (Table 7.6). Phase 2 respondents were most satisfied with exponential smoothing (72%), followed by regression (66%) and decomposition (61%). Respondents were most dissatisfied with straight line projections (42%).

As for contrasts, Phase 2 respondents were less satisfied with jury of executive opinion and moving average than were Phase 1 respondents. Phase 2 respondents also were more satisfied with exponential smoothing and somewhat more satisfied with simulation, life cycle analysis, decomposition, and Box-Jenkins analysis. These differences suggest that quantitative techniques are more successful in forecasting today than they were in the 1980s.

In Phase 1, only 7.80% of respondents were familiar with and satisfied with Box-Jenkins analysis. In Phase 2, 16.72% of respondents were familiar and satisfied with this approach. Although this increase probably is indicative of improved Box-Jenkins software, the consistently low level of application and satisfaction led us to give limited treatment in Chapter 3 to Box-Jenkins as an OMTS technique.

TABLE 7.6 Satisfaction

Technique	Sample Size		Percentage Satisfied		Percentage Neutral		Percentage Dissatisfied	
	Phase 1	Phase 2	Phase 1	Phase 2	Phase 1	Phase 2	Phase 1	Phase 2
Qualitative								
Jury of executive opinion	118	131	54*	35*	24*	36*	22	29
Sales force composite	112	140	43	34	25	27	32	39
Customer expectations	95	130	45	46	23	32	32	22
Quantitative								
Moving average	112	179	58*	40*	21*	35*	21	25
Straight line projection	93	169	32	28	31	30	37	42
Exponential smoothing	104	172	60*	72*	19	24	21*	4*
Regression	99	156	67	66	19	29	14*	5*
Trend line analysis	40	14	5	58	48	28	40	15
Simulation	65	100	54	50	18*	42*	28*	8*
Life cycle analysis	52	99	40	36	20*	46*	40*	18*
Decomposition	71	84	55	61	14*	28*	31*	11*
Box-Jenkins (open-model time series)	47	78	30	44	13*	45*	57*	11*
Expert systems		66		45		47		8
Neural networks		37		38		49		13

*Statistically different at $p \leq .05$.

Usage

Table 7.7 reveals statistically significant differences in usage for all given techniques except simulation. The direction of these differences suggests that firms in Phase 2 have a greater tendency to forecast 3 months to 2 years in advance. Phase 1 did not reflect such a tendency.

Table 7.7 also indicates the popularity of techniques across time horizons. In the 3 months to 2 years time horizon, the majority of respondents preferred exponential smoothing (92%), jury of executive opinion (77%), sales force composite (77%), regression (69%), and trend line analysis (57%). In the greater than 2 years time horizon, the majority of respondents preferred jury of executive opinion (55%).

Analysis across forecast levels found few statistically significant differences between Phases 1 and 2 (Table 7.8). This suggests that forecasters are applying techniques to the same forecast levels as they were in 1984. There were only three significant differences: greater use of exponential smoothing

TABLE 7.7 Usage Across Time Horizons (percentages of respondents)

Technique	Less Than 3 Months		3 Months to 2 Years		More Than 2 Years	
	Phase 1	Phase 2	Phase 1	Phase 2	Phase 1	Phase 2
Qualitative						
Jury of executive opinion	37*	4*	42*	77*	38	55
Sales force composite	37*	4*	36*	77*	8*	21*
Customer expectations	25*	5*	24*	38*	12	15
Quantitative						
Moving average	24*	9*	22*	45*	5	11
Straight line projection	13*	5*	16*	35*	10	10
Exponential smoothing	24*	8*	17*	92*	6	16
Regression	14*	4*	36*	69*	28	30
Trend line analysis	21*	2*	28*	57*	21	22
Simulation	4	1	9	6	10	12
Life cycle analysis	1	1	5*	24*	12	18
Decomposition	9*	2*	13*	40*	5	10
Box-Jenkins (open-model time series)	5	2	6*	19*	2	7
Expert systems		1		6		8
Neural networks		2		17		6

NOTE: Sample sizes: Phase 1 = 160; Phase 2 = 186.
*Statistically different at $p \leq .05$.

for corporate-level forecasts, greater use of life cycle analysis for product line forecasts, and less use of customer expectations for product forecasts. Note that the categories of forecast level vary slightly from those used in Phase 1. The categories used in Phase 2 were preferred by managers in the pretest and, thus, were incorporated into the questionnaire.

Application

The overall degree of forecast accuracy (defined in both studies as 1 minus the mean absolute percent error [*MAPE*] experienced) across both phases is almost equivalent, reflecting weighted averages of 85% for Phase 1 and 84% for Phase 2 (see Table 7.9). There is a noticeable difference in accuracy (i.e., greater than 10%) for product forecasts in the greater than 2 years time horizon. This indicates that respondents in Phase 2 are experiencing greater accuracy when forecasting long term for individual products. Although there also is a noticeable difference for corporate-level forecasts in the

TABLE 7.8 Usage Across Forecast Level (percentages of respondents)

Technique	Industry		Corporate		Product Group in Phase 1	Product Line		Product		Stock Keeping Units by Location in Phase 2
	Phase 1	Phase 2	Phase 1	Phase 2		Phase 1	Phase 2	Phase 1	Phase 2	
Qualitative										
Jury of executive opinion	26	26	41	47	32	32	37	22	17	11
Sales force composite	5	5	20	31	25	27	29	24	22	18
Customer expectations	8	5	12	15	18	18	16	23*	12*	10
Quantitative										
Moving average	4	3	9	12	18	19	17	20	20	15
Straight line projection	6	5	10	11	11	10	12	11	12	9
Exponential smoothing	4	8	6*	23*	14	14	28	23	34	25
Regression	18	17	22	26	21	19	24	12	22	16
Trend line analysis	13	9	20	19	20	21	21	22	20	14
Simulation	7	4	9	5	7	4	5	4	3	2
Life cycle analysis	4	8	4	12	4	4*	14*	6	6	3
Decomposition	2	4	4	12	8	7	12	9	14	13
Box-Jenkins (open-model time series)	2	3	3	9	3	2	7	6	5	4
Expert systems		4		4		2		3	2	
Neural networks		3		5		5		6	5	

NOTE: Sample sizes: Phase 1 = 160; Phase 2 = 186.
*Statistically different at $p \leq .05$.

TABLE 7.9 Percent Accuracy

Forecast Level	Less Than 3 Months		3 Months to 2 Years		More Than 2 Years	
	Phase 1	Phase 2	Phase 1	Phase 2	Phase 1	Phase 2
Industry	92	90	89	88	85	87
n	61	1	61	16	50	36
Corporate	93	72	89	90	82	88
n	81	2	89	64	61	42
Product group	90		85		80	
n	89		96		61	
Product line	89	90	84	86	80	88
n	92	4	95	83	60	25
Product	84	82	79	79	74	86
n	96	14	88	89	54	10
Stock keeping units by location		76		75		87
n		17		58		5

NOTE: Weighted averages: Phase 1 = 85; Phase 2 = 84. Weighted average calculated by weighting each cell accuracy by the number responding.

less than 3 months time horizon, the cell's small sample size in Phase 2 prohibits any general conclusions.

In a related question, Phase 2 investigated how firms measured forecast accuracy (see Table 7.10), which Phase 1 did not explore. It was revealed that the majority of respondents relied on *MAPE*. A quarter of respondents relied on mean absolute deviation (*MAD*).

Akin to the findings of Phase 1, the majority of Phase 2 respondents identified accuracy (92%) and credibility (92%) as top criteria for evaluating sales forecasting effectiveness (see Table 7.11). The majority of Phase 2 respondents also identified customer service performance (77%), ease of use (75%), and inventory turns (55%) as criteria for evaluating sales forecasting effectiveness. Interestingly, Phase 2 respondents considered cost (41%) and return on investment (35%) as lesser criteria to evaluate forecasting effectiveness. This suggests that forecasting techniques often are not evaluated based on financial measures.

Conclusions From Comparing Phases 1 and 2

This comparison sought to answer the question, "Have sales forecasting practices changed over the past 10 years?" With regard to the issue of

TABLE 7.10 Measures of Forecast Accuracy

	Number and Percentage of Respondents in Phase 2
Mean absolute percent error	122 (52)
Mean absolute deviation	59 (25)
Mean squared error	23 (10)
Deviation	9 (4)
Percentage error	8 (3)
Forecast ratio	2 (< 1)
Inventory statistic	2 (< 1)
Standard deviation	2 (< 1)
Other	9 (4)

NOTE: Percentages are in parentheses. Some respondents listed more than one measure.

familiarity, forecasting executives are more familiar with quantitative techniques than they were 10 years ago. Practitioners are, in particular, more familiar with the technique of exponential smoothing. Practitioners were less familiar with the qualitative technique of jury of executive opinion than they were 10 years ago. This finding is especially noteworthy in light of other studies indicating higher familiarity with the jury of executive opinion technique (Dalrymple, 1987; Wilson & Daubek, 1989).

Findings concerning satisfaction somewhat parallel findings associated with familiarity. Forecasting executives were more satisfied with exponential smoothing, indicating that exponential smoothing was a more successful technique than it was 10 years ago. Conversely, respondents in Phase 2 were less satisfied with jury of executive opinion, suggesting that it was a less successful technique. Although this would suggest a positive relationship between familiarity and satisfaction, this was not always the case. Respondents in Phase 2 were quite familiar with the technique of moving average but were less satisfied with this technique.

As for usage, Phase 2 respondents appear to be concentrating on sales forecasting in the 3 months to 2 years time horizon. This contrasts with the Phase 1 findings, in which respondents were generally likely to use techniques across all time horizons. The most popular (i.e., greatest degree of usage) forecasting technique was exponential smoothing applied in a 3 months to 2 years time horizon. Within this same time horizon, a majority of respondents also used jury of executive opinion, customer expectations, regression, and trend line analysis. Interestingly, jury of executive opinion was shown to be a

TABLE 7.11 Criteria for Evaluating Sales Forecasting Effectiveness

Criterion	Sample Size in Phase 2	Percentage Important
Accuracy	205	92
Credibility	206	92
Customer service performance	199	77
Ease of use	206	75
Inventory turns	198	55
Amount of data required	205	46
Cost	205	41
Return on investment	199	35

popular technique in this time horizon, as it was in Sparkes and McHugh (1984) and Drury (1990). However, jury of executive opinion reflected less satisfaction than did any of the other four "popular" techniques. This is further evidence that satisfaction is an important factor.

Accuracy still remains a top criterion for evaluating sales forecasting effectiveness. With particular regard to achieved accuracy, the Phase 2 study found little change in the accuracy of forecasting techniques over the past 10 years. This finding suggests that the forecasting techniques discussed in the first few chapters of this book will not, alone, necessarily improve accuracy. Managers should consider other issues associated with forecasting including the forecast environment, data collected, computer systems used, and management of the forecasting process.

Although part of the intent of Phase 2 was to assess changes in sales forecasting practices since the early 1980s, it also provides a new baseline or benchmark for sales forecasting practices. With this benchmark goal in mind, a number of questions were asked in Phase 2 that were new since Phase 1. It is these results that are discussed next.

Phase 2 Results

Although the previous studies we reviewed in Tables 7.1, 7.2, and 7.3 examined sales forecasting technique issues, no study prior to Phase 2 had looked at the broader sales forecasting issues regarding the types of systems used to support the sales forecasting techniques or how the sales forecasting function is managed. This is surprising given that (as we discuss throughout this book) forecasting systems and management have as much, if not more, potential to affect the ultimate effectiveness of sales forecasts as does the proper selection of the forecasting technique.

Thus, although the systems within which sales forecasts are developed and the management processes by which the role of sales forecasting is defined are integral parts of the sales forecasting function, previous surveys of sales forecasting have largely ignored these topics. This led to the questions that drove part of Phase 2: "What are the characteristics of sales forecasting systems and management approaches to sales forecasting?" and "What is the level of management satisfaction with these systems and management approaches?" To address the two components of the research question, the findings are divided into the two main areas of interest: sales forecasting systems and sales forecasting management.

Sales Forecasting Systems

Companies on average employed 1.82 sales forecasting computer systems. In other words, many companies have more than a single computer system for developing sales forecasts. In 30% of the responding companies, these systems were contained entirely on personal computers; in 29%, they were contained entirely on mainframes. More often, however, these systems consisted of both a personal computer system and a mainframe system (41% of respondents). This probably is indicative of the proliferation of personal computer-based sales forecasting software packages, combined with the availability of much of the necessary information still residing on the mainframe.

The majority of respondents' systems were not on distributed data networks (55%). This indicates a lack of electronic integration of the sales forecasting function with the various functions using the sales forecasts (marketing, sales, finance, production, and logistics) and the function providing information (management information system [MIS]). This finding was reinforced by the fact that almost half (44%) of the responding companies did not have electronic connections between forecasting systems and the production and inventory planning (distribution requirements planning [DRP]/materials requirements planning [MRP]) systems and that more than one third (36%) were not even electronically linked to the MIS. These findings indicate the potential for "islands of analysis." As discussed in Chapter 6, islands of analysis exist when the different areas involved in the sales forecasting process make their calculations/analyses on separate systems and, therefore, may inadvertently not share all this information with other systems. Islands of analysis often lead to contradictory assumptions, analyses, and results.

For the companies whose sales forecasting systems were electronically linked to the MIS, less than half of the respondents had access to the type of information that could be used for regression-based forecast modeling (see Table 7.12). In fact, the only information that was electronically available in a majority of companies was sales history and/or demand history. Particularly disturbing were the number of companies trying to forecast with no access to market research information (89% of responding companies).

Computer systems software was divided between commercial software (48%) and software that was custom built for the company either internally (41%) or by an outside developer (11%). This indicates that about half of the responding companies find software that is customized to their particular sales forecasting needs to be more effective than generalized software. This provides growing support for the idea expressed in Chapter 6 of letting the tool fit the problem instead of the other way around.

All of these findings, taken in aggregate, indicate a typical forecasting function in which a personal computer is available, some access to the mainframe is possible, but the type of information readily available for analysis is limited. Perhaps more important, electronic access to the users of the forecast is severely limited, and, in an alarmingly large number of companies, no vehicle for electronically transmitting the resultant forecasts to the users is possible. Clearly, the forecasting function has a long way to go in the area of computer systems integration.

Of particular interest were two recent innovations in channels of distribution that have been touted as providing more accurate and timely information to the forecasting system (Kahn & Mentzer, 1996): electronic data interchange (EDI) and direct customer forecasts. Responses, however, indicate that most companies' sales forecasting systems do not have access to EDI from suppliers (82%) or customers (69%). Also, most companies (77%) do not receive forecasts directly from customers (i.e., the customers' forecasts of what their customers plan to buy). These results would indicate that although there does seem to be potential for improving channel-wide forecast accuracy through EDI and direct customer forecast information, these innovations currently are not being realized.

Another aspect of forecasting systems that has considerable potential for improving forecast accuracy is the simple expedient of making it easy for forecasters to adjust technique forecasts based on their qualitative judgments. This potential is being realized in most (76%) of the responding companies.

The departments most likely to make changes to the forecast were marketing, sales, planning, and product management (See Table 7.13). Not surprisingly, these results largely follow the functions with knowledge of

TABLE 7.12 Types of Information Input From Management Information
Systems to the Sales Forecasting System

	Number and Percentage of Respondents
Sales	94 (72)
Demand	77 (59)
Orders	58 (44)
Price changes	49 (33)
New product introduction information	36 (27)
Advertising/promotional information	25 (19)
Competitive information	17 (13)
Market research information	15 (11)
Economic information	14 (11)
Other	11 (8)

NOTE: Percentages are in parentheses. Data are based on 131 companies responding to the question. There are multiple responses.

TABLE 7.13 Functional Personnel With Access to the Sales Forecasting
System to Make Changes to the Forecasts

	Number and Percentage of Respondents
Marketing	95 (49)
Sales	61 (31)
Planning	53 (27)
Product management	50 (26)
Logistics	46 (24)
Finance	18 (9)
Production	15 (8)
Research and development	2 (1)

NOTE: Percentages are in parentheses. Data are based on 194 companies responding to the question. There are multiple responses.

customers and markets. However, combined with the earlier findings of limited electronic integration, this access apparently is interpersonal. These results in combination seem to indicate that ease of access for other functional areas means that they can tell the forecaster the changes they want made but that they cannot directly enter these changes into the sales forecasting system.

Various functional areas may need ongoing information on forecasts and forecasting accuracy (i.e., the ability to review the forecasts being developed), even if these individuals are not actually allowed to make changes to the forecasts. In the responding companies, the departments allowed to review but not make changes to the forecasts most often included marketing, finance, production, sales, and planning (See Table 7.14). Again, these typically are personnel with a need for ongoing knowledge of the developing sales forecasts. However, it is interesting to note that for every function listed in Tables 7.13 and 7.14, more companies allow these functions review access to their forecast systems (Table 7.14) than allow actual access to make changes (Table 7.13). This would indicate that most companies see these functions as users of, rather than as developers of, the sales forecasts.

Overall, respondents were neutral about their satisfaction with their existing sales forecasting systems; the average response was 4.20 on a scale from 1 (*extremely dissatisfied*) to 7 (*extremely satisfied*) with 4 being neutral (see Table 7.15). This, again, could be a function of system improvements brought over the years by improved personal computer-based software but still limited information and functional area electronic access.

Sales Forecasting Management

To investigate how the sales forecasting process is managed, respondents were asked which of the four fundamental approaches to forecasting management outlined in Chapter 6 were used by their companies:

1. In the first approach, each functional department involved in the sales forecasting process develops its own forecast for its own internal uses, independently of all other departments. Because this is a self-contained approach, it is called the *independent* approach. This is a narrow approach to forecasting that ignores the synergistic advantages of input from various perspectives. Furthermore, it lacks any form of coordination of plans based on the sales forecasts.

2. In the second managerial approach, one department is assigned the responsibility for developing the sales forecast, and all other departments must use the resultant forecast. Because the responsibility for the forecast is held in one department, this is called the *concentrated* approach. Although it solves some of the coordination problems of the Independent approach, the concentrated approach gives the sales forecast a definite bias toward the orientation of the department developing it. For example, if residing in logistics, the forecast will tend to be stock keeping unit by location (SKUL) oriented. If residing in marketing, the forecast will tend to be product line oriented. If residing in sales, the forecast will tend to be sales territory oriented. If

TABLE 7.14 Functional Personnel With Access to the Sales Forecasting System to Review, but not Make Changes to, the Forecasts

	Number and Percentage of Respondents
Marketing	128 (66)
Finance	120 (62)
Production	111 (57)
Sales	105 (54)
Planning	104 (53)
Logistics	97 (50)
Product management	90 (46)
Engineering	34 (17)
Research and development	20 (10)

NOTE: Percentages are in parentheses. Data are based on 195 companies responding to the question. There are multiple responses.

TABLE 7.15 Satisfaction With Existing Sales Forecasting System

Scale	*Number of Responses*	*Percentage*
1 = very dissatisfied	13	6.0
2	22	11.0
3	30	14.5
4 = neutral	33	16.0
5	70	34.0
6	30	14.5
7 = very satisfied	8	4.0

NOTE: Average = 4.20, SD = 1.54.

residing in production, the forecast will tend to be stock keeping unit (SKU) oriented. If residing in finance, the forecast will tend to be dollars oriented. Of course, each of these functional areas has a different time horizon orientation that will, in turn, affect the orientation of the forecast.

3. In the third managerial approach to sales forecasting, for each product grouping, each functional area makes its own independent forecast, but representatives from each functional area come together each forecasting period to reach a negotiated final forecast. Thus, this is called the *negotiated* approach and overcomes some of the bias problems of the concentrated approach. However, the fact that each function brings its own orientation does create an environment of politics that can bias the results.

4. Finally, in the fourth approach, for each product grouping, a committee is formed with representatives from various functional areas, and one person is placed in charge of the forecast committee. This committee develops forecasts that have the input of all functional areas. This is called the *consensus* approach and overcomes some of the bias problems of the concentrated approach as well as some of the political problems of the negotiated approach. Although superior sales forecasts can result from this management approach, it often requires more personnel resources and more interfunctional coordination than is possible within many companies.

It is a measure of the improved sophistication of sales forecasting management that few companies still follow an independent approach (see Table 7.16). However, almost half of the responding companies have one department responsible for developing sales forecasts (a concentrated approach). A number of companies (more than half) are trying some form of the negotiated or consensus approach; those companies that are indicate they are more satisfied with the results (see Table 7.17).

Managerial responsibility for inventory (having it available for customer access but not overstocking) should affect involvement in, and responsibility for, development of tactical forecasts. As indicated in Table 7.18, the production department usually is responsible for raw material inventory (65% of responding firms) and work-in-process inventory (78% of responding firms). Logistics was designated as responsible for finished goods inventory for 46% of responding companies, followed by production with 32%. Combined with earlier results on access to the sales forecasting system (Table 7.13) and review of the sales forecasts (Table 7.14), these results indicate that production, planning, and logistics responsibility for inventory does not seem to create a great need to have access to the sales forecasting system, but it does create a strong review-based involvement in the development of the forecast.

With regard to the role that management plays in the forecasting process, middle managers appear to actually be involved in developing the sales forecasts in a majority of companies (68%), followed by 23% of the responding companies in which middle managers only review the forecasts and 6% in which they only approve the developed forecasts. This "hands-on" involvement indicates a recognition of the importance of sales forecasting to middle management planning and a recognition of the value of middle management qualitative input to the development of the forecasts. Such recognition appears to carry over to upper management, which has actual involvement in 27% of the companies, review responsibilities in 27%, and approval responsibilities in 38%. However, in many responding companies (34%), the planning process is backward; that is, the business plans are used to develop the forecasts

TABLE 7.16 Approaches Used to Develop Sales Forecasts

	Number and Percentage of Respondents
1. Each department develops and uses its own sales forecasts (independent approach)	25 (12.2)
2. One department is responsible for developing sales forecasts (concentrated approach)	97 (47.3)
3. Each department develops its own forecasts, but a committee coordinates a final forecast (negotiated approach)	59 (28.8)
4. A forecast committee/task force is responsible for developing sales forecasts (consensus approach)	55 (26.8)

NOTE: Percentages are in parentheses. Some of the 205 companies responding to this question selected more than one approach; that is, they were using different approaches in different areas of their companies.

instead of the other way around. Apparently, management in these companies is more concerned with the business plans than with the sales forecasts, even though the latter should drive the former.

To obtain an overall picture of the sales forecasting management process in responding companies, five statements were presented to respondents, who rated each statement on a scale of 1 (*strongly disagree*) to 5 (*strongly agree*). A significant majority of respondents agreed that their forecasts were prepared via a formal/routine process with clear and precise instructions (Table 7.19). However, a significant majority disagreed with the statement that forecasting performance is formally evaluated and rewarded. A significant number of respondents also disagreed with the statement that their sales forecasting budgets were sufficient. Taken in combination, this produces some interesting conclusions. Apparently, a large number of companies have a formal and documented sales forecasting process, but this process lacks the fundamental aspect of performance measurement. Such a deficiency ignores the management maxim we introduced in Chapter 2: "What gets measured gets rewarded and what gets rewarded gets done." If sales forecasting performance is not measured or rewarded, then there is little motivation to improve it. Combined with an insufficient budget, these results alone have more potential to negatively affect forecast performance than does the entire process of technique selection.

As an example of the impact of such a lack of motivational incentive to improve forecasting effectiveness, a large number of responding companies (28%) still use shipments as their best measure of demand. Although ship-

TABLE 7.17 Satisfaction With Approach to Developing Sales Forecasts

	n	Percentage Dissatisfied	Percentage Neutral	Percentage Satisfied
1. Independent approach	25	44.0	28.0	28.0
2. Concentrated approach	96	22.9	17.7	59.4*
3. Negotiated approach	59	25.4	13.6	61.0*
4. Consensus approach	53	13.2	17.0	69.8*

*$p < .05$.

TABLE 7.18 Department Responsible for Inventory (numbers and percentages)

	Raw Materials	Work in Process	Finished Goods
Production	95 (65)	110 (78)	51 (32)
Planning	38 (26)	32 (23)	45 (29)
Logistics	25 (17)	24 (17)	73 (46)
Product management	16 (11)	11 (8)	41 (26)
Purchasing	9 (6)	—	—
Research and development	9 (6)	4 (3)	6 (4)
Finance	8 (6)	7 (5)	15 (10)
Engineering	5 (3)	10 (7)	4 (3)
Marketing	3 (2)	6 (4)	46 (30)
Sales	3 (2)	2 (1)	42 (27)
Number of responding firms	146	141	158

NOTE: Percentages are in parentheses.

ments clearly are an inadequate surrogate for demand (shipments data do not capture the amount of demand that the company received but could not fulfill due to inadequate previous forecasts, that is, shipments equal demand minus lost sales), the lack of incentive to improve the sales forecasting process by gathering this more valuable demand information exists in more than one fourth of the responding companies.

In terms of the qualifications for a sales forecaster (Table 7.20), respondents identified forecasting experience as most important (77%). More than half of the respondents also identified experience in statistics (64%), computer

TABLE 7.19 Statements About Company Sales Forecasting Process

	n	Percentage Disagree	Percentage Neutral	Percentage Agree
The forecast is prepared via a formal/routine process with clear and precise instructions	204	27	18	55*
Forecasting performance is formally evaluated and rewarded	205	56*	19	25
The final sales forecast is believed by all concerned	204	40	29	31
The sales forecasting budget is sufficient	201	38*	39	23
There are enough people assigned to develop the sales forecasts	205	37	21	42
Too much money is spent in this company to manage around forecasting error	202	37	27	36

$*p < .05.$

systems (61%), marketing (56%), and logistics (51%) as important. A significant number of respondents also viewed experience in sales and managing inventory as important. Although respondents were provided with the opportunity to mention other important qualifications, no others were listed.

Forecasting in Consumer Markets Versus Industrial Markets

Consumer markets and industrial markets are inherently different. Consumer markets encompass individual consumers and families/households "that buy or acquire goods and services for personal consumption" (Kotler, 1991, p. 196). Conversely, industrial markets consist of organizations "that acquire goods and services to use in the production of other products or services that are sold, rented, or supplied to others" (Kotler, 1991).

These inherent differences influence the market structure characteristics of firms in each of these markets. Firms in industrial markets normally have fewer buyers, whereas firms in consumer markets contend with greater numbers of buyers. Industrial market firms reflect a closer relationship between customers and sellers because close relationships are critical for maintaining customers in such a small customer base. Close customer relationships are more difficult in consumer markets due to the sheer volume of customers.

TABLE 7.20 Sales Forecaster Qualification Importance

	n	Percentage Unimportant	Percentage Neutral	Percentage Important
Forecasting experience	204	7	16	77*
Statistics experience	202	17	19	64*
Computer systems experience	203	14	25	61*
Marketing experience	203	17	27	56*
Logistics experience	202	25	24	51*
Sales experience	203	22	32	46*
Inventory experience	201	31	23	46*

*$p < .05$.

Industrial market firms also experience inelastic demand in the short run, whereas consumer market firms traditionally reflect more demand elasticity. Demand in industrial markets frequently is derived from demand in consumer markets. Therefore, the effects of short-term fluctuations in consumer demand can be multiplied back up the channel.

Due to varying market structure characteristics, firms in consumer markets and industrial markets typically differ in their marketing activities. Consumer market firms often rely more on broad-based advertising across various media outlets. Industrial market firms have more specific advertising aimed at fewer outlets and tend to rely on sales forces because there are fewer customers who can be more easily identified and directly contacted. Industrial market firms also handle larger order quantities that require greater storage capacity. Consumer market firms contend with smaller quantities that often must be delivered faster, thereby requiring operations that can handle greater throughput. Because of higher volume, industrial market firms offer quantity discounts and negotiate price per contract. Pricing in consumer market firms typically is more stable because the firms themselves often set the prices to be offered.

Because of varying business practices as a consequence of varying market patterns, it often has been suggested that sales forecasting practices also differ between firms in consumer markets and those in industrial markets. In fact, there is some evidence for such differences.

Dalrymple (1987) found that industrial market firms have a stronger preference for the sales force composite method than do consumer firms. He speculated that the close relationship between industrial salespeople and their customers encourages industrial firms to use their sales forces to forecast. Dalrymple also found industrial market firms to have greater preferences for leading indicators, econometric models, and multiple regression techniques.

Herbig, Milewicz, and Golden (1993) supported Dalrymple's (1987) findings by reporting that industrial market firms prefer to use the sales force composite method more than do consumer market firms. These authors also found that industrial market firms rated their forecasting processes as easier to understand, whereas consumer market firms rated their processes as harder to comprehend. Interestingly, consumer market firms expressed the belief that their forecasting processes were more accurate, whereas industrial market firms felt that their forecasting processes were less accurate.

Along with the issues of technique usage and accuracy, other conceivable differences could distinguish the forecasting practices of consumer market firms versus industrial market firms. Firms may differ on technique familiarity as a result of standard sales forecasting practices within consumer markets versus industrial markets. Satisfaction with techniques also may differ across firms in each market as a result of greater success in predicting market fluctuations; those techniques that can adapt quickly to market fluctuations will provide more satisfaction to consumer markets because demand fluctuates more rapidly at the individual consumer level. In addition, there may be differences in the roles of EDI, DRP, MRP, and MIS in the forecasting process and how these technologies affect the forecasting process. It is believed that EDI, MRP, DRP, and MIS should be more prevalent in consumer markets because the volatility of consumer markets places a premium on demand foresight.

Phase 2 Findings

To compare the responses of consumer market firms and industrial market firms in Phase 2, t tests were used. Those responses with statistical levels of $p \leq .05$ were deemed significant to highlight as key differences between firms in consumer markets versus industrial markets.

Overall, there were few differences between firms in consumer markets and those in industrial markets. It appears that (except where otherwise noted) technique familiarity, satisfaction, usage, and accuracy are independent of market type. It does, however, appear that the information technologies of EDI, MRP, DRP, and MIS are used to varying degrees in forecasting for consumer markets versus industrial markets. Results of the t test analyses for each of these issues are discussed in the following subsections.

Technique Familiarity

As shown in Table 7.21, there were three significant differences between consumer firms and industrial firms regarding technique familiarity. Two of these differences indicate that forecasting executives in consumer firms are significantly more familiar with straight line projections than are their counterparts in industrial firms. A third difference indicates that significantly more consumer firms are somewhat familiar with Box-Jenkins analysis than are industrial firms. However, no difference was found between the numbers of consumer firms and industrial firms that were unfamiliar or familiar with Box-Jenkins analysis. Thus, this difference, although statistically significant, seems somewhat minor.

Technique Satisfaction

As shown in Table 7.22, three significant differences also were found across consumer firms and industrial firms with regard to technique satisfaction. Two of these differences indicate that forecasting executives in consumer firms are much more dissatisfied with the sales force composite technique than are their counterparts in industrial firms. This finding corresponds to the findings of Dalrymple (1987), who noted that sales force composite forecasting was more prevalent in industrial firms. In light of greater satisfaction, it appears that the sales force composite technique is more successful in industrial settings. As also indicated by Dalrymple (1987), this probably is the result of more direct and frequent contact between most industrial firms and their customers compared to that between most consumer market firms and their customers.

A third difference indicated that industrial firms were more satisfied with trend line analysis. It is possible that industrial market trends may be more stable and lasting than consumer market trends and, thus, may be the reason for the superior success of trend line analysis in industrial firms.

Technique Usage

Consumer firms and industrial firms appear to contrast on their usage of forecasting techniques across time horizons. However, they do not appear to contrast much across forecast levels.

Most usage differences between consumer firms and industrial firms occurred in the 3 months to 2 years time horizon (see Table 7.23). Consumer firms relied on regression analysis, jury of executive opinion, decomposition,

TABLE 7.21 Familiarity

Technique	Sample Size Consumer	Sample Size Industrial	Percentage Familiar Consumer	Percentage Familiar Industrial	Percentage Somewhat Familiar Consumer	Percentage Somewhat Familiar Industrial	Percentage Not Familiar Consumer	Percentage Not Familiar Industrial
Qualitative								
Customer expectations	108	65	64	65	22	15	14	20
Jury of executive opinion	107	65	68	63	15	12	17	25
Sales force composite	108	64	71	67	17	14	12	19
Quantitative								
Box-Jenkins (open-model time series)	108	65	35	39	28*	15*	37	46
Decomposition	108	65	49	38	18	20	33	42
Expert systems	107	65	34	26	31	31	35	43
Exponential smoothing	106	63	88	89	7	5	5	6
Life cycle analysis	108	65	52	45	23	25	25	30
Moving average	108	62	92	90	5	7	3	3
Neural networks	105	64	21	14	26	22	53	64
Regression	109	65	75	76	11	12	14	12
Simulation	108	65	47	48	28	26	25	26
Straight line projection	108	64	89*	77*	10	12	1*	11*
Trend line analysis	108	65	71	74	17	14	12	12

NOTE: Consumer = consumer market firms; Industrial = industrial market firms.
*Statistically different at $p \leq .05$.

straight line projections, and life cycle analysis more than did industrial firms. Conversely, industrial firms relied on sales force composite and Box-Jenkins analysis more than did consumer firms, although neither group had a large number using Box-Jenkins analysis. These findings, again, support Dalrymple's (1987) conclusion that industrial firms rely heavily on their sales forces for forecasting.

In the less than 3 months time horizon, significantly more consumer firms used regression analysis and straight line projections (although, again, the numbers were small). Because these techniques also were found to be preferred by consumer firms in the 3 months to 2 years time horizon and in the

TABLE 7.22 Satisfaction

Technique	Sample Size		Percentage Satisfied		Percentage Neutral		Percentage Dissatisfied	
	Consumer	Industrial	Consumer	Industrial	Consumer	Industrial	Consumer	Industrial
Qualitative								
Customer expectations	69	40	40	57	35	28	25	15
Jury of executive opinion	72	38	35	34	36	40	29	26
Sales force composite	76	41	26*	49*	24	24	50*	27*
Quantitative								
Box-Jenkins (open-model time series)	38	25	42	48	45	36	13	16
Decomposition	50	23	62	61	24	35	14	4
Expert systems	37	16	46	38	49	50	5	12
Exponential smoothing	91	51	70	73	23	25	7	2
Life cycle analysis	54	28	37	36	48	46	15	18
Moving average	98	54	39	46	36	30	25	24
Neural networks	21	9	24	56	62	33	14	11
Regression	80	47	66	68	29	28	5	4
Simulation	50	29	52	55	36	41	12	4
Straight line projection	93	47	27	28	30	30	43	42
Trend line analysis	75	46	41*	65*	44	31	15	4

NOTE: Consumer = consumer market firms; Industrial = industrial market firms. Some familiar respondents did not provide satisfaction ratings.
*Statistically different at $p \leq .05$.

greater than 2 years time horizon (although not significantly), it appears that regression analysis and straight line projections are more favored by consumer firms. This finding contrasts with that of Dalrymple (1987), who found regression to be more popular with industrial firms. It is possible that regression is becoming more popular with consumer firms due to greater accessibility of consumer demographic databases and more firms specializing in individual consumer behavior research. Information from these two sources may provide more independent variables from which to determine regression models.

TABLE 7.23 Percentage Usage Across Time Horizons

Technique	Less Than 3 Months		3 Months to 2 Years		More Than 2 Years	
	Consumer	Industrial	Consumer	Industrial	Consumer	Industrial
Qualitative						
Customer expectations	3	3	31	35	13	17
Jury of executive opinion	4	2	86*	65*	68*	45*
Sales force composite	2	5	70*	87*	20	25
Quantitative						
Box-Jenkins (open-model time series)	3	0	12*	32*	6	8
Decomposition	3	0	49*	30*	12	12
Expert systems	2	0	9	2	10	2
Exponential smoothing	11	3	91	98	18	12
Life cycle analysis	0	0	28*	7*	17	17
Moving average	12	5	49	42	6	15
Neural networks	0	3	15	13	2*	10*
Simulation	1	0	4	7	12	10
Regression	7*	0*	77*	60*	34	22
Straight line projection	7*	0*	46*	22*	10	8
Trend line analysis	4	0	61	58	26	20

NOTE: Consumer = consumer market firms ($n = 99$); Industrial = industrial market firms ($n = 60$).
*Statistically different at $p \leq .05$.

In the greater than 2 years time horizon, more consumer firms employed jury of executive opinion, whereas more industrial firms employed neural networks. Because jury of executive opinion also was favored by consumer firms in the 3 months to 2 years category and in the less than 3 months time horizon (although not significantly), it appears that consumer firms generally have a greater preference for jury of executive opinion. Because consumer markets do not have as strong salesperson-to-customer relationships as do industrial markets, it is possible that there is a need to rely more on executive opinion than on salesperson opinion when making a judgmental forecast.

As Table 7.24 shows, there were four significant differences in technique usage across forecast level. At the corporate level, more industrial firms preferred using sales force composite than did consumer firms. Again, it appears that industrial salespeople are bestowed higher esteem when forecasting. The other three differences were at the SKU level and indicate that consumer firms use regression analysis, jury of executive opinion, and decomposition more than do industrial firms. As mentioned previously, greater amounts of data on individual consumers may facilitate the use of regression by consumer firms at the SKU level. As for jury of executive opinion, it is somewhat surprising to see executive opinion popular for forecasting at the SKU level; almost one quarter of the consumer firms surveyed use jury of executive opinion at the SKU level. Given the large number of SKUs in consumer firms, it was expected that executives would spend more time on strategic forecasting (industrial, corporate, or product line forecasting) than on tactical forecasting at the SKU level. However, this does not appear to be the case in the consumer firms of Phase 2. It is possible that executives in these firms are using other quantitative techniques to make individual SKU forecasts and are then using executive opinion to make broad adjustments to groups of SKUs such as all SKUs in a product line. Even so, this possible explanation seems to be an inordinate use of valuable executive time involved in tactical forecasting. It is left to future research to determine whether this is the case and, if so, what effect this procedure has on accuracy and cost.

Accuracy

As Table 7.25 indicates, the accuracy performances experienced by consumer firms and industrial firms across time horizons and forecast levels were very similar. The only significant difference was forecasts made in the 3 months to 2 years time horizon at the SKUL level. This difference showed that industrial firms experience significantly greater accuracy than do consumer firms. Although other cells in Table 7.25 reflect differences of greater than 5%, these differences were not significant due to large variances or small sample size.

Even if these other cells had reflected significant differences, the weighted average accuracy collapsed over all cells shows that consumer firms and industrial firms achieve similar levels of forecasting accuracy. Hence, the market structure unique to each of the two types of companies does not appear to significantly affect forecasting accuracy performance.

Information Technology Use in the Forecasting Process

A significantly greater proportion of consumer firms have integrated their forecasting process with EDI information from their customers (Table 7.26). Industrial firms did not appear to be linking their forecasting and EDI systems. Also, a significantly greater proportion of consumer firms have integrated

TABLE 7.24 Percentage Usage Across Forecast Level

Technique	Industry		Corporate		Product Line		Product (SKU)		SKU by Location	
	Consumer	Industrial	Consumer	Industrial	Consumer	Industrial	Consumer	Industrial	Consumer	Industrial
Qualitative										
Customer expectations	4	5	11	18	11	15	13	5	8	12
Jury of executive opinion	30	23	50	47	43	28	23*	7*	14	7
Sales force composite	3	5	24*	40*	26	35	23	18	19	20
Quantitative										
Box-Jenkins (open-model time series)	4	2	7	13	5	12	3	8	2	5
Decomposition	5	3	15	12	16	10	20*	8*	15	8
Expert systems	5	0	5	2	3	2	5	0	3	0
Exponential smoothing	7	7	25	18	28	28	37	33	27	28
Life cycle analysis	7	5	11	7	16	7	8	3	4	2
Moving average	1	5	11	13	16	18	24	13	18	12
Neural networks	1	3	4	5	4	5	5	7	3	7
Regression	20	17	24	27	26	17	28*	13*	21	10
Simulation	4	3	5	3	4	5	3	3	1	2
Straight line projection	5	3	12	8	17	7	16	8	13	5
Trend line analysis	11	7	19	20	22	20	26	17	16	17

NOTE: SKU = stock keeping units; Consumer = consumer market firms ($n = 99$); Industrial = industrial market firms ($n = 60$).
*Statistically different at $p \leq .05$.

TABLE 7.25 Accuracy

	Less Than 3 Months		3 Months to 2 Years		More Than 2 Years	
Forecast Level	*Consumer*	*Industrial*	*Consumer*	*Industrial*	*Consumer*	*Industrial*
Industry	10	—	85	92	86	85
n	1	0	9	5	19	14
Corporate	73	—	90	91	87	86
n	2	0	34	22	20	15
Product line	92	—	85	89	92	80
n	3	0	40	32	16	6
Product (SKU)	80	89	78	82	91	83
n	10	3	56	24	5	4
SKU by location	77	69	73*	81*	90	78
n	11	3	35	20	2	2

NOTE: SKU = stock keeping units; Consumer = consumer market firms ($n = 99$); Industrial = industrial market firms ($n = 60$). Weighted averages: consumer markets = 83; industrial markets = 85.
*Statistically different at $p \leq .05$.

their forecasting systems and their DRP/MRP systems. On the other hand, significantly more industrial firms are taking input directly from their MIS's than are consumer firms. Taken together, these findings suggest that more consumer firms develop forecasts from EDI information and then electronically transmit these forecasts to the DRP and/or MRP systems. Industrial firms use their MIS's to develop forecasts and then apply these forecasts where necessary.

Conclusions: Industrial Forecasting Versus Consumer Forecasting

Although a surprising number of similarities were found, there are certain differences between consumer forecasting practices and industrial forecasting practices that warrant discussion. As found by previous research and reaffirmed in Phase 2, industrial firms favor the sales force composite technique more than do consumer firms. Hence, industrial companies should allot more training time to the implementation of the sales force composite technique when training their sales forces and forecasting personnel. Furthermore, industrial companies should pay special attention to facilitating the collection and aggregation of sales force data through new programs (e.g., greater collaboration between forecasting personnel and the sales force) and new

TABLE 7.26 Use of Information Technologies (percentages responding *yes*)

Technology	Consumer Market Firms	Industrial Market Firms
Does your sales forecasting system have access to EDI from your suppliers?	21	12
Does your sales forecasting system have access to EDI from your customers?	41*	17*
Is the output from your sales forecasting system electronically transmitted to a DRP/MRP system?	64*	43*
Is the input to your sales forecasting system electronically transmitted from your MIS?	29*	45*

NOTE: EDI = electronic data interchange; DRP = distribution requirements planning; MRP = materials requirements planning; MIS = management information system.

technologies (e.g., the sales force using portable computers to provide daily updates to composite forecasts on a central computer).

This study also found that consumer firms employ regression, straight line projections, and jury of executive opinion more than do industrial firms. It appears that the lack of direct customer information forces consumer firms to identify extrinsic factors that correspond to sales, extrapolate sales history to predict future sales, and depend on company executives for qualitative forecasts. Conversely, the direct contact with a smaller customer base that is common in industrial markets allows industrial firms to rely primarily on sales force forecasts. The implication of these findings is that consumer firms should highlight the techniques of regression, straight line projections, and jury of executive opinion in their training of forecasting personnel. This implies different training (i.e., the more quantitative procedures of regression analysis) in quantitative techniques and different individuals (i.e., executives instead of the sales force) involved in the training process for qualitative forecasts.

A particularly interesting difference concerns the use of information technologies. More consumer firms appear to integrate EDI, DRP, and MRP into the forecasting process, whereas more industrial firms rely on MIS. By using EDI, DRP, and MRP, consumer market firms are becoming more dependent on quick response systems, which require faster forecasting processes and greater levels of accuracy. The interesting point is that consumer market firms and industrial market firms are almost alike in their technique usage patterns (aside from the differences already discussed) and achieved forecasting accuracy. It is possible that forecasting techniques are not being applied properly in consumer markets and/or the volatility of customer demand of consumer markets inhibits better achieved accuracy. In light of consumer firms' greater involvement in quick response systems, a key concern for these firms should be how to integrate, and possibly improve, forecasting techniques for use in quick response systems.

Conclusions From Phase 2

The results of Phase 2 lead to some interesting conclusions about the state of sales forecasting techniques, systems, and management. With regard to our use of techniques over the past two decades, the surprise is in the lack of real changes. Companies in the 1990s are largely applying the same techniques in the same situations and are getting the same results (satisfaction and accuracy) as did companies in the 1980s. The challenge is to improve this forecasting technique application process to match the proper techniques with the situations in which they perform best. We addressed this topic partially in Chapter 6 and will return to it in Chapter 9.

On a positive note, companies are improving the sophistication of the process by which the sales forecasting function is managed. Less than one out of eight responding companies uses an Independent approach to sales forecasting management, with the majority using a negotiated or consensus approach. These latter two approaches require a greater commitment of managerial resources (indicating an increase in the importance of the sales forecasting function) but can more than compensate for this with sales forecasts improved by a broader range of input from various other functional areas. Recognition of this positive cost-benefit relationship in such a large number of responding companies is encouraging.

What is less than encouraging is the lack of sales forecasting performance evaluation in more than half of the responding companies. In any area of management, a lack of performance evaluation and reward for improved performance will lead to a lack of motivation for continuous improvement. Given this maxim of management, it is not surprising that respondents also showed little enthusiasm for training sales forecasting personnel, for gathering the more valuable but more difficult demand numbers instead of the easier but less accurate shipment numbers as input to the sales forecasting process, or for providing adequate budgets for the sales forecasting function.

This lack of performance motivation is exacerbated by the fact that management in many respondent companies views the sales forecasting process backward. The sales forecasts should be developed (based on market and channel information), and, from this base, the sales and financial plans for the companies should be derived. Unfortunately, in one out of three responding companies, management first develops the sales and financial plans and then uses these plans to derive the forecast.

With regard to sales forecasting systems, improvements seem to have come largely in the area of technology (related strongly to the increased effectiveness of personal computers and the sales forecasting software that operates on them). Regardless of these technological innovations, however, the islands of analysis that still exist, the lack of access to the information necessary to make informed sales forecasts, and the lack of direct demand input from channel members have left respondents largely neutral on their satisfaction with sales forecasting systems.

This, combined with the lack of electronic integration between functional areas involved in the development or use of the sales forecast or between suppliers and customers, leads to a number of challenges for improvements in sales forecasting systems. First, companies need to eliminate islands of analysis in the sales forecasting process. This implies increasing system integration for all the personnel involved in developing the sales forecasts. This will eliminate the use of different numbers as input to the sales forecasts, minimize disparate assumptions in each step in the sales forecasting process, and encourage more closely reconciled final forecasts.

Second, sales forecasting system access for marketing, sales, planning, product management, and logistics should be increased. The first four typically have information on the marketplace, and the fifth has information on the distribution channel disposition and movement of inventory, and all of this information is valuable input to the sales forecasting process. Rather than just having these functional areas advise sales forecasting personnel, they should be able to make their adjustments directly to the sales forecasting system, with the effect of their changes on sales forecasting performance tracked over time. This would allow more consistent input and allow these functional areas to track their impact on forecast accuracy over time.

Increasing sales forecasting system integration with suppliers or customers also is important. With the advent of EDI and vendor-managed inventory systems, it is possible to reduce much of sales forecasting uncertainty created by channel mismanagement. When the retailer orders product based on its attempt to forecast demand, the wholesaler orders based on its attempt to forecast retailer demand, and the manufacturer orders based on its forecasts of wholesaler demand, much "slack" is built into the channel in the form of product ordered in anticipation of incorrect forecasts. When the manufacturer has access to retail point-of-sale demand and can back up that demand through the channel all the way to its suppliers, significant reductions in channel-wide inventory may result.

Finally, each company is a complex system of customer demand, suppliers, channel members, and competitors. The idea that a canned sales forecasting system will deal with myriad nuances is unlikely. As companies strive to become more effective in sales forecasting, they will need to move more toward systems that are customized to their unique requirements.

In this chapter, we have tried to provide insight into the characteristics of sales forecasting techniques, systems, and management approaches as well as sales forecasting managers' satisfaction with these techniques, systems, and management approaches. The findings indicate moderate sophistication in the area of techniques, but we have a long way to go in sales forecasting to reach the same level of managerial sophistication achieved in other functional areas of business. In addition, the systems that support these techniques and management processes need considerable refinement. We will achieve this potential only if more managerial attention is focused not only on the techniques of sales forecasting but also on the management of its processes and the systems that support these processes.

To increase this focus, we undertook Phase 3 of the benchmarking studies to delve more in-depth into the sales forecasting management practices of a select group of companies. It is the results of this phase that are dealt with in the next chapter.

References

Armstrong, J. S. (1988). Research needs in forecasting. *International Journal of Forecasting, 4,* 449-465.

Conference Board. (1970). *Sales forecasting.* New York: Author.

Conference Board. (1971). *Planning and forecasting in the smaller company.* New York: Author.

Dalrymple, D. J. (1975, December). Sales forecasting methods and accuracy. *Business Horizons,* 69-73.

Dalrymple, D. J. (1987). Sales forecasting practices: Results from a United States survey. *International Journal of Forecasting, 3,* 379-391.

Davidson, T. A. (1987). Forecasters: Who are they? Survey findings. *Journal of Business Forecasting, 6*(1), 17-19.

Drury, D. H. (1990). Issues in forecasting management. *Management International Review, 30,* 317-329.

Fildes, R., & Lusk, E. J. (1984). The choice of a forecasting model. *Omega, 12,* 427-435.

Herbig, P., Milewicz, J., & Golden, J. E. (1993). Forecasting: Who, what, when, and how. *Journal of Business Forecasting, 12*(2), 16-21.

Kahn, K. B., & Mentzer, J. T. (1994). The impact of team-based forecasting. *Journal of Business Forecasting, 13*(1), 18-21.

Kahn, K. B., & Mentzer, J. T. (1995). Forecasting in consumer and industrial markets. *Journal of Business Forecasting, 14*(2), 21-28.

Kahn, K. B., & Mentzer, J. T. (1996). EDI and EDI alliances: Implications for the sales forecasting function. *Journal of Marketing Theory and Practice, 4*(2), 72-78.

Kotler, P. (1991). *Marketing management: Analysis, planning, implementation, and control* (7th ed.). Englewood Cliffs, NJ: Prentice Hall.

Lowenhar, J. A. (1984). Fortune 500 firm revamps system after 32% forecasting error. *Journal of Business Forecasting, 3*(3), 2-6.

Mentzer, J. T., & Cox, J. E., Jr. (1984a). Familiarity, application, and performance of sales forecasting techniques. *Journal of Forecasting, 3,* 27-36.

Mentzer, J. T., & Cox, J. E., Jr. (1984b). A model of the determinants of achieved forecast accuracy. *Journal of Business Logistics, 5,* 143-155.

Mentzer, J. T., & Kahn, K. B. (1995). Forecasting technique familiarity, satisfaction, usage, and application. *Journal of Forecasting, 15,* 465-476.

Mentzer, J. T., & Kahn, K. B. (1997). State of sales forecasting systems in corporate America. *Journal of Business Forecasting, 16*(1), 6-13.

Pan, J., Nichols, D. R., & Joy, O. M. (1977). Sales forecasting practices of large U.S. industrial firms. *Financial Management, 6*(3), 72-77.

Reichard, R. S. (1966). *Practical techniques of sales forecasting.* New York: McGraw-Hill.

Sales forecasting: Is five percent error good enough? (1967, December 15). *Sales Management,* 41-48.

Sparkes, J. R., & McHugh, A. K. (1984). Awareness and use of forecasting techniques in British industry. *Journal of Forecasting, 3,* 37-42.

Wheelwright, S. C., & Clarke, D. G. (1976, November-December). Corporate forecasting: Promise and reality. *Harvard Business Review, 54,* 40-42.

Wilson, J. H., & Daubek, H. G. (1989). Marketing managers evaluate forecasting models. *Journal of Business Forecasting, 8*(1), 19-22.

CHAPTER 8

Benchmarking Studies: In-Depth Analysis

*D*uring the analysis of Phase 2 of the benchmarking studies, we frequently asked the question, "I wonder what the respondent meant by that answer?" Equally often, the comment was made, "It would be great to be able to ask a follow-up question so that we could really understand how this company manages this aspect of forecasting."

We were finding that, although Phases 1 and 2 yielded a wealth of information about the forecasting practices of several hundred responding companies, it also generated a great deal more questions that we wanted answered. These questions also were occurring to companies using the results from Phase 2; companies were reading the results and coming back to us with in-depth questions that we could not answer.

Therefore, in 1994, to gain greater insight into the sales forecasting process and to find out what constituted best practices with regard to sales forecasting management, a research team at the University of Tennessee, with the support of Anheuser-Busch, Andersen Consulting, AT&T Network Systems, and Pillsbury, began Phase 3 of the benchmarking studies.

This chapter discusses the results of Phase 3 of the benchmarking studies. The research in Phase 3 began with the selection of 20 companies from those that responded to the survey in Phase 2. We were interested in including companies that had reputations as top performers, although not necessarily top performers in sales forecasting. To understand the variations in sales forecasting management performance, we wanted top-performing companies that might still have varying degrees of success in forecasting sales. In addition, we wanted to include companies at various levels of the supply chain.

Site visits were arranged with 15 manufacturers, 3 distribution firms, and 2 retailers: Anheuser-Busch, Becton-Dickinson, Coca Cola, Colgate Palmolive, Federal Express, Kimberly Clark, Lykes Pasco, Nabisco, J. C. Penney, Pillsbury, ProSource, Reckitt Colman, Red Lobster, RJR Tobacco, Sandoz, Schering Plough, Sysco, Tropicana, Warner Lambert, and Westwood Squibb.

For each company, any documentation of its sales forecasting, management practices was first requested. This documentation included any reports, documentation of systems and/or management procedures, and informal protocols. Once this information was analyzed, an interview schedule was arranged with anyone in the company affiliated with sales forecasting including developers and users of the sales forecasts. Prior to visiting the company to conduct the interviews, a detailed 11-page protocol was sent to each person to be interviewed (a copy of this protocol is included in the appendix to this chapter). The interviews were conducted on-site by the research team with two interviewers in each interview to ascertain interjudge reliability. Interviews were tape-recorded, and the transcripts from these interviews were analyzed for sales forecasting management content.

This in-depth analysis of the documentation and the interview contents of these 20 companies led us to conclude that sales forecasting management can be divided into four dimensions: *functional integration, approach, systems,* and *performance measurement.* These four dimensions of forecasting management revealed by the analysis of Phase 3 of the benchmarking studies also are the four major parts of this chapter. Within each dimension, we identify and discuss four stages of sophistication with regard to sales forecasting management. In addition to identifying stages within each dimension, we provide guidelines to enable companies to progress toward a higher level of sophistication for each forecasting dimension. Following these four sections, some general conclusions with respect to Phase 3 are addressed.

The reader should keep in mind that although all four of these dimensions are discussed separately, they are inextricably intertwined, and discussion of one dimension sometimes refers to aspects of another dimension. Furthermore, although we refer to companies in certain stages, it is important to remember that a particular company can be in one stage on a certain dimension and in a completely different stage on another dimension. However, progress in one dimension usually is related to progress in the others. Finally, there were no companies that were in Stage 4 on all four dimensions.

For managers involved in forecasting, this chapter facilitates determination of what stages their companies are in on each forecasting dimension and also provides guidelines on what actions are necessary to progress to higher stages on each dimension. For students studying forecasting, this chapter provides an in-depth understanding of the processes involved in correctly managing the forecasting function.

Functional Integration

Effectively managing sales forecasting with respect to functional integration requires that a company implement a concept we term Forecasting C^3—communication, coordination, and collaboration. Communication encompasses all forms of written, verbal, and electronic communication among the functional business areas—marketing, sales, production, finance, and logistics (including purchasing). Coordination is the formal structure and requires meetings between two or more functional business areas. Collaboration is an orientation among functional areas toward common goal setting and working together. See Figure 8.1 for a summary of the characteristics of the functional integration stages.

Functional Integration Stages

Stage 1 companies allow each functional area to have its own forecast for its own purposes. As we discussed in Chapter 1, marketing tends to want yearly product line forecasts, sales wants quarterly forecasts by salesperson territory, finance wants yearly dollar forecasts, production wants stock keeping unit (SKU) forecasts tied to the production cycle, and logistics wants stock keeping unit by location (SKUL) forecasts tied to the replenishment cycle. These disparate goals for forecasting cause major communication breakdowns among functional areas and, as a result, lack of any coordinated or collaborative sales forecasting effort. As a further result, there is no accountability for discrepancies in sales forecasts among functional areas. As might be expected, forecasting accuracy and effectiveness are low in Stage 1 companies.

Stage 2 companies have progressed to a recognition of the need for coordinated sales forecasts through formal meetings among the functional

Stage 1

- Major communication breakdowns among marketing, finance, sales, production, logistics, and forecasting
- Each area has its own forecasting effort
- No accountability among areas for forecast accuracy

Stage 2

- Coordination (formal meetings) among marketing, finance, sales, production, logistics, and forecasting
- Forecasting located in a certain area—typically operations oriented (located in logistics or production) or marketing oriented (located in marketing or sales)—that dictates forecasts to other areas
- Planned consensus meetings, but meetings dominated by operations, finance, or marketing (i.e., no real consensus)
- Performance rewards for forecasting personnel only

Stage 3

- Communication and coordination among marketing, finance, sales, production, logistics, and forecasting
- Existence of a forecasting champion
- Recognition that marketing is a capacity-unconstrained forecast and that operations is a capacity-constrained forecast
- Consensus and negotiation process to reconcile marketing and operations forecasts
- Performance rewards for improved forecasting accuracy for all personnel involved in the consensus process

Stage 4

- Functional integration (C^3—collaboration, communication, and coordination) among marketing, finance, sales, production, logistics, and forecasting
- Existence of forecasting as a separate functional area
- Needs of all areas recognized and met by reconciled marketing and operations forecast (finance = annual dollar forecasts; sales = quarterly dollar sales territory-based forecasts; marketing = annual dollar product-based forecasts; production = production cycle unit stock keeping unit forecasts; logistics = order cycle unit stock keeping unit by location forecasts)
- Consensus process recognizes feedback loops (e.g., constrained capacity information is provided to sales, marketing, and advertising; sales, promotions, and advertising can drive demand)
- Multidimensional performance rewards for all personnel involved in the consensus process

Figure 8.1. Forecasting Benchmark Stages: Functional Integration

areas, with forecasting housed in a specific functional area. The problem with this approach is that the location of forecasting gives the forecasts a decidedly biased "flavor." When forecasting is located in production or logistics, the forecasts are more operational in nature, whereas companies that locate forecasting in marketing or sales have more marketing-oriented forecasts. The difficulties encountered by companies in this stage are due to the fact that marketing and sales find short-range SKU and SKUL forecasts of little use in determining yearly and quarterly product and product line forecasts, whereas production and logistics have little use for longer term dollar forecasts. Furthermore, marketing and sales tend to look on forecasts as capacity unconstrained, whereas production and logistics are constantly aware of and bound by supply chain capacity constraints that limit the potential demand that can be fulfilled.

Coordination in this stage often is accomplished through "consensus forecast" meetings, but the lack of common goal setting (i.e., collaboration) causes these meetings to be dominated by either operations or marketing/finance, to the detriment of the other functions. Because forecasting is a recognized area within a specific business function, its personnel are evaluated solely on their contributions to the goals of the function in which forecasting is housed. For example, forecasting personnel located in marketing/sales are evaluated on sales goals, whereas forecasting personnel located in operations are evaluated on production/distribution scheduling goals.

Stage 3 companies follow more of a true consensus forecasting approach, with more effective communication and coordination between the functional areas and a recognized forecasting champion. This leads to more effective negotiation among the various functional areas to reach a consensus forecast that recognizes the goals of marketing/sales/finance and the capacity constraints of operations. To achieve more commitment from all personnel involved in reaching the consensus forecast, all consensus team members receive performance rewards for improved forecasting effectiveness.

Stage 4 companies achieve functional integration that stresses Forecasting C^3—communication, coordination, and collaboration. Stage 4 companies structure forecasting as a separate functional area, coordinating the forecasting needs of all functional areas and thereby reducing the adversarial negotiation approach exhibited by Stage 3 companies, that is, a true consensus approach. This is augmented by systems that provide full access to information that affects the forecasting process and outcomes (e.g., capacity constraints, promotions, advertising campaigns). Performance rewards are based on the multidimensional nature of these feedback loops. For example, instead of rewarding on forecasting accuracy alone, rewards are based on division or corporate profitability and customer service goals.

Improving Functional Integration

Figure 8.2 summarizes the directions necessary to improve functional integration in the sales forecasting process. Companies seeking to improve forecasting effectiveness on the dimension of functional integration can facilitate this improvement by recognizing forecasting as a separate functional area. The primary responsibility of the forecasting function is to bridge the gaps among the orientations of the functional areas within the company (marketing, sales, finance, production, and logistics) by providing sales forecasts at the levels and time horizons required by these functional areas. Improving functional integration also requires that common goal setting with regard to forecasting be encouraged across functional areas. This common goal setting can be facilitated by communication and information access across functional areas.

Finally, improving functional integration requires that performance rewards for personnel involved in the forecasting process be based not merely on forecast accuracy but also on the consequences of forecasting accuracy (e.g., business unit or corporate profitability, meeting customer service goals).

Approach

The dimension of approach encompasses what is forecast and how it is forecast. See Figure 8.3 for a summary of the characteristics of the approach stages.

Approach Stages

Stage 1 companies have forecasting approaches that are driven by the business/profit plan, that is, top-down forecasts. They concentrate primarily on the profit plan with little recognition of the impact of economic factors, marketing efforts, or stage in the product life cycle of their product mix. Forecasting is seen principally as a tactical function (e.g., "How do we obtain the sales this month to meet the plan?") with little impact on the development of their business plans.

Rather than forecasting actual demand for their products, Stage 1 companies forecast shipments from their facilities. No recognition is given to the

***To improve forecasting effectiveness on the dimension of functional
integration, companies should do the following:***

- Recognize forecasting as a separate functional area whose responsibility is to provide forecasts at levels and time horizons that are useful to marketing, sales, finance, production, and logistics
- Encourage communication, coordination, and collaboration by enabling access to relevant information across functional areas
- Provide performance rewards to all personnel involved in the forecasting process based on the impact of forecasting accuracy

Figure 8.2. Improving Functional Integration

fact that such an approach ignores what actually was demanded and considers only the company's past ability to fulfill demand. Also, no recognition is given to the differences in forecasting needs of different products. Forecasting techniques usually are some type of naive forecasts and/or statistical approaches with little or no understanding by personnel of how the techniques work, that is, a "black box" approach. Often, personnel involved in forecasting receive no training in forecasting techniques or in understanding their company's environment, and little or no documentation of the forecasting process is available.

Stage 2 companies take more of a bottom-up (SKUL up to corporate forecast) approach to forecasting demand, where demand is determined by what is recorded in invoices or corporate reports. This approach does improve on the approach of Stage 1 companies by recognizing that some demand cannot be fulfilled by shipments, but it does not capture the demand that could not be filled and, as a result, simply was never recorded. Time-series forecasting techniques are prevalent, but more for their simplicity than for their appropriateness in all forecasting situations encountered.

There is greater recognition of the interrelationship between the business plan and forecasting and the effect of marketing/promotion efforts and seasonality on demand. However, the plan still takes precedence over the forecasting process. More emphasis is placed on some documentation of the forecasting process and statistical training for personnel, but little emphasis is placed on activities to help forecasting personnel understand the business environment.

Stage 3 companies recognize the importance of top-down and bottom-up forecasting approaches but do little to reconcile these approaches. Having moved beyond shipments forecasts or self-recorded demand forecasts, Stage 3 companies use some point of sale (POS) demand and supply chain timing/

Stage 1

- Plan-driven, top-down forecasting approach (failure to recognize the interaction among forecasting, marketing, and the business plan)
- Forecast shipments only
- Treat all forecasted products the same
- Naive and/or simple statistical approach to forecasting, often with little understanding of the techniques used or the environment ("black box forecasting")
- Fail to see the role of forecasting in developing the business plan (forecasting viewed solely as a tactical function)
- No training of forecasting personnel in techniques or understanding of the business environment
- No documentation of the forecasting process

Stage 2

- Bottom-up, stock keeping unit by location-based forecasting approach
- Forecast self-reported demand (demand recognized by the organization) or adjusted demand (invoice keyed demand)
- Recognize that marketing/promotion efforts and seasonality can drive demand
- Recognize the relationship between forecasting and the business plan, but the plan still takes precedence over the forecasts
- Limited training in statistics, with no training in understanding the business environment
- Limited documentation of the forecasting process

Stage 3

- Both top-down and bottom-up forecasting approaches
- Forecast point-of-sale demand and back this information up the supply chain and/or use key customer demand information ("uncommitted commitments")

Figure 8.3. Forecasting Benchmark Stages: Approach

inventory information to forecast demand at their position in the channel. Some customers of Stage 3 companies provide projections of future demand needs and current inventory levels, enabling this information to be used for separating these key customers' forecasts from overall forecasts. However, these customers are not required to accept shipments based on their previously projected demands (i.e., "uncommitted commitments"); therefore, the uncommitted nature of these projections does not allow for vendor-managed inventories.

- Use ABC analysis or some other categorization for forecasting accuracy importance
- Identification of categories of products that do not need to be forecast (e.g., two-bin items, dependent demand items, make-to-order items)
- Use of regression-based models for higher level (corporate to product line) forecasts and a "suite" of time-series techniques for operational (product to stock keeping unit by location) forecasts
- Recognize the importance of subjective input from marketing, sales, and operations to the forecast
- Forecasting drives the business plan
- Training in quantitative analysis/statistics and an understanding of the business environment—a strong manager/advocate of the forecasting process

Stage 4

- Top-down and bottom-up forecasting approaches with reconciliation
- Vendor-managed inventory factored out of the forecasting process
- Full forecasting segmentation of products (ABC, two-bin, dependent demand, make-to-order, product value, seasonality, customer service sensitivity, promotion driven, life cycle stage, shelf life, raw material lead time, production lead time)
- Understand the "game-playing" inherent in the sales force and the distribution channel (motivation for sales to underforecast and for distributors to overforecast)
- Develop forecasts and business plan simultaneously, with periodic reconciliation of both (e.g., consideration of capacity constraints as part of long-range plan and forecasts)
- Ongoing training in quantitative analysis/statistics and an understanding of the business environment
- Top management support of the forecasting process

Figure 8.3. Continued

ABC analysis is used to identify categories of important products that require more accurate forecasts. This categorization of product forecasts is further expanded by Stage 3 companies to include products that do not need to be forecast. Examples include the following:

1. *Products that move so slowly that they are considered two-bin items.* For such a product, inventory is kept in two locations (bins). When one bin is empty, a replenishment bin is ordered. Because the item moves so slowly,

the new order arrives long before the second bin is empty, thus eliminating the need to forecast.

2. *Products with dependent demand, that is, products that are sold to manufacturing locations that use a constant and predictable amount per day over a long production scheduling cycle.* Such products allow for planned production/procurement and eliminate the need for forecasting.

3. *Products that are made to order.* Customers expect no inventory and are willing to wait through the production order cycle to receive delivery, eliminating the need to forecast these products.

Stage 3 companies recognize that regression-based forecasting works better for longer range forecasts at levels higher in the corporation, that a "suite" of time-series forecasts (discussed in Chapters 6 and 9) works better for shorter range SKU and SKUL forecasts, and that experienced business qualitative input is an important component of all forecasts. As a result, more emphasis is placed on training in understanding the business environment and in quantitative analysis/statistics. The latter includes training in statistics but also encompasses analysis of business, environmental, and channel relations and their impact on the forecasts.

With such increased insight into the relationships in which the business is involved comes an increased tendency to allow the forecasts and their root explanations to drive the business plan instead of the other way around.

Stage 4 companies recognize that top-down and bottom-up forecasting approaches are not two independent processes but rather are interdependent. Thus, any changes to one forecast are reconciled with forecasts at the same level from the other approach. Stage 4 companies also are more involved in vendor-managed inventory for key customers, and forecasts for these customers are managed separately. Furthermore, a full range of segmentation factors are considered in determining the level of forecasting sophistication and accuracy required for each product. These include the factors of ABC analysis, two-bin designations, dependent demand products, and make-to-order products mentioned in previous stages but also include the following:

1. Dissimilar seasonal patterns
2. Products whose demand is largely promotion driven and, thus, should be forecast with regression-based promotional models
3. Different stages in the product life cycle that affect the importance of forecasting and the predictability of demand
4. Whether or not the product has a short shelf life because the shorter the shelf life, the greater the product obsolescence due to forecasting error

5. The value of the product because more valuable products are more costly to hold in inventory, thereby increasing the inventory cost of forecasting error

6. The customer service sensitivity of the product because the higher the customer service sensitivity, the higher the customer service cost of stockouts due to forecasting error

7. The raw material lead time because different forecasting horizons (and, consequently, different forecasting techniques) are required for products whose raw materials can be procured in a matter of weeks compared to products whose raw materials may take more than a year to obtain

8. The production lead time because, similar to raw material lead times, the length of the lead time for the production schedule and how often this schedule can be changed affect the forecasting time horizon and techniques

With a full appreciation of the intricacies of the business environment comes a recognition that a certain amount of "game-playing" will occur in any forecasting process. For instance, salespeople will underforecast to obtain lower quotas, and distributors will overforecast to cause greater quantities to be produced and held in inventory to be available for their use. Subjective modification of forecasts generated by these groups based on an understanding of the business greatly increases forecasting accuracy.

Stage 4 companies recognize that the business plan and forecasts are intertwined and should be developed together rather than allowing one to drive the other. This final point is achieved in Stage 4 companies only through top management's recognition of the importance of forecasting both to the business plan and to operational planning.

Improving Forecasting Approach

Figure 8.4 summarizes the actions that will facilitate improvement in forecasting approach.

Companies seeking to improve forecasting effectiveness on the dimension of approach should, first and foremost, understand and reconcile their top-down and bottom-up forecasting processes. Related to this is an understanding of the interaction between the business plan and the forecasts, that is, how to use forecasting to facilitate business planning. To promote this understanding and improvement, the support of top management is essential.

When striving to improve the forecasting approach, it also is important for a company to have initial and ongoing training in quantitative analysis/

To improve forecasting effectiveness on the dimension of approach,
companies should do the following:

- Obtain top management support for the forecasting/business plan process
- Reconcile forecasts and the business plan
- Reconcile top-down and bottom-up forecasting approaches
- Train forecasting personnel in quantitative analysis/statistics and an understanding of the business environment
- Incorporate an understanding of forecasting "game-playing" into the forecasting process
- Segment out of the forecasting process key customers who can be forecast separately or will participate in vendor-managed inventory programs
- Segment products by their demand patterns, their importance to the company, the importance of promotions, stage in the life cycle, shelf life, product value, customer service sensitivity, and raw material and production order cycles

Figure 8.4. Improving Forecasting Approach

statistics and the business/industry environment in which the firm operates. This training will help forecasting personnel develop an appreciation of the complex nature of their business environment and give them the tools needed to incorporate these factors into their forecasts. Understanding the nature of the environment also fosters a recognition that a certain amount of game-playing will occur in any forecasting process and enables forecasting personnel to subjectively modify forecasts accordingly so that forecasting accuracy is improved.

The forecasting approach also can be improved by investigating the possibility of segmenting out key customers and forecasting them separately—or, better yet, instituting a vendor-managed inventory program with these customers.

Finally, companies should consider segmenting products by demand patterns, importance to the company, how responsive product demand is to promotions, product life cycle stage, product shelf life, product value, customer service sensitivity, and raw material and production order cycles. These factors can guide the degree of forecasting effort expended on a product as well as the degree of forecasting accuracy the company attempts to achieve.

Systems

The dimension of systems encompasses computer and electronic communications hardware and software used in forecasting. See Figure 8.5 for a summary of the characteristics of the systems stages.

Systems Stages

Stage 1 companies have a number of separate information systems that are not interconnected, a situation that we refer to as "islands of analysis." As a result, information is transferred from one functional area to another via printed reports. This information must be input manually to the receiving function's computer system, which can result in the same data being input over and over again in these isolated systems. This inhibits productivity and results in considerable data entry errors.

Few people outside Management Information Systems (MIS) understand the functionality of the systems, and no forecasting performance metrics are captured or reported.

Stage 2 companies have electronic links among the functional areas involved in generating and/or using the forecasts, thus eliminating the need for manual transfer and input of information. On-screen reports of forecasting performance metrics are available, as are periodically printed reports. However, these reports frequently are quite large and contain a great deal of extraneous information.

Stage 3 companies have moved to a client-server system architecture with improved system user interfaces, which allow changes and subjective input to the forecasts to be easily entered and communicated to all functional areas. This is augmented by a common ownership of information, that is, a "data warehouse." Reports can be customized and are available on-screen or printed on demand.

Stage 4 companies have taken their open-systems architecture to key customers and suppliers so that electronic data interchange (EDI) linkages allow supply chain staging of inventory based on POS demand forecasts. Companies at this stage have been found to achieve considerable savings in supply chain inventories through the added EDI information (Kahn & Mentzer, 1996).

Stage 1

- Corporate management information systems, forecasting software, and distribution requirements planning systems are not linked electronically
- Printed reports, manual transfer of data from one system to another, lack of coordination between information in different systems
- Few people understand the systems and their interaction (all systems knowledge held in Management Information System)
- "Islands of analysis" exist
- Lack of performance metrics in any of the systems or reports

Stage 2

- Electronic links among marketing, finance, forecasting, manufacturing, logistics, and sales systems
- On-screen reports available
- Measures of performance available in reports
- Reports periodically generated

Stage 3

- Client-server architecture that allows changes to be made easily and communicated to other systems
- Improved system-user interfaces to allow subjective input
- Common ownership of databases and information systems
- Measures of performance available in reports and on-screen
- Reports generated on demand and performance measures available on line

Stage 4

- Open-systems architecture so that all affected areas can provide electronic input to the forecasting process
- Electronic data interchange linkages with major customers and suppliers to allow forecasting by key customer and supply chain staging of forecasts (i.e., real-time point-of-sale forecasts to plan key customer demand ahead of supply chain cycle)

Figure 8.5. Forecasting Benchmark Stages: Systems

Improving Forecasting Systems

Figure 8.6 provides a summary of how to improve the sales forecasting function on the dimension of systems.

Companies seeking to improve the effectiveness of their forecasting systems should move to a client-server architecture. The client-server struc-

To improve forecasting effectiveness on the dimension of systems, companies should do the following:

- Eliminate "islands of analysis" by moving to a client-server architecture that allows all functional areas involved in and/or affected by the forecast to have input to the process
- Develop a common ownership of databases and information systems
- Provide the ability to obtain customized on-screen and printed reports on demand
- Enfold key customers and suppliers into the forecasting information system to allow supply chain staged inventory based on point-of-sale demand forecasts

Figure 8.6. Improving Forecasting Systems

ture eliminates islands of analysis and allows all of the functional areas involved in and/or affected by the forecast to have access and input to the forecasting process. Implementation of client-server architecture also fosters the development of a common ownership of databases and information systems involved in the forecasting effort. The client-server structure also facilitates those involved in forecasting by allowing them to obtain customized reports in both on-screen and printed formats.

Finally, to improve the sales forecasting function on the dimension of systems, look for opportunities to enfold key customers and suppliers into the forecasting information system. This allows supply chain staged inventory that can make use of POS information in the formulation of demand forecasts.

Performance Measurement

The dimension of performance measurement addresses what metrics are used to measure forecasting effectiveness and the information gathered to explain that performance. See Figure 8.7 for a summary of the characteristics of the performance measurement stages.

Performance Measurement Stages

Stage 1 companies do not have the systems or the understanding of the forecasting process to even measure accuracy. Although forecasts are developed and used, no measure of accuracy exists and, not surprisingly, accuracy is not tied to performance evaluation. Typical performance evaluation criteria

Stage 1

- Accuracy not measured

- Forecasting performance evaluation not tied to any measure of accuracy (often tied to meeting plan, reconciliation with plan, etc.)

Stage 2

- Accuracy measured, primarily as Mean Absolute Percent Error, but sometimes measured inaccurately (e.g., forecast, rather than demand, used in the denominator of the calculation)

- Forecasting performance evaluation based on accuracy with no consideration for the implications of accurate forecasts for operations

- Recognition of the impact on demand of external factors (e.g., economic conditions, competitive actions)

Stage 3

- Accuracy still measured as Mean Absolute Percent Error, but more concern given to the measurement of the supply chain impact of forecast accuracy (e.g., lower acceptable accuracy for low-value, noncompetitive products, recognition of capacity constraints in the supply chain and their impact on forecasting and performance)

- Graphical and collective (throughout product hierarchy) reporting of forecast accuracy

- Forecasting performance evaluation still based on accuracy, but there is a growing recognition that accuracy has an effect on inventory levels, customer service, and achieving the marketing and financial plans

Stage 4

- Realization that exogenous factors affect forecast accuracy and that unfulfilled demand is partially a function of forecasting error and partially a function of operational error

- Forecasting error treated as an indication of the need for a problem search (e.g., point-of-sale demand was forecast accurately, but plant capacity prevented production of the forecast amount)

- Multidimensional metrics of forecasting performance; forecasting performance evaluation tied to the impact of accuracy on achievement of corporate goals (e.g., profitability, supply chain costs, customer service)

Figure 8.7. Forecasting Benchmark Stages: Performance Measurement

are based on meeting the business plan or reconciliation of the forecast to the business plan.

Stage 2 companies use some measure of forecast accuracy, generally Mean Absolute Percent Error (*MAPE*), as the sole metric of forecasting performance. However, limited understanding of forecasting at this stage leads some Stage 2 companies to incorrectly specify the *MAPE* formula (a phenomenon discussed more fully in Chapter 2), using forecast rather than demand in the denominator, a formulation that incorrectly inflates the accuracy measure (i.e., the higher the forecast, the lower the *MAPE* value, regardless of whether the forecast was accurate or not). In this stage, some companies begin to recognize the impact of external factors such as economic conditions, weather, and competitive actions on demand and, thus, on forecast accuracy.

Stage 3 companies still use *MAPE* as a measure of forecast accuracy, but concern shifts more to measuring the impact of forecast accuracy on marketing and supply chain activities. The former includes acceptance of lower forecast accuracy for products that are less important to the strategic marketing plan (i.e., lower profit margins and/or customer service sensitivity). The latter includes the consideration of supply chain capacity constraints and the recognition that high levels of forecast accuracy are not as important for low-value products that are cheaper to carry in inventory.

The actual reporting of accuracy measures in Stage 3 companies becomes more sophisticated, with graphical presentations of accuracy and the ability to look at accuracy at various levels in the product hierarchy (from SKUL unit demand all the way up to corporate dollar demand).

Stage 4 companies realize that forecasting error is partially a function of incorrect forecasts and partially a function of the inability of the supply chain to deliver the products when and where they are demanded. It is interesting that this concept was explored in depth almost 20 years ago (Bowersox, Closs, Mentzer, & Sims, 1979) but still is a characteristic only of Stage 4 companies. This recognition leads to treating forecasting error not as an end result but rather as a symptom of a problem to be investigated further. For instance, investigation of a forecasting error may indicate that POS demand was forecast accurately, but a lack of communication with production failed to alert the forecast system that the demand forecast was beyond the production capacity of the supply chain. The solution to the forecasting "error" in this case is an adjustment to the forecasting information system.

Finally, Stage 4 companies have moved beyond measuring forecasting performance by the unidimensional metric of accuracy (e.g., *MAPE*). Multidimensional metrics are used that tap accuracy as well as the impact of the forecast on profitability, competitive strategy, supply chain costs, and customer service.

Improving Forecasting Performance Measurement

Figure 8.8 provides a summary of how to improve sales forecasting performance measurement.

Improvement of sales forecasting performance measurement requires measuring forecast accuracy at all the levels relevant to the functional areas using the forecast. If each functional area using the forecast is not able to track the accuracy of the forecast in terms that are relevant to that area (e.g., product line, SKUL), then the forecasting function will not be relevant to that area's business processes. When measuring forecast performance, it is important to use a measure of accuracy with which management is familiar and comfortable. We found that *MAPE* is the most popular of such measures because it overcomes some of the problems inherent in other measures of forecast accuracy. (For a discussion of other measures of forecast accuracy including mean absolute error, mean squared error, and percent error, see Chapter 2.)

Another important step to take when trying to improve sales forecasting performance measurement is to provide graphical, as well as statistical, measures of accuracy. At the risk of using a cliché, a picture really is worth a thousand words. Graphical representations of sales forecasts against actual demand enable users and developers of the sales forecasts to understand forecast performance quickly and clearly.

Finally, companies seeking to improve sales forecasting performance measurement must realize the importance of not only measuring forecasting accuracy but also understanding and measuring the impact of forecast accuracy on profitability, competitive strategy, supply chain costs, and customer service.

Conclusions

All companies that participated in Phase 3 of the benchmarking studies had some dissatisfaction with their sales forecasting processes. Particular areas of dissatisfaction were new product forecasting and the forecasting of low-volume, sporadic products. The companies that were at higher stages of sophistication on the four forecasting dimensions were attempting to remedy these problems, whereas companies in lower stages of sophistication accepted these problems as "part of the business." This observation demonstrates that companies that have relatively high levels of sophistication regarding their

To improve forecasting effectiveness on the dimension of performance measurement, companies should do the following:

- Measure forecast accuracy at all the levels relevant to the functional areas using the forecast
- Use a measure of accuracy with which management is comfortable but recognize that Mean Absolute Percent Error is the most popular of such measures
- Provide graphical, as well as statistical, measures of accuracy
- Provide a multidimensional metric of forecasting performance that includes accuracy as well the impact of the forecast on profitability, competitive strategy, supply chain costs, and customer service

Figure 8.8. Improving Forecasting Performance Measurement

forecasting functions also can be characterized as continuously improving, that is, learning organizations.

No one company was found to be in Stage 4 on all of the forecasting dimensions. It was surprising how often companies that performed well on other measures of business success (e.g., profitability, market share) were Stage 1 or Stage 2 companies when it came to forecasting. However, the companies whose sales forecasting functions were identified as being relatively sophisticated realized that failing to improve their sales forecasting processes led to problems in the long term (e.g., tactical inventory and production problems, strategic marketing and planning problems).

This benchmark study provides clear steps of progression within each dimension to move a company to a level of excellence in forecasting, a progression that is indicative of the learning organization orientation just mentioned. The rewards of such an orientation and the forecasting excellence it encourages are considerable and include lower inventory levels, lower supply chain costs, higher customer service levels, and higher morale.

Appendix

Sales Forecasting
Audit Protocol

Questions About Sales
Forecasting Administration

Start with a general request, which may answer many of the specifics given below:

Please describe the process you go through to develop each sales forecast.

Specific Questions

To what extent are various functional departments involved in the development of sales forecasts? (Examples: engineering, finance, logistics, marketing, planning, product management, production, research and development [R&D], sales, sales forecasting)

What approach is used by these functional departments to develop sales forecasts?

1. Do these departments develop and use their own separate forecasts?

2. Does one department develop a single forecast that all departments use?

3. Does a forecast committee develop a single forecast that all departments use?

4. Does each department develop its own forecast and a committee develops a final compromise forecast?

If No. 2, which department develops the forecast?

If No. 3 or 4, which departments are on the committee?

How satisfied are you with this approach?

What is middle management's role in developing sales forecasts? (Examples: review only, approval only, actual involvement, combination of these)

What is upper management's role in developing sales forecasts? (Examples: review only, approval only, actual involvement, combination of these)

At the beginning of each forecasting period, how does the sales forecasting process begin? (Examples: sales forecasts developed by computer system, sales force, both computer system and sales force, marketing, forecasting/planning group)

Is the business plan based on the sales forecast, or is the sales forecast based on the business plan? To what degree do you make the forecast agree with the business plan?

Which department(s) is (are) responsible for managing inventory? (Examples: engineering, finance, logistics, marketing, planning, product management, production, R&D, sales, sales forecasting)

Do you think the process for preparing a forecast is clear and routine with precise instructions available? Please be specific.

Is forecasting performance formally evaluated and rewarded? How?

Is the sales forecasting budget sufficient for the personnel, computer hardware/software, and training required?

Too much money is spent in this company to manage around forecasting error. Do not specifically ask this, but look for examples to be pursued in the conversation.

Are the sales forecasts developed and reported in:
Units, then converted to dollars?
Units only?
Dollars, then converted to units?
Dollars only?

What is forecast? (Examples: distributor orders, shipments, sales, customer demand)

How do you deal with the following special events:
New products?
Promotions?
Variety in product/package details?

What percentage of your business is in the following categories:
Consumer products?
Industrial products?
Consumer services?
Industrial services?

Company type—To be determined from company documents and general discussion:
Manufacturer
Logistics/transportation
Telecommunications company
Wholesaler
Utility
Retailer
Health care company
Publisher

What is the length and variability of production lead times for your company?

What is the length and variability of raw material lead times for your company?

What is the length and variability of cycle times to your customers?

Are products primarily made to order or made to forecast?

Do you have a specified goal for level of logistics customer service?

Inventory turns?

What is the achieved level for both of these?

How would you describe the level of competition in your industry?

Is the demand for your products primarily driven by marketing efforts of your company and its competitors?

Describe the typical channel of distribution for your products (length).

What is the shelf life for your products?

To what degree do you use the same forecasting management processes in different countries?

If the answer is low, is this something you are trying to accomplish?

Questions About Sales Forecasting Systems

Start with a general request, which may answer many of the specifics given below:

Please describe the information systems and forecasting computer systems you use to develop each sales forecast.

Specific Questions

The number and type (hardware, software) of forecasting systems?

How long has each been in use?

Is your forecasting system on a distributed data network (LAN/WAN)?

Is your forecasting system on personal computers, a mainframe, or both?

Was your software (1) developed by vendor, (2) custom built by your company, or (3) a commercial software package?

If No. 1, who was the vendor and please describe the development process?

If No. 3, what is the name of the package?

Is the output from the forecasting system electronically transmitted to a distribution requirements planning (DRP)/materials requirements planning (MRP) system for production and inventory planning? Are forecasts used to determine ROP and OQ?

Is the input to your forecasting system electronically transmitted from the corporate management information system (MIS)?

With what other systems does the forecasting system interact?

How automated is the integration?

What information is input from the MIS to the sales forecasting system? (Examples: sales, demand, orders, price changes, new product introduction information, advertising/promotional information, competitive information, market research information, economic information, past forecast accuracy)

Does the sales forecasting system have access to electronic data interchange (EDI) information from suppliers?

Does the sales forecasting system have access to EDI information from customers?

Does the sales forecasting system receive demand information directly from customers?

If yes, are forecasts adjusted based on this information?

How easy is it for users to enter adjustments to sales forecasts directly into the forecasting system?

Which functional personnel have access to the sales forecasting system to review, but not make changes to, the forecasts?

Which have access to the sales forecasting system to make changes to the forecasts? (Examples: engineering, finance, logistics, marketing, planning, product management, production, R&D, sales, sales forecasting)

To what degree are your forecasting systems in different countries compatible?

If the answer is low, is this something you are trying to accomplish?

How satisfied are you with your existing sales forecasting system?

A copy of all system specifications, reports, and graphs should be requested.

Questions About Sales Forecasting Techniques

At what level of product detail do you forecast? Why? (Examples: stock keeping unit [SKU], stock keeping unit by location [SKUL], product, product line, division, corporate)

For what forecast interval do you forecast? Why? (Examples: weekly, monthly, quarterly, yearly)

For what time horizons do you forecast? Why? (Examples: 6 months, 9 months, 12 months, 2 years)

For what geographic breakdown?

For each of the levels, intervals, horizons, and geographic breakdowns just described, what forecasting technique(s) is (are) used? (Examples: regression, jury of executive opinion, exponential smoothing, moving average, sales force composite, Box-Jenkins, trend line analysis, decomposition, straight line projections, customer expectations, life cycle analysis, simulation, expert systems, neural networks)

How credible are the subjective technique values you receive from:
Salespeople?
Channel members?
Executives?

To what degree do each "game-play" in providing forecasts?

How do you forecast "slow movers," "spikes," and "blips"?

Questions About Sales Forecasting Performance

We will need documented information on the following:
Percent error (PE) by forecasting level
PE goal by time horizon
PE by time horizon and level
PE goal by time horizon and level

What criteria are used for evaluating sales forecasting effectiveness? (Examples: accuracy, ease of use, credibility, cost, amount of data required, inventory turns, customer service performance, return on investment, impact of forecast error on safety, stock/logistics customer service, operating costs of forecast error)

Are performance statistics weighted by volume?

What graphical reports are available? (Example: plot of PE over time)

What measures of forecast error are used? (Examples: mean absolute percent error, mean absolute deviation, mean squared error, deviation, PE, forecast ratio, inventory statistics, standard deviation)

References

Bowersox, D. J., Closs, D. J., Mentzer, J. T., & Sims, J. R. (1979). *Simulated product sales forecasting.* East Lansing: Michigan State University, Bureau of Business Research.

Kahn, K. B., & Mentzer, J. T. (1996). EDI and EDI alliances: Implications for the sales forecasting function. *Journal of Marketing Theory and Practice, 4*(2), 72-78.

CHAPTER 9

MULTICASTER Book Version

*A*lthough we were involved in developing a number of mainframe-based sales forecasting systems back in the 1970s, in 1982 we developed one of the first PC-based, commercial sales forecasting software packages. This system, called *EASY CASTER, worked on the old two-floppy disk computers; hard disks were not even available yet. The system had eight different time-series techniques as well as simple and multiple regression analysis. To use the system, you put the EASY CASTER diskette in the A drive and your data disk in the B drive. You could select one technique at a time, and it took a considerable amount of time to make one forecast.*

Because the system was designed to make one forecast at a time for one product at a time, it really was designed to analyze techniques to help the user decide which techniques to use in larger, mainframe-based systems. In fact, the analytical capabilities of EASY CASTER made it very popular for teaching forecasting techniques in college courses.

EASY CASTER led to us working with a number of companies in the 1980s to develop customized, in-house, PC-based sales forecasting systems, which eventually led to the development of the customizable system, MULTICASTER, discussed in Chapter 6.

> *We have now come full circle by going from a*
> *PC-based system designed to analyze and forecast a*
> *small number of products (EASY CASTER), to a*
> *large-scale, PC-based system designed to forecast many*
> *products (MULTICASTER Forecasting System [MFS]),*
> *and back to a PC-based system for analyzing a small*
> *number of products (MULTICASTER Book Version*
> *[MBV]), a supplement for this book.*
>
> *During this circle, of course, the system has become*
> *much more powerful. MBV has built into it all the*
> *sophistication of the large-scale MFS version but is*
> *available for you to try what you have learned in this*
> *book on your own demand data.*

This chapter is really a "walk-through" of how to use the software that accompanies this book. The purpose of this software is to allow you to read the book, turn to your computer, and try what you have learned to forecast some of your own data. Rather than use the cumbersome term MULTICAS-TER Book Version, we simply abbreviate this to MBV for the rest of the chapter.

MBV has four major components: a set of data files, the worksheet, the Settings screen, and the Notes screen. These four components are used together in a straightforward process to produce forecasts of your data. This process is described first, followed by an in-depth explanation of how to use each of these four components.

MBV Process

As illustrated in Figure 9.1, MBV starts with installing the system on your computer (instructions for installing MBV on your computer can be found in Appendix A) or simply using MBV directly from the system disk that accompanied this book, although MBV runs much faster when installed on a computer.[1] The next step is loading your data into a MBV Template spreadsheet data file. This is one of two ".csv" files that are included on your MBV diskette. You may access this data file through your spreadsheet package (e.g., Lotus 123, Excel) and replace the sample data with your own data. We discuss the format of this data sheet later, but the purpose of this step is to enter your data in an environment that is readily available and easy to use.

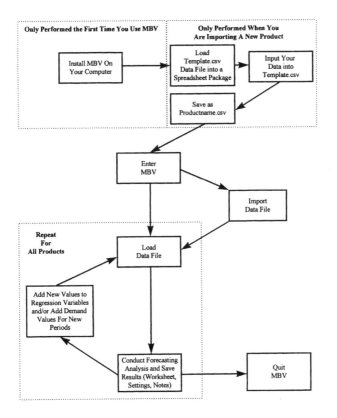

Figure 9.1. MULTICASTER Book Version Process

Once the data are correctly entered into the spreadsheet, this file should be saved as a comma-delimited (or .csv) file—with the name of the file associated with the name of the product (i.e., productname.csv)—in the same directory where you have previously installed MBV. If you do not wish to install MBV on your computer, then simply save the spreadsheet data file to the MBV system diskette. However, due to the storage capacity of the diskette, this will limit the number of product files you can create and save.

If you have already followed the installation procedure in Appendix A, then you enter MBV by double-clicking on the MBV icon on your desktop screen. To run MBV from the system diskette in the A drive, click on the Start button that appears on the lower left corner of Windows 95, click on Run, and then enter "a:\MBV."

When you enter MBV, you will see a screen like the one in Figure 9.2. Click on the OK button, and you will then be asked to enter one of the

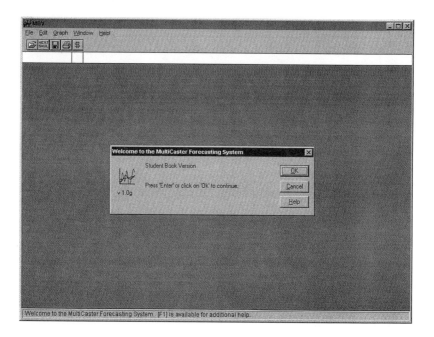

Figure 9.2. MULTICASTER Book Version Opening Screen

passwords from Appendix B of this chapter. Once you have successfully entered the password, the next screen (shown in Figure 9.3) will offer you the option of loading a file you have already imported (by clicking on the right mouse button or pressing the F5 button) or importing a new file. The MBV system disk comes with data files for products already imported; among these, some files have only histories of demand for those products (i.e., for 25 products from a variety of companies), and some files have the demand histories for various products of a furniture manufacturer and regression variables that might be useful for forecasting demand for these products.

To import a new file, click on the File I Import menu, and the screen in Figure 9.4 will appear. Click on the Import Product button, then select the .csv file you wish to import from the screen shown in Figure 9.5. When you are finished importing data files, you may click on the Done button, and you will be returned to the screen in Figure 9.3.

If you wish to load a file you have already imported, click on the right mouse button from the screen shown in Figure 9.3, or hit the F5 button, and then indicate the file you wish to load. Once you have loaded a file, you will see a screen similar to that in Figure 9.6. This is the worksheet component mentioned in the introduction to this chapter. From this screen, you can make

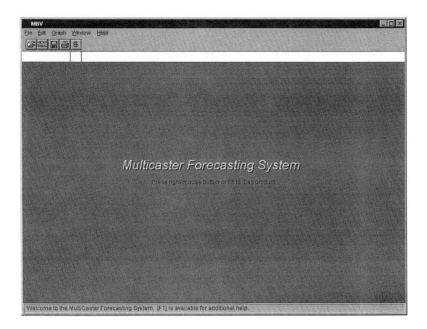

Figure 9.3. MULTICASTER Book Version File Load Selection Screen

adjustments to forecasts, analyze graphs, and perform various other functions we discuss later. Also, notice that in the lower left corner of Figure 9.6 are buttons labeled Worksheet, Settings (Figure 9.7), and Notes (Figure 9.8). By clicking on any of these three buttons, you can move among these three components of MBV.

Briefly, the settings screen is used to specify how you wish to forecast this particular product and to create the forecast. (When you first import and load a data file, there will be no forecast numbers in the worksheet until you access the Settings screen and "Reforecast.") The Notes screen is available to keep notes on the logic you used to make any forecasts.

When you have finished analyzing a particular product, you can save your changes from the File | Save menu, close the worksheet with the File | Close menu, and move on to any other products you wish to load and forecast. At this point, you also can add new future values to any of the regression variables by typing those values directly into the worksheet. To make these new values a permanent part of the worksheet, again follow the File | Save menu.

When you are finished forecasting all of your products for the current period and wish to move on to the next period (i.e., load a new period's demand for each product), you must access each product's Settings screen and select

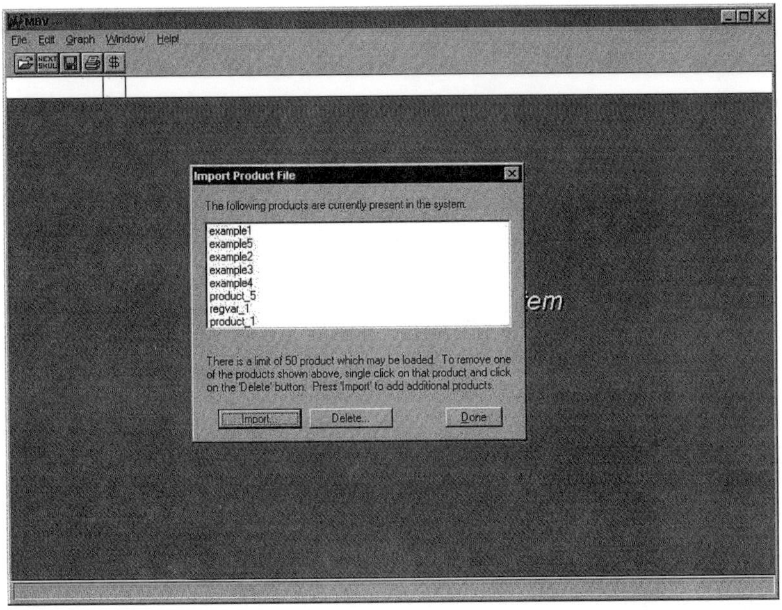

Figure 9.4. MULTICASTER Book Version File Import Screen

"Advance to Next Period." Because this process will "lock" all information in the current period, MBV will ask you to confirm that you wish to continue. If you select "Continue," then MBV will ask you to enter the demand value for the new "current period." You need to repeat this procedure for every product. Note that because the production version of MULTICASTER (i.e., MULTICASTER Forecasting System [MFS]) is designed to deal with a much larger number of products, this procedure for updating each period is automatic.

When you have finished forecasting and updating all the products you wish, you simply exit the system through the File I Quit menu.

Data Files

Our intention in creating the data files in a spreadsheet environment was to make it easy for the user to create, change, and import into MBV any of his or her own data.

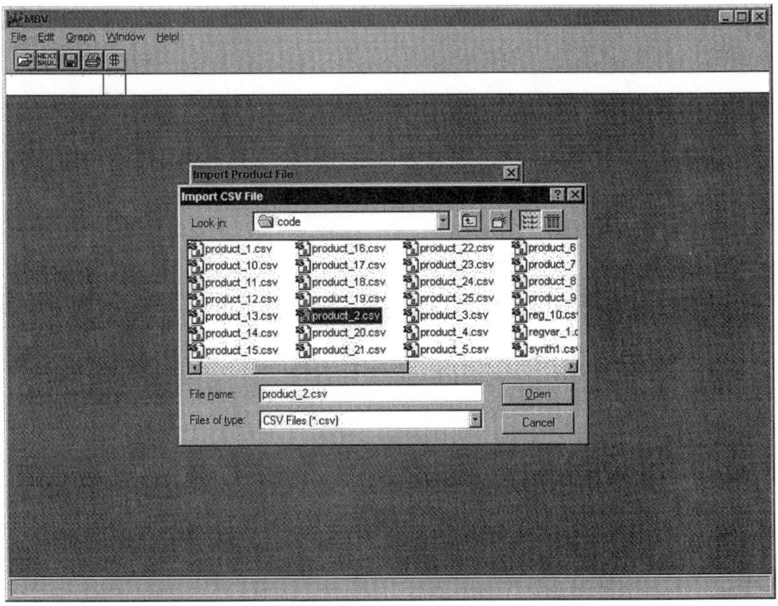

Figure 9.5. MULTICASTER Book Version File Import Selection Screen

To create you own data file, use Lotus 123 or Excel to access one of the MBV template spreadsheet data files (.csv file) included on your MBV diskette. Your data file should have the generic form illustrated in Figure 9.9. Your company name, your name, and ID are optional. However, it is important to enter in this data file the number of periods per year (12 if the data are monthly, 4 if quarterly, 52 if weekly), the period in which you are presently developing a forecast (the Current Period is 1 period past the last period with actual demand data), how many periods into the future you wish to forecast (Forecast Horizon), and the price per unit of the product.

You need to label the periods (columns) because these labels will be imported into the MBV worksheet. The next row is the actual history of demand that is to be forecast, followed in the regression template by the names and values per period of any regression variables (up to a total of 10) you wish to try. Again, it is important to include the regression variable names because these will be imported into MBV.

The data, which start in the second column, should be the information for the first period of the first year in which you have demand history that you wish to include in the forecasting analysis. For example, if your data begin in

units	Oct-96	Nov-96	Dec-96	Jan-97	Feb-97	Mar-97	Apr-97	May-97	Jun-97	Ju
Level	677	672	668	659	659	659	659	659	659	
Trend	-7	-6	-6	-6	-14	-21	-29	-36	-44	
Seasonality	17	10	3	-1	-10	-15	-15	-16	-9	
Predictor Effect	0	0	0	0	0	0	0	0	0	
MBV Forecast	687	676	665	652	635	623	615	607	606	
Analyst Adjustment										
Mgt Adjustment										
Adjusted Forecast	687	676	665	652	635	623	615	607	606	
Forecast Override										
Final Forecast	687	676	665	652	635	623	615	607	606	
Quarterly Forecast			2,028			1,910			1,828	
Annual Forecast (♦)	7,583	7,494	7,406	7,315	6,663	6,028	5,405	4,790	4,183	
Actual Demand	687	684	662							
Quarterly Demand			2,033							
Annual Demand (×)	8,510	8,418	8,313							
MBV:										
Percent Error	0.0%	-1.2%	0.5%							
MAPE	1.5%	1.5%	1.5%							
YTD MAPE	1.1%	1.2%	1.1%							

Figure 9.6. MULTICASTER Book Version Worksheet

August 1994, then the second column should start with January 1994, with blanks in the columns until you reach the column for August 1994 (where the actual demand values will begin). Ordinarily, the more history, the better, especially because regression and some of the time-series techniques need at least 2 years of data to work well. The total number of periods of history, in addition to the months into the future to forecast, can be up to 256. This is a deviation of MBV from MFS. Because MBV uses spreadsheet packages to import the data, it is limited to the number of columns allowed in such packages (i.e., 256) and, thus, has an upper limit to the number of periods that can be considered. There is no such limit in MFS.

The regression values must be entered as integers. For example, to enter price (which normally would be recorded in dollars), it must be entered in cents (e.g., $235.10 should be entered as 23510). This will not affect the accuracy of regression forecasting. Again, this is a limitation of MBV that does not exist in the larger production version (MFS).

When you have included all the information into your new spreadsheet, simply save it as a .csv file and it is ready to be imported into MBV.

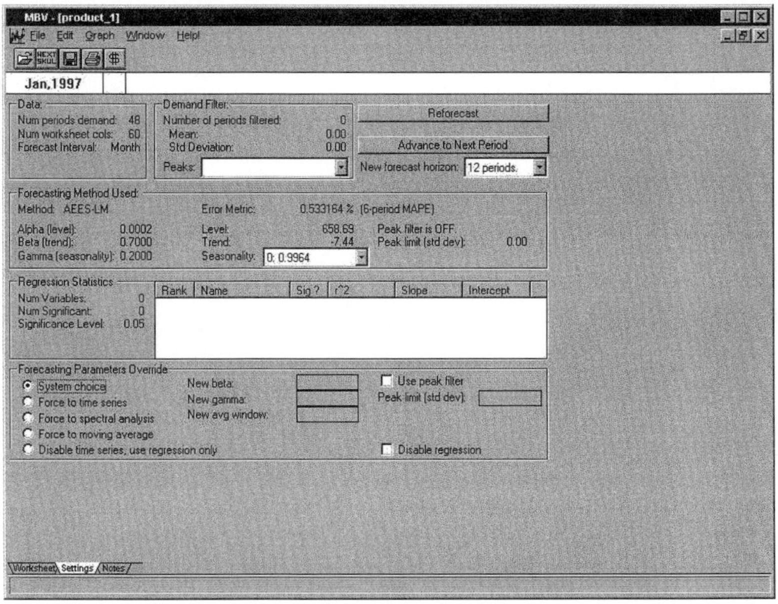

Figure 9.7. MULTICASTER Book Version Settings Screen

Worksheet

The worksheet (Figure 9.6) is an environment in which the forecast specified in the Settings screen can by qualitatively analyzed, adjusted, and/or overridden. If time series is used and level, trend, and/or seasonal components are identified, then they are placed in the corresponding first three rows in the worksheet. Even though the formulas in Chapter 3 described multiplying together the various components to get the forecast, to take advantage of the convenience of a worksheet, these three components are displayed in a fashion that allows them to be added together to arrive at a forecast (thus showing the impact of each component on the forecast).

The effects of all the significant regression variables for any given period are added together and placed in the fourth row of the worksheet (labeled Predictor Effect). Under this row, all regression variables that were included in the data file can be displayed. For each regression variable in each period, both the value of that variable in that period and the effect that value has on the forecast can be displayed. If the value of the variable is displayed but the

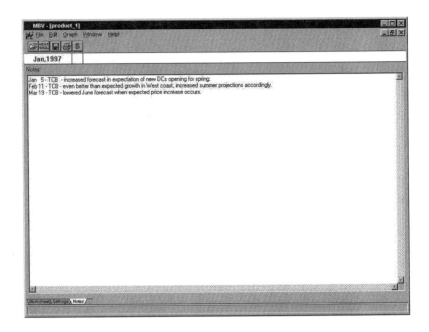

Figure 9.8. MULTICASTER Book Version Notes Screen

line below it is blank (the line for the effect on the forecast), it means that this variable did not have a significant effect on the forecast and, therefore, was not used. By default, this detailed information is displayed in the worksheet. If you wish to suppress this detail, then click on the green arrow in the Predictor Effect row label. If you wish to bring this detailed information back, then click again on the same arrow.

For each period, the Level, Trend, Seasonality, and Predictor Effect are added together to arrive at the MBV Forecast. For all periods previous to the current period (i.e., all periods for which actual demand exists), the forecast recorded is the forecast made 1 period before the period in question. In other words, for each of the previous periods, the recorded forecast was a forecast of 1 period into the future. This is the forecast on which the error statistics are calculated. For future periods, you can forecast as far forward as you want (and as specified in the data file). This is a deviation of MBV from MFS. In MFS, the user can specify how far into the future each forecast is important and calculate the error statistics based on this "critical forecast horizon."

As we discussed in Chapter 5, different individuals within a company may make different qualitative adjustments to forecasts; therefore, it is impor-

Company Na	ABC Inc		Notes: This example contains eight demand points, ten					
User Name	John Nemo		regression variables, and will produce forecasts out					
User ID	42		through Feb 97 (6 period forecast horizon).					
			An actual product would typically contain at least 2					
Number peri	12		or 3 years of demand points.					
Current Peri	9		Only cells shown in bold-italics are used by the program,					
Forecast Ho	6		other cells may contain notes, other numbers, graphs, etc.					
Unit Price	1.23							
Period	1	2	3	4	5	6	7	
	Jan-96	Feb-96	Mar-96	Apr-96	May-96	Jun-96	Jul-96	
Demand (u	12	43	21	23	65	23	45	
RegVar 1	2	3	4	6	7	4	3	
RegVar 2			4				4	
RegVar 3			3	2	1	4	6	
RegVar 4	6		1			2		
RegVar 5	1	3	4	6	2	3	4	
RegVar 6	2		1					
RegVar 7	1	1	4	6			4	
RegVar 8	1	2	2	3	3	2	2	
RegVar 9	3	2	1	3	4	6	2	
RegVar 10	4		2		1			

Figure 9.9. Example of .csv File to Be Imported Into MULTICASTER Book Version

tant to capture the impact of those adjustments separately. For this reason, three rows are provided in the worksheet to make changes to the systems forecast. Notice that if you try to make changes on any of these rows during previous periods, a "padlock" icon appears reminding you that you cannot make changes to forecasts in periods where the actual values are already known. (Sorry, but this would be cheating.)

In an actual company, the first adjustment row (Analyst Adjustment) typically would be made by a forecast analyst and constitutes adding or subtracting from the system forecast. The second row (Mgt Adjustment) typically would be made by a forecasting manager (hopefully, considering a broader range of factors as discussed in Chapter 5) and, again, constitutes adding or subtracting from the total of the system and the analyst forecast. The third row is an override of the system forecast and any adjustments that have been made to it. The result of these qualitative adjustments or overrides is the Final Forecast. Again, this is a deviation of MBV from MFS; MBV has only two adjustment rows and the override row, whereas MFS can have as many adjustment rows as the user wishes to specify, and only certain people can make adjustments on certain rows.

The next two rows in the worksheet provide a summation of the last 3 months or 13 weeks (the Quarterly Forecast row) and the next 12 months or 52 weeks (the Annual Forecast row).

The next three rows in the worksheet provide the same detail of information for the actual demand. If the actual demand in any period has been "filtered" (explained later in the "Settings" section), a green triangle will appear in the upper left corner of the actual demand cell for that period.

The rest of the worksheet displays error statistics discussed in Chapter 2: (a) for the MBV forecast, (b) for the forecast as adjusted by the analyst, and (c) for the final forecast (which includes either the management adjustment or the override).

A considerable amount of additional options and information is available in the pull-down menus and toolbar. The File menu allows new worksheets to be loaded (also possible from the toolbar), saving or quitting presently loaded worksheets (also possible from the toolbar), importing additional data files, printing a copy of the worksheet (also possible from the toolbar), exporting the existing file to Excel for more sophisticated graphing options, and quitting the MBV environment.

From the File | Load Product menu, two options exist. The user can select the list of all the products loaded into MBV and select the product to analyze (Directly option). The Directly option typically is sufficient for MBV, but MFS often has thousands (or hundreds of thousands) of products to forecast, so this list can become unwieldy. For this reason, the From Exception List option is provided. The Exception List contains products in decreasing order of a metric (called the Weighted PE [percent error]) which is equal to the total demand volume for that product for the last 3 periods times its 3-period mean absolute percent error (*MAPE*). The higher this error metric (or the worse the error), the earlier the product appears on the list. In MFS, this Exception List is adapted so that only those products with error rates higher than what is considered acceptable by management appear on the list. Remember the seventh principle from Chapter 6; you tell the system which forecasts are important (in this case, through the Exception List).

Because many popular spreadsheet packages have much more sophisticated graphing options than does MBV, it may be desirable to export the worksheet (once you have completed your analysis). As with most worksheet-like environments, MBV allows you to "copy" and "paste" to and from other spreadsheet packages. To select a range of cells to copy, first move to the first cell in the range, then press the period (.) key. Continue to move the cursor using the arrow keys. A black rectangle will surround a range of cells. When you have the range that you wish to copy selected, select the Copy option in the Edit menu. The cells will revert to the normal, nonhighlighted appearance, and the range will be copied to the clipboard. Now you can switch to another application and select Paste from *that application*'s Edit menu. The range selected will appear.

The preceding process also may be used to bring a range of cells from another package into MBV. However, because MBV permits changeable values only in the adjustment and override rows, only these rows will be affected. Because you cannot paste something that has not already been defined, the Paste option in the Edit menu will be able to be selected only if the clipboard already contains a "cut" or "copy" from another application.

If you would prefer to create a copy of the current worksheet and save it as a file, then you can select the Export option in the File menu. You can select either a text or an Excel format. The text format uses commas or tabs to separate the columns of worksheet information and may then be read into a word processing package. The Excel format permits you to create a file, which may be loaded using Microsoft Excel.

Either format allows you to select a subset or range of rows and columns of the entire worksheet. To select only a few columns to be exported, click on the All button below the Column Start/End section of the Export to File dialogue box. After clicking, you will be able to select a start column and an end column. Because the Microsoft Excel format will permit only up to 256 columns to be exported, this may limit the size of a weekly forecast export. Individual rows may be chosen similarly. Click on the All button below the Row(s) section. Again, after clicking, you may single-click to highlight individual rows to be exported.

If you choose to export all rows or columns, you may still click on the All button and select all rows and columns.

When you have completed selecting the worksheet range to export, click on the Export. . . button. A dialogue box will appear allowing you to choose the file name and location for the exported file. Click on the OK button to generate the file.

Although most of the toolbar buttons are self-explanatory, one toolbar button needs explanation. If the data loaded in the data (.csv) file consisted of units and a dollar value was entered in the file (in Cell B8 of the .csv file), then the forecasts will be developed in units, but the toolbar button with the dollar sign on it allows quick conversion of all numbers to dollars. Thus, users (such as production personnel) can look at forecasts in units or can quickly convert the forecasts to dollars if desired (as it might be by marketing and/or finance personnel). In MFS, this option is expanded to also allow quick conversion to product volume (a form in which a logistics manager might want to see the forecast for distribution center capacity planning), weight (a form in which a transportation manager might want to see the forecast for transportation vehicle planning), price, cost, or gross margin (forms in which financial managers and/or accounting managers might want to see the forecast).

If we are in a large worksheet with hundreds of columns, it can be tedious to look for the current month, that is, the one in which we are developing the next forecast. To alleviate this inconvenience, the Jump to Current Period option in the Edit menu moves the cursor to the month in which we are trying to develop the forecast. (You can accomplish the same thing directly by pressing Ctrl and N keys simultaneously.)

Under this same Edit menu is the option for forecasting new products through the Looks-Like option. Selecting this option produces the screen shown in Figure 9.10. This option produces a forecast for a user-specified number of periods (up to a maximum of all the periods in the first year). Once the number of periods is specified, you also must enter several qualitative assessments:

1. Your forecast of the total demand for these initial periods
2. Your qualitative assessment of what the growth in demand per period (trend) will be during these periods
3. Your assessment of when this demand will begin (the Insert at section of the screen)
4. Your assessment of the initial seasonal pattern

You have several options for specifying the initial seasonal pattern. The Product button allows you to select the seasonal pattern of any other products loaded into MBV. The next three options are variations on a seasonal pattern that follows a normal curve. The Clear Prior Models button removes any Looks-Like settings that have been previously saved for this product; that is, it gives you a "clean slate" from which to start reevaluating this new product. When you have completed your analysis, press the Apply button to apply the results to this product in the worksheet. This will cause the Looks-Like results to be displayed on the MBV Forecast row with a green triangle in the upper left corner of each affected cell. These Looks-Like forecasts will override any MBV forecasts for the affected periods (those displaying the green triangles).

By accessing the Graph menu (or pressing the Alt and # keys simultaneously), any of nine graphs can be displayed. These are the various graphs that sales forecasters typically use to assist in their analyses of system forecasts to

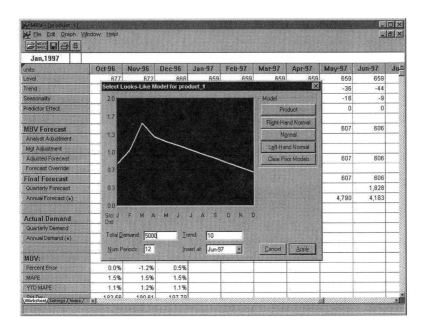

Figure 9.10. Looks-Like New Product Forecasting Screen

make qualitative adjustments. Users should familiarize themselves with each of these graphs and decide which are the most helpful to them.

A particular feature of Graph 5 should be discussed. When in this graph, if the user "feels" the forecast needs to be adjusted, it is not necessary to flip back to the worksheet, make an entry, and then flip back to the graph to see its effect. If you simply place the cursor on the Final Forecast line for the month you wish to change, click the left mouse button, and then move the cursor to where you think the forecast should be, the system will redraw the graph, calculate your change, and put that change in the Forecast Override cell for that period. In this way, you can "pick and point" your forecast changes.

You will notice when you do this (or when you make any qualitative adjustment, for that matter), the worksheet will display an icon of a finger with a string tied around it. This is to remind you to enter the Notes screen and record your logic for making this qualitative adjustment.

Settings

This component provides various forecasting status information and allows selection of forecasting methods and options through the screen illustrated in Figure 9.7. The Data section of this screen provides information on the number of periods in which actual demand data are available. The number of worksheet columns adds to this the number of periods in the initial year that have no actual demand values and the number of periods specified to forecast into the future (i.e., the forecast horizon). The Forecast Interval should be in weeks, months, quarters, or years.

The Demand Filter section of this screen is used only if you specify a peak filter in the lower right box on this screen. A peak filter is used when there are large peaks or troughs in the data that are not representative and, therefore, should not be included in the MBV forecast. When you enable the peak filter (by specifying the filter in terms of the number of standard deviations of the demand from the average), MBV will take any period in which demand is outside this range and "filter" the demand; that is, MBV still will record the actual demand value, but it will use the value that is the specified number of standard deviations above or below (depending on whether it is a peak or a trough, respectively) the average up to that period in the forecasting calculations. MBV will display in the Demand Filter section the number of periods in which demand was filtered and the mean and standard deviation as of the current period. The specific periods in which this filtering occurred, the actual demand value, and the filtered value also are displayed. Furthermore, MBV will indicate the filtered periods in the worksheet by placing a green triangle in the upper left corner of the Actual Demand cell for that period.

The Forecasting Method Used section displays information on the forecasting method currently being used in the MBV forecast. Method simply indicates the technique chosen either by MBV or the user. When you allow MBV to pick the "best" forecast, MBV tries a variety of techniques and selects the "best" based on the lowest *MAPE* for the last half year (the Error Metric). The Error Metric achieved for the technique chosen is displayed in this section. The lower left corner of this section displays parameters relevant to the technique chosen. The center of the section displays information on the level, trend, and seasonality values, and the right side of the section displays the peak filter status.

If regression variables were included in the data file and regression analysis is enabled (at the bottom of this screen), then the Regression Statistics screen will display relevant information on each regression variable. The left side of this section displays the number of variables that were included and the number that were found to be significant through stepwise regression at the .05 level of significance. The remainder of this section displays information on each variable included. Rank is the order in which the significant variables were selected during the stepwise process, followed by the nonsignificant variables in order of decreasing r^2. Slope is the b_1 value and intercept is the b_0 value in Equation 4.2.

The Forecasting Parameters Override section is where the user specifies how MBV should forecast this particular product. Selection of the System Choice option allows MBV to try the following:

1. Moving average (with the different numbers of periods included in the average ranging from 2 to the number of periods in a year)
2. Naive (a moving average with an N of 1)
3. Exponential smoothing
4. Exponential smoothing with trend
5. Exponential smoothing with seasonality
6. Exponential smoothing with trend and seasonality
7. Adaptive smoothing of 3, 4, 5, and 6
8. Open-model time series (OMTS) in the form of spectral analysis
9. Stepwise regression analysis

All of these techniques are defined in Chapter 3 or 4. MBV selects which of Techniques 1 through 8 produces the lowest error metric and then uses Technique 9 to forecast the residual.

You can select "Force to time series" if you want to try only exponential smoothing techniques (Techniques 3, 4, 5, 6, and 7). Because the values of beta and gamma must be between 0 and 1 in exponential smoothing, you can "turn off" a certain time-series component by setting the smoothing constant for that component equal to 0. In other words, to use exponential smoothing only (Technique 3), set the values of beta and gamma both equal to 0. This turns off trend (beta = 0) and seasonality (gamma = 0). Similarly, trend or seasonality can be left on or turned off to obtain Technique 4 or 5. If you do not enter anything for beta and gamma, MBV will find the optimal values of each (i.e., the values that minimize the error metric). Thus, when the "Force to time series" option is chosen, you still can allow MBV to find the best values of beta and gamma, you can enter your own values (between 0 and 1), or you can simply turn off the trend component and/or seasonality component. The reason for doing either of the latter two is to analyze the effect of each of these on forecasting accuracy.

You can select "Force to spectral analysis" if you want to try only OMTS (Technique 8). When this option is chosen, you still can allow MBV to find the best values of beta (smooths annual trend) and gamma (smooths season-ality), or you can enter your own (analyzing the effect of each of these on forecasting accuracy).

You can select "Force to moving average" if you want to try Technique 1 or 2. When this option is chosen, you still can allow MBV to find the best number of periods to include in the moving average (from 1, which is really the naive technique, to the number of periods in a year), or you can enter your own (analyzing the effect of each of these on forecasting accuracy).

For any of these options, you can enable regression analysis, which allows regression analysis to forecast the part of the demand that the time series could not (i.e., the noise or residual) in the same way as described for MFS in Chapter 6, or disable regression analysis. The option of "Disable time series, use regression only" is the converse of this; that is, MBV will not try to forecast demand with any of the time-series techniques. Rather, the actual demand is analyzed and forecast with regression analysis. The value of this option is that the information displayed in the Regression Statistics section pertains to how strongly each regression variable is related to the actual demand, not the residual after time series has forecast actual demand.

Notes

Any time a qualitative forecast is made or a qualitative adjustment is made to a quantitative forecast, it is crucial for sales forecasters to document their logic. The value of this is to review this logic when similar situations occur at later dates and/or to learn from the documented logic of other sales forecasters.

The Notes component of MBV assists in this documentation by providing a notebook attached to each product (Figure 9.8). Whenever you make qualitative adjustments and/or overrides, we encourage you to fully describe the logic that went into that change. For guidance in the types of factors to consider in this logic, you can review Chapter 5.

Conclusions

MBV is a special version of MFS created to accompany this book. As such, the passwords to enter MBV are related to Appendix B of this chapter. (We do not encourage anyone to use MBV without first learning the advantages and disadvantages of different forecasting techniques as described in this book.)

Although MFS is designed to handle a much larger number of product forecasts, MBV has the same analytical power of the larger production version. The intent of MBV is to allow readers of this book to quickly and easily apply what they have learned to their own products in a realistic forecasting system environment.

Appendix A
MBV Installation

The MBV program is sufficiently compact that you may run the program directly from the floppy disk that came with this book. However, many users prefer the increased performance/speed obtained by installing the program and associated data files on their computers' hard drives. You may choose to use the installation script or to copy the files manually. Each procedure is described in the following sections.

Installation Script

The installation script will make a copy of all product worksheets from the floppy disk to the hard drive. Therefore, any forecasting work performed using the example products on the floppy diskette also will be copied. Once installed, however, any new work or changes will reside only on the installed computer and will not be transferable back to the floppy or to another computer (unless files are copied manually, as described in the subsequent "Manual Installation" section).

To install MBV on your computer, place the MBV system diskette in the A drive, click on the Start button in the lower left corner of your screen, click on Run, and then enter "a:\setup" and press the Enter key.

A series of screens will appear, on which you will be asked to read a license agreement and then to select the subdirectory on which you wish to install the MBV system (typically "c:\MBV"). The setup program then creates the named subdirectory on your hard drive, copies the needed files, and creates shortcuts on your desktop to run the program.

After installation, if you wish to remove MBV from your computer, click on the Start button and then Settings and Control Panel. . . Double-click on the Add/Remove Programs icon, click on MBV from the list of installed programs, and then click on the Add/Remove button. Removing the MBV program also will remove any associated MBV forecasting worksheets on your computer.

Manual Installation

This section describes the manual version of the automatic one just described. It is intended for use in the unusual circumstances where the preceding script is not successful.

The MBV system consists of a single executable program (MBV.exe) and a single data file for each program imported into the system with a name of product.dta, where product is the name of the forecast item. The system may have up to 100 imported products (and therefore ".dta" files). In addition, a single MFS_list.dta contains the list of imported products.

Both the executable program and all the .dta files should reside in the same subdirectory, whether on a floppy diskette or on a hard drive. Loading these files on the chosen subdirectory is accomplished by the copy commands that are normal for your computer.

No registry variables or associated .dll files are used, and the program may be removed by simply deleting the MBV and .dta files.

Appendix B
MBV Passwords

We do not encourage anyone to use MBV without first reading this book. It is inadvisable to try forecasting with a system such as MBV without first understanding the logic of the sales forecasting techniques used. For this reason, we have provided a password screen in MBV that is tied to the book.

Each time you enter MBV, you will be asked for one of the passwords listed below. Simply type in the password that corresponds to the number below and continue to use MBV.

1 = system	21 = reason
2 = number	22 = without
3 = button	23 = continue
4 = addition	24 = phrase
5 = spread	25 = sheet
6 = continue	26 = windows
7 = procedure	27 = import
8 = product	28 = particular
9 = chapter	29 = briefly
10 = directly	30 = click
11 = done	31 = screen
12 = finish	32 = month
13 = larger	33 = version
14 = production	34 = forecast
15 = select	35 = marketing
16 = update	36 = label
17 = finance	37 = columns
18 = detail	38 = logistics
19 = multiply	39 = stepwise
20 = sales	40 = application

Note

1. MBV is designed to operate on any machine running Windows 95 or Windows NT 4.0 or greater.

CHAPTER 10

Managing the Sales
Forecasting Function

*W*e were trying to explain the intricacies of
*managing the sales forecasting function in the
company to the new CEO of a large retail chain—a new
CEO whose background was in marketing for a consumer
products manufacturer.*

*"I don't understand why this is such a big deal," he
said. "Just select the right technique and, where it needs
adjustment, let my marketing folks make the necessary
adjustments."*

*"That's fine at the product level," we answered, "but
you have to realize the magnitude of the number of
forecasts needed to run the stores. It doesn't help the
stores at all if we accurately forecast the demand for
men's white shirts, size 15/35, at the national level; the
store manager needs to know the demand at each store
for each shirt, in each style, in each size."*

*Recognition began to dawn on his face. "You know,
my background is in marketing. I never thought about
forecasting in terms of anything except the product. Just
how many variations of our products do we carry in each
store?"*

*The answer (given different products, sizes, and
styles) was 62,000!*

> *He gulped, "And we have 1,100 stores? Why, that*
> *means we have a DBN of forecasts to make each week!"*
> *"A DBN?" we asked.*
> *"Yeah, a darn big number."*
> *How this CEO learned to manage this DBN of*
> *weekly forecasts is largely the subject of this final chapter.*

Managing the sales forecasting function is concerned with more than just realizing how many forecasts we need to make to satisfy the planning needs of all the business functions. It also includes an understanding of the sales forecasting process, managing how the sales forecasting function interacts with other functional areas of the company, the interaction between sales forecasting processes and systems, the interaction between sales forecasting and business planning, what is forecast, the orientation of the sales forecasting function, the role of a sales forecasting champion, and how and where we measure the performance of this business function.

Before we address these aspects of sales forecasting management, however, there are a number of questions (listed in Table 10.1) that you should ask yourself about your company prior to embarking on defining and refining the sales forecasting function. How to find the answers to these questions is largely contained in the experience of the people within the company and in the first nine chapters of this book, but they must be answered for each company in its unique way before going on to the sales forecasting management issues mentioned in the previous paragraph and addressed more fully in the latter part of this chapter.

Sales Forecasting Management Questions

The answers to these questions should tell you much about how the sales forecasting function should operate to efficiently and effectively help your company conduct the business of developing and using sales forecasts.

Narrow or Broad Customer Base

The first question to ask is the following: Is your company's customer base narrow or broad? A narrow customer base simply means that the sales of the company (regardless of the unit or dollar volume) go to a relatively small number of customers. An example of a broad customer base is the consumer markets served by packaged goods manufacturers, whereas an example of a

TABLE 10.1 Sales Forecasting Management Questions

---

1. Customer base narrow or broad?
2. Data characteristics (shipments/sales/demand, age, detail, external data, quality)?
3. Number of forecasts (horizons and intervals, products, channels, locations)?
4. Number of new products?
5. Regional differences?
6. Seasonality?
7. Sophistication of personnel (systems and forecasting) and systems?
8. Sales forecasting budget?
9. Accuracy needed?

---

narrow customer base is that served by a manufacturer of specialized industrial components. One company with which we have worked produces a product that is only sold directly to automobile assembly plants in North America. Thus, even though this is a company with annual dollar sales in excess of $50 million, its customer base is only 56 customers (the number of automobile assembly plants in North America).

The narrower the customer base, the more likely a company can rely on direct customer contact information to produce more qualitatively oriented sales forecasts. In the example just given, the sales forecasting function calls the production scheduling department of each of its 56 customers each month and asks for the schedule of car production (which is sent by electronic data interchange [EDI]). From this information, a very accurate qualitative sales forecast can be derived.

Contrast this example to a large manufacturer of consumer products that sells to all of the 45 million households in the United States. Such a broad customer base makes any appreciable customer contact impossible (even if we surveyed 1 million homes, we still would have contacted only about 2% of our customers!) and causes more reliance on quantitative forecasting (i.e., time-series and regression) techniques. Thus, the narrower the customer base, the more a company can rely on direct customer contact qualitative techniques (discussed in Chapter 5), and the broader the customer base, the more reliance will be placed on quantitative techniques (Chapters 3 and 4), with qualitative adjustments.

Data Characteristics

The second set of questions concerns the type, availability, and qualtiy of data:

1. What data are available to your company for use in the forecasting function? Specifically, do you have data available on shipment history, order history, and/or customer demand (e.g., point-of-sale [POS] data)?
2. How old are the data (i.e., How many weeks, months, or years are contained in the data)?
3. At what level of detail are the data?
4. What data external to your company can you obtain to facilitate sales forecasting (i.e., external factors that might affect product demand for use in a regression model)?
5. How accurate are the data that are available?

Sales, shipments, and demand. The answer to the first question determines what we will forecast. It is important to distinguish among sales, shipments, and demand. Although called sales forecasting, this function really is about forecasting demand. Demand is what our customers want to buy from us, sales is our ability to accept orders from our customers, and shipments is what our operations system can actually deliver to our customers. Suppose, for example, that demand for one of our products next month is 10,000 but that our salespeople (due to uncertainty about delivery time commitments) can confirm only 9,000 units in actual sales. Suppose, further, that our production/logistics system can produce and deliver only 7,500 units of those ordered (sold). If our information system only collects and records shipments, then our historical record of this month will show shipments of 7,500 units *and nothing else*! What will be lost is the fact that we actually sold 1,500 units more and could have sold 2,500 units more if the capacity to produce and deliver had been available. With only this shipments history available to the forecasting function, we will continue to forecast "demand" to be 7,500 units per month, never recognize the lost sales each month, and never increase capacity to capture this extra true demand. However, if the only data we have are a history of what we have shipped in the past, then these are the data we will have to use until more meaningful demand data can be gathered. However, the commitment should be made immediately to begin gathering these more accurate sales and demand data.

Data age. How much historical data are available largely defines the sales forecasting techniques that can be used. If less than 1 year of data are available, then only the more simplistic fixed-model time-series (FMTS) techniques are going to work; any time-series technique that considers seasonality needs at least 2 years of data (so that it can identify two complete seasonal patterns) to begin forecasting effectively. Open-model time-series (OMTS) techniques typically need at least 4 years of data, whereas regression analysis typically needs at least 5 periods of data for each variable in the regression equation (so that if we had sales as 1 variable and had advertising, price, and trade promotions as the 3 independent variables, we would need at least 4 variables times 5, or 20 periods of data). Of course, many companies have such short life cycles for their products that many of these techniques are simply never practical.

Data level. The level of detail of the data refers to the planning detail required. If we are forecasting annual dollar sales by product line for a marketing plan, then data at the same level and time horizon are fine. However, if we also need weekly unit forecasts by stock keeping unit by location (SKUL), then annual product line data will be of little help. Because we need sales forecasts for a number of different functional plans, data at the level of detail corresponding to each of these planning needs are necessary.

This level of detail is called the *forecasting hierarchy* and is defined as all the planning levels and time horizons/intervals at which forecasts are needed. Table 10.2 illustrates one such forecasting hierarchy for a company with which we have worked. In this company, the logistics function needs forecasts weekly by SKUL, the production and purchasing functions need forecasts biweekly by stock keeping unit (SKU), the sales function needs dollar sales quarterly by product, the marketing function needs annual dollar sales for the next year by product line and for the next 5 years by division, and finance needs annual dollar sales for the next 5 years by strategic business unit (SBU) and for the overall corporation. The data detail required for developing a forecast for each of these functions must match each planning level, horizon, and interval.

External data availability. Finally, the availability of data on factors external to the actual sales history determines whether or not regression analysis can be used. If the only data available are concerned with sales, shipments, or demand history, then there is no information on which to build a regression model. To complete the variable selection stage discussed in Chapter 4, historical data on factors such as price, advertising, trade and consumer promotions, economic activity, and competitive actions (for just a few examples) must be available.

Data quality. Corporate records are not always as trustworthy as we would like them to be. Invoices sometimes do not get entered, they can be

TABLE 10.2 Example Forecasting Hierarchy

Corporate (Years 1-5 annual, dollar)
↑
Strategic business unit (Years 1-5 annual, dollar)
↑
Division (Years 1-5 annual, dollar)
↑
Product line (annual, dollar)
↑
Product (quarterly, dollar)
↑
Stock keeping unit (biweekly, unit)
↑
Stock keeping unit by location (weekly, unit)

---

entered with errors when they do get entered, and demand may be recorded in the wrong period. All of these are examples of data quality problems.

One company with which we have worked was quite proud of its EDI system of recording its distributors' POS demand. However, when we interviewed distributors for this company, we found that these POS orders actually were taken and filled by a paper system and were entered into the electronic system later. During high-demand months, distributors "simply do not have the time to keep the system up to date; we are too busy selling." The result was that many orders did not get entered into the system until the month after the demand occurred. Of course, this resulted in inaccurate data on monthly demand patterns.

Number of Forecasts

The third set of questions concerns how many forecasts you need, and this is a function of the following:

1. At what levels, time horizons, and intervals are forecasts required?
2. How many products (i.e., product lines and product items [SKUs]) must be forecast?
3. In how many distribution channels are your products marketed?
4. How many product/location combinations (e.g., by sales regions, distribution centers, individual customers) must be forecast?

Levels, horizons, and intervals. We have said many times in this book that the different functional areas require forecasts at different levels, time horizons, and intervals. Examination of Table 10.3 (which is really a reproduction of Table 1.1) to determine how the various functional areas in your company fill in the bottom three rows begins to answer this question of how many forecasts are required and how often they are required (i.e., defining the forecasting hierarchy).

Number of products. To understand the impact of forecasting different numbers of products, contrast the forecasting process for a company that manufactures a group of specialized industrial components with the forecasting process for an apparel manufacturing company that must forecast the numerous SKUs generated by multiple size, color, style, and fabric combinations. Limited product line companies can devote considerably greater attention to any one forecast than can broad line companies that have literally thousands of products to forecast for each of the levels, horizons, and intervals mentioned in the previous question. For example, one telephone company with whom we worked in the 1980s had essentially only one product to forecast—new phone installations. With no local competition, this was the only forecast relevant to all the planning functions; thus, a team of three people devoted its full attention to developing one forecast each month. This team could put considerably greater time into using sophisticated OMTS and regression analysis than could a company such as Brake Parts, Inc., which has several hundred thousand products to forecast each month (Mentzer & Schroeter, 1993).

Distribution channels. The third question in this set considers companies that have multiple channels for the same product. For example, an automotive parts manufacturer may market a certain product directly to original equipment manufacturers, through a separate channel under its own brand name, and through a large retailer channel under the brand name of that retailer. Thus, this one product is now marketed through three separate channels, each with its own demand patterns and, therefore, its own forecasting needs.

Production/location combinations. Similarly, the difference between the number of SKUs and the number of SKULs can dramatically change the number of forecasts that are required. As the example at the beginning of this chapter illustrates, the number of forecasts needed to meet the planning needs of all business functions is determined by the number of products we produce *and* the number of locations at which they are shipped or sold.

TABLE 10.3 Forecasting Requirements of Various Managerial Functions

	Marketing	Sales	Finance/ Accounting	Production: Long Term	Production/ Purchasing: Short Term	Logistics: Long Term	Logistics: Short Term
Needs	Annual plans (updated monthly or quarterly) for new and existing products or product changes, promotional efforts, channel placement, and pricing	Setting goals for the sales force and motivating salespeople to exceed those goals	Projecting cost and profit levels and capital needs	Planning the development of plant and equipment	Planning specific production runs	Planning the development of storage facilities and transportation equipment	Specific decisions of what products to move to what locations and when
Level	Product or product line	Product by territory	Corporate, division, product line	Product (SKU)	Product (SKU)	Product by location (SKUL)	Product by location (SKUL)
Horizon	Annual	1-2 years	1-5 years	1-3 years	1-6 months	Monthly to several years	Daily, weekly, monthly
Interval	Monthly or quarterly	Monthly or quarterly	Monthly or quarterly	Quarterly	Weekly or monthly	Monthly	Daily, weekly, monthly

NOTE: SKU = stock keeping unit; SKUL = stock keeping unit by location.

New Products

Similarly, the number of new products introduced in a given planning horizon affects how we will forecast. Are these variations on existing products or truly new products? Not surprisingly, we have found that the forecasting of genuinely new products is cited by many companies as one of the most difficult forecasting problems they face. At its best, new product forecasting is a leap into the future with little or no historical information to tell us which way to leap. New product forecasting can take a great deal of sales forecasting personnel time, can hurt the credibility of the forecasting group through poor new product forecasting accuracy, and can reduce the morale of the forecasting group. It is, however, a necessary function in a competitive environment and should be augmented by procedures such as those discussed in Chapters 5, 6, and 9.

Regional Differences

Regional differences in how the product is purchased will increase the number of forecasts to be made and the analysis required. For example, manufacturers of agricultural chemicals have a very different market in the United States as compared to that in Canada. The much shorter growing season in Canada creates entirely different market behaviors that must be forecast differently.

Seasonality

Similarly, the degree of seasonality of the products we market affects the techniques used to forecast. Many FMTS techniques and regression do not consider seasonality and, thus, either should not be used in high seasonal situations or should be used in conjunction with techniques that do consider seasonality.

Personnel and Systems Sophistication

How sophisticated are the personnel involved in the sales forecasting function? Do they have educational backgrounds in statistics or econometrics? What is their level of experience and knowledge regarding the industry in which your company does business? If the answers to these questions are on the lower side, then additional training of sales forecasting personnel probably is in order (statistical/quantitative analysis training for those with business experience and business experience/qualitative analysis training for those with statistical backgrounds), and the sophistication of the techniques used should be limited until such training is obtained.

How sophisticated are the hardware and software systems available for use in forecasting? Are there electronic interfaces among the systems (hardware and software applications) in use by producers and users of the sales forecasts? Without such interconnectivity, many of the benefits that accrue from the sales forecasting system principles discussed in Chapter 6 cannot be realized.

Budget

Similarly, without a commitment to the sales forecasting budget, these training and systems problems probably will not get fixed. Interestingly, we found in Phase 2 of the benchmarking studies that few companies felt their sales forecasting budgets were adequate.

Accuracy Needed

Finally, what level of accuracy is required for the various forecasts? That is, what are the consequences of forecasting error at various levels (e.g., SKUL), time horizons, and time intervals? We have found that forecasting accuracy often is considered to be like customer service—the more, the better. However, true analysis of sales forecasting management sometimes produces the conclusion that the benefit of improved accuracy is not worth the cost. *All* the dimensions of sales forecasting performance measurement discussed in Chapter 2 should be taken into consideration to conduct a return-on-investment (ROI) analysis of any changes to sales forecasting management. The costs of training, new systems, and improved techniques all should be weighed against the improvements in supply chain costs, planning costs, and customer service levels. In most cases, the ROI on such investments is dramatic, but it still should be evaluated to determine what is an acceptable level of sales forecasting accuracy for each business function in each level, horizon, and interval.

The Sales Forecasting Process

With these questions in mind, it is important to review the sales forecasting process in its entirety before we try to manage it. Figure 10.1 illustrates the components of the sales forecasting process. Linking the *environment* in which the sales forecasting process exists and the resultant *sales forecasting performance* are *sales forecasting management, systems, techniques,* and *users.* Sales forecasting management encompasses the approach taken to manage the sales forecasting process (discussed later in this chapter). Sales forecasting techniques encompass the selection between the time-series, regression, and qualitative alternatives discussed in Chapters 3, 4, and 5, respectively. Sales forecasting systems (discussed in Chapter 6) are the analysis and communications template that is laid over the sales forecasting management processes (also discussed later in this chapter). How skillfully a company coordinates this sales forecasting process ultimately determines the success of the sales forecasting function.

On the outer ring of Figure 10.1 is the environment in which the demand for the company's products (and, consequently, the uncertainty faced by the sales forecasting function) exists. As one of the questions earlier in this chapter indicated, this environment also encompasses the availability of a history of orders, shipments, or demand, that is, the data that can be used to help determine sales forecasts. The state of the economy and the level of competition in the industry and the supply chain, as well as possible competitive responses to company marketing policies (e.g., advertising), also are factors that affect the sales forecasting process.

On the inner circle of Figure 10.1 are the *sales forecast users,* which include marketing, sales, finance/accounting, production/purchasing, and logistics. Before examining the managerial approach, the differing forecasting requirements of various business functions within the organization must be considered. Effectively and efficiently managing the sales forecasting function requires recognition of these varied requirements because, as we discussed in Chapter 1, different functions within the organization have different needs from the sales forecast as input to their planning processes (see Table 10.3).

Because marketing focuses on annual plans for products (e.g., brands) and/or product lines that are updated on a monthly or quarterly basis, they need dollar forecasts of product and/or product lines with a yearly time horizon and monthly or quarterly intervals.

The sales function focuses on setting sales quotas and motivating the sales force to meet or exceed these quotas. The sales forecast level required by sales is determined by how the sales force is organized in the company (e.g., by geographic sales territory, by industry, by customer) and is generally some combination of product by location, product by industry, and product by customer. Because sales managers' planning horizons (which depend on the structure of the compensation plan) often are yearly, and because individual

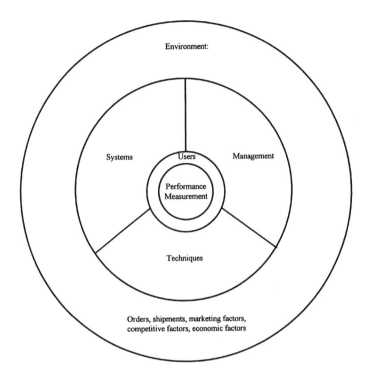

Figure 10.1. The Sales Forecasting Management Process

salespeople frequently receive quarterly commissions, the sales forecasts required by the sales function typically have a time horizon of 1 year with quarterly interval updates.

Because the planning process for finance is concerned with predicting costs (provided by accounting), revenues, profits, and capital resource requirements, it generally requires relatively long-term dollar forecasts (e.g., a 1- to 5-year time horizon with monthly or quarterly updates). Similarly, because finance is concerned with resource planning for a corporation or division, the forecast level required typically is at the corporate or perhaps divisional or SBU level.

The production function must generate both long- and short-term plans. Long-term plans are required for planning plant and equipment development, whereas short-term plans are required for production scheduling and purchasing. Because plant and equipment planning requires information about what product items or mixture of product items will be produced when facilities are brought on line, the sales forecasts must be at the SKU level with a time horizon sufficient for bringing new production facilities on line (e.g., 1 to 3 years) and updated at intervals (typically quarterly) to ensure that the plans remain in line with market developments.

Production scheduling and purchasing require sales forecasts at the SKU level so that production of specific product items (and the scheduling of the materials to produce them) can be planned. Furthermore, because production planning is generally accomplished on a 1- to 6-month time horizon with weekly or monthly updates, both production scheduling and purchasing require sales forecasts at the corresponding time horizons and intervals.

The responsibility of logistics is to ensure the timely shipment of product items to required locations. To accomplish this, logistics, similar to production, must generate long- and short-term plans, both of which require sales forecasts at the SKUL level. Long-term plans are required to develop storage and/or transportation facilities, and short-term plans are required to construct inventory and transportation schedules. The forecasting horizon required for long-term logistics planning depends on how long it takes to bring distribution facilities (e.g., distribution centers, transportation equipment) on line and can vary from 1 month (e.g., for rented facilities) to 2 years (e.g., for custom-built transportation equipment or distribution centers) with monthly forecast intervals for plan updating. The forecasting horizon for short-term logistics plans, which depends on the company's order cycle time (e.g., from manufacturing plant to distribution center or customer), requires monthly, weekly, or, in some cases, daily sales forecasts with weekly or daily intervals for updating.

As the preceding discussion illustrates, sales forecasting requirements can range from the SKUL to the corporate level, from weekly to multiple-year time horizons, and from daily to quarterly time intervals. The managerial approach has a significant effect on the success in meeting these diverse requirements.

Sales Forecasting Managerial Approaches

Based on our research and experience with hundreds of companies, we have found that companies typically organize their sales forecasting function in one of four ways: the *independent approach,* the *concentrated approach,* the *negotiated approach,* or the *consensus approach* to sales forecasting management.

Furthermore, we also have found that the efficiency and effectiveness of a company's sales forecasting organization depend on the degree of functional integration that exists within the company. The components of functional integration are defined as Forecasting C^3—communication, coordination, and collaboration. Communication is the written, verbal, and electronic information shared among the functional areas. Coordination is the formal structure and required meetings between two or more functional areas. Collaboration is an orientation among functional areas toward common goal setting (in this case, common sales forecasting performance goals). The four managerial approaches, as well as the degree of functional integration each approach entails, are now discussed with regard to the implications of these two concepts for the success of a company's sales forecasting function.

The Independent Management Approach

Companies that use the *independent* approach to sales forecasting tend to be quite naive in their approaches to organizing their sales forecasting functions. Each functional department in a company develops a sales forecast geared to its specific requirements; for example, finance develops a corporate-level dollar forecast 1 to 5 years out, production develops 6-month product item (SKU) forecasts for production scheduling, logistics develops monthly product/location (SKUL) forecasts for distribution planning, and so forth.

The problem with this approach is not necessarily that each department develops a forecast in the format that fits its particular requirements; rather, the problem is the lack of functional integration that characterizes this approach. With the independent approach to forecasting management, there is little (if any) communication, no coordination, and no collaboration among the functional areas with regard to the forecasting process. The lack of communication prevents input into each department's forecasting process from perspectives other than its own, thereby hindering each department's effort to develop an accurate forecast. How can production or logistics possibly develop an accurate forecast for its production or distribution planning without being aware of marketing's promotional schedule? Even more important, however, is the fact that the absence of coordination and collaboration among the departments developing separate forecasts hinders the departmental sales forecasts being used as a contribution to the planning functions in various departments as well as corporate-level planning.

The Concentrated Management Approach

The *concentrated* form of sales forecasting organization assigns forecasting responsibility to one department (e.g., logistics or marketing). Our research and experience have revealed that this managerial approach at least partially addresses the communication and coordination aspects of functional integration more effectively than does the independent managerial approach. Oral, written, and sometimes electronic communications generally take place among the various departmental users of the sales forecast developed by the responsible department, and these communications provide information that can be incorporated into the official forecast. Furthermore, formal meetings frequently are scheduled, or there is some structure in place for distributing the official forecast to all departments. However, this managerial approach does not address the collaboration aspect of functional integration, as evidenced by the fact that the forecast developed by the responsible department is heavily biased by that department's forecasting and planning requirements. If logistics is the department responsible for developing the sales forecasts, then the forecast will be at the SKUL level with a time horizon of 1 month to several years and daily, weekly, or monthly updating intervals. If marketing develops the sales forecast, then it will be in product/brand dollars or product line dollars with a yearly time horizon and monthly or quarterly updates.

Furthermore, we have found that sales forecasting concentrated in marketing tends to lead to capacity-unconstrained forecasts. In other words, marketing tends to develop forecasts that are solely based on market demands and do not consider the capacity constraints of the production and logistics systems. Conversely, sales forecasting concentrated in an operations area (production or logistics) tends to develop forecasts that are based on capacity constraints and ignore the demands of the company's markets. The problem with either form of concentration is that because of the lack of a collaboration among departments, the orientation of the sales forecasts tends to ignore information from other departments and the form of the official sales forecast ignores the requirements of some departments. Therefore, this managerial approach seldom provides effective input to all the planning processes.

The Negotiated Management Approach

A company that uses a *negotiated* approach to manage its sales forecasting process develops sales forecasts in each functional department and then assembles representatives from each department during each forecasting interval to negotiate an official sales forecast for each forecasting level and horizon. In terms of functional integration, the negotiated approach overcomes some of the bias problems of the concentrated approach by encouraging communication and, particularly, coordination among departments. However, because each department initially develops its own sales forecasts to bring to the negotiation process, there is no real collaboration in terms of the forecasting process; that is, the development of the sales forecasts is guided not by common goals and information but rather by the separate goals, information, and requirements of each individual department.

In addition, the negotiation process intrinsic to this approach is plagued with political pressures among departments that can bias the negotiated forecast. Remember, each department brings its own forecast to the negotiation process, a forecast that was developed on the basis of its own requirements. Particularly when there is a power imbalance among departments that allows one or more departments to dominate the negotiation process, these separate orientations can bias the final forecast.

The Consensus Management Approach

In the *consensus* form of sales forecasting organization, a committee consisting of representatives from each functional department, as well as a member designated to be in charge of the forecasting committee, is responsible for developing sales forecasts using input from each department. A genuine consensus forecasting approach incorporates high levels of Forecasting C^3 by asking the forecasting committee to develop a common forecast— one that is based not on the individual forecasts of different departments but rather on informational input from each department to develop a common forecast. This degree of functional integration can assist in overcoming the biased forecasts produced by the focus on individual departmental requirements in the concentrated form of sales forecasting organization. If commitment to common goals (i.e., collaboration) is sufficiently evolved, then this can aid in overcoming the political problems that tend to bias forecasts developed under the negotiated form of sales forecasting organization. Companies contemplating this managerial approach should understand that it is resource intensive in terms of both time and personnel. However, if a company has the resources to encourage the necessary functional integration, then the consensus form of organization can result in superior sales forecasts.

Processes and Systems

Many companies with which we have worked have asked us to advise them on the sales forecasting system they should use. Invariably, when we are asked this question, we ask them to describe the management process by which the sales forecasts are developed. Often, there are no answers; the companies are trying to develop systems solutions without an understanding of the management process. This is a backward approach to sales forecasting management.

In many companies in the benchmarking studies, there was no one person in the company who understood the entire sales forecasting process. Many individuals understood bits and pieces of the process, but few understood the *entire* process. Without such an understanding, it is not possible to design and implement a system to augment this process.

In fact, the sales forecasting system should be a communication and analysis framework (template) that can be laid over the sales forecasting management process. The company has to define the process first. An example should help illustrate this concept.

One global manufacturer of industrial products with which we have worked has multiple product lines sold all over the world by a direct sales force. Many of these products are sold to customers in numerous industries. Thus, we may have a product that is sold by one salesperson in Australia to a particular industry and another salesperson in Europe who sells the same product for a different use in another industry. This has led to a worldwide sales force that specializes in certain products, in certain industries, and in certain geographic areas.

Given this multifaceted complexity of the sales forecasting environment, the company wanted a system that allowed development of a quantitative forecast with qualitative adjustment by geographic territory by industry by the sales force, with adjustment by product line by marketing managers, and with overall planning adjustments by upper management. This led to a definition of the company's sales forecasting process that is illustrated in Figure 10.2. The process starts with a computer model-generated forecast. These sales forecasts are broken down by product, industry, and geographic territory and are sent electronically to the sales force. Each salesperson is provided with a quarterly report of economic and market trends in his or her industry and is asked to make adjustments to the quantitative forecasts. When adjustments are made, the salesperson is asked to electronically record the logic behind the adjustments.

All of the sales force adjustments are electronically transmitted back to the forecasting group, where they are combined. Each marketing manager then receives the adjusted forecasts for his or her product lines and markets. Again, the marketing managers are asked to qualitatively adjust these forecasts and record their logic.

These forecast adjustments are received and compiled by the forecasting group and are transmitted to management for adjustment at the divisional level. Once the upper management adjustments are received, the forecasts are

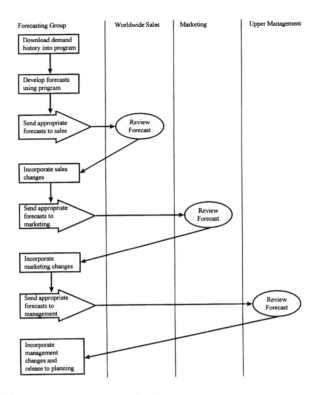

Figure 10.2. Example Sales Forecasting Process

broken down to the level and horizon appropriate for each functional planning area and are transmitted electronically for use in planning.

Notice that this process has laid over it the systems template to transmit all information electronically, pull information necessary for the computer model forecasts from appropriate data sources within the company and the supply chain, aggregate and disaggregate to the level and horizon needed at each step, and compare each forecast and adjustment to the actual demand once it is received (more on this last point later in this chapter).

Sales Forecasting and Planning: An Iterative Process

What is not captured in this example but is an integral part of any sales forecasting process is an implementation of the iterative process of sales forecasting and planning. As we discussed in the benchmarking studies chapters, many Stage 1 companies use their business plans to drive the sales forecasts—a naive approach given that the forecasts should be driven by the realities of the marketplace, not the financial needs of the corporations. More sophisticated companies develop sales forecasts independently of their business plans, but when the forecasts and the plans diverge, the forecasts are made to "fit" the plans.

In fact, companies that are effective at sales forecasting and business planning start with the sales forecasting process. Remember our definition of a sales forecast back in Chapter 1: *a projection into the future of expected demand given a stated set of environmental conditions.* Given expected economic and competitive conditions *and* initial marketing/sales/production/logistics plans, we make a projection of future expected demand. From this base, the business plan can be developed. When the resultant business plan does not meet the financial needs/goals of the company, we iterate back to the sales forecast and examine what additional efforts in marketing and/or sales can be undertaken to increase the demand forecast and what additional efforts can be undertaken by production/logistics to increase capacity to the level necessary to meet the business plan. It is this iterative process of sales forecast to business plan and then back to sales forecast to business plan, and so on, that ensures a business plan that is based on the financial *and* marketplace realities facing the company.

Functional Silos

Much has been written in recent years about the functional "silos" of management and how important it is to "tear down the walls" between these silos to integrate the information, goals, and strategies of the various business functions. If we look at finance/accounting, marketing, sales, production/purchasing, and logistics as separate management functions/silos, we find that two additional business functions are actually the integrating forces in the company. Figure 10.3 illustrates this concept.

All five of the business planning functions that we have discussed throughout this book can be represented by the vertical, separate silos, whereas information systems and sales forecasting are diagonal, integrating silos. The integrating role of information systems comes from the fact that information systems need to take in information from all five of these business functions *and* that all five of these business functions need information from

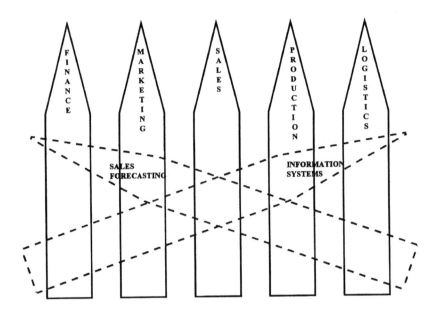

Figure 10.3. The Integrating Force of Sales Forecasting Management

information systems. Finance/accounting takes in information on marketing expenditures, sales commissions, production costs, and so forth *and* reports performance metrics back to each of these functions. In addition, information systems provide *coordinating information*—information that crosses functional silo boundaries to coordinate the planning of each business function with the plans of the other business functions.

In a like manner, sales forecasting needs information on marketing plans, sales plans, production/purchasing schedules, and logistics capacities to develop informed forecasts. In addition, each of these functions needs sales forecasts at the appropriate level and horizon and updated at the appropriate intervals to develop effective plans. Sales forecasting depends on information systems to provide this information and to communicate the forecasts back to the other functions. In this manner, the five traditional functional silos are actually brought together by information systems and sales forecasting. In fact, to effectively manage the business, information systems and sales forecasting should be inextricably intertwined with each other and the other business functions.

A Forecasting Champion

One factor that we have noticed in common among all the companies with which we have worked that are successful at sales forecasting is the existence of a *sales forecasting champion.* Whether the heads of recognized forecasting groups, part of loose collections of forecasters within different departments, or users of the sales forecasts who do not actually develop them, forecasting champions have several characteristics in common. First, they have an appreciation of the managerial/planning role that sales forecasting plays within the corporation (e.g., the importance of managing the sales forecasting function in conjunction with the other business functions, the iterative role of sales forecasting and business planning, the different sales forecasting needs of the other business functions). Second, they are strong, clear advocates for the role of sales forecasting in business planning to anyone who will listen, especially upper management. Third, they may or may not have strong statistical training, but they always have a strong understanding of the environment in which the company operates and an appreciation of the advantages and disadvantages of different statistical approaches. We call this latter trait *quantitative analysis strength,* rather than statistical strength, because it means much more than just the ability to analyze a stream of numbers with statistics. Rather, it is an appreciation of where certain statistical techniques do and do not work and where qualitative (informed business environment) analysis is superior to, or can augment, statistics.

As a career path, many forecasting champions become the heads of forecasting groups, often with the title of forecasting manager or director of forecasting, and continue with this as a career for many years. Many in such positions move on to higher roles in the business planning function of their companies. Still others move into the more traditional business functions while keeping their understanding and appreciation of the sales forecasting/business planning ability to leverage corporate effectiveness. Regardless of the eventual career path that will be taken, however, the challenge to anyone reading this book is to answer the question: Are you willing to become the forecasting champion in your company?

A Final Word on Performance Measurement

We could not end this book without revisiting the management principle we introduced in Chapter 2:

What gets measured gets rewarded
and
What gets rewarded get done.

Sales forecasting management is no exception. To implement this principle, as managers, we need to look at it backward. What do we want to get done? If we look at the example in Table 10.2, we see that this company needs to achieve improved planning at the weekly SKUL level (for logistics planning), at the biweekly SKU level (for production scheduling and purchasing planning), at the quarterly dollar sales by product level (for sales management), at the annual dollar sales for the next year by product line and the next 5 years by division level (for marketing), and at the annual dollar sales for the next 5 years by SBU and the overall corporation level (for finance). If we add the information in Figure 10.3 (actually, Table 10.2 and Figure 10.3 are adapted from the same company), we see that this company also needs to achieve accurate forecasts from the model developed by the forecasting group and accurate adjustments to these forecasts by the sales force, the marketing managers, and upper management.

These details tell us what we want to get done. The next step is to reward the forecasting group for producing forecasts that are accurate at the various levels and horizons in the forecasting hierarchy of Table 10.3. In addition, members of the sales force should be rewarded for their adjustments to these forecasts at the level and horizon at which they are comfortable making such adjustments. The same can be said for rewarding marketing managers and upper management. Of course, to fairly provide these rewards, we need to go back to the first step in our principle and measure the accuracy (and the cost and customer service implications of improved accuracy discussed in Chapter 2) of the forecasts and adjustments at each of these levels and horizons and base rewards on these performance metrics.

One company that embraced this concept is actually the company that was the example at the beginning of Chapter 1 (we have now come full circle with our examples). Once the roles of each functional area in developing the sales forecasts had been clearly defined in a monthly schedule that described what had to be done to develop the sales forecast on each day and who was responsible for its completion (a chart much like Figure 10.3), a forecasting champion was named with the sole responsibility of seeing that each daily step was completed. Finally, as a recognition of the principle just discussed, the vice president of marketing changed the reward structure for the product managers; fully 25% of their performance appraisals (and, consequently, their bonuses) became based on improving forecasting accuracy over the previous forecasting period. Of course, to accomplish this, we had to institute a performance evaluation system to track the effect of their adjustments on forecasting accuracy. Where product managers previously had spent an average of a half day each month developing their forecasts, with this change the average grew to 4 days per month. The selection by the forecasting group of the proper forecasting techniques for each product had a profound impact on accuracy. However, the largest improvements in forecasting performance came not from techniques but rather from improvements in the systems and management of the sales forecasting function and the extra time the product managers devoted to adjusting the forecasts—extra time that was the result of rewarding the effect of this effort on performance.

Conclusions

We began the preface of this book by stating that this effort had been a labor of love. Well, sometimes love hurts. It was an enjoyable, yet gut-wrenching, process to bring together the experiences of three decades of work with hundreds of companies, all between the covers of one book. We profoundly hope this effort assists you in better managing the sales forecasting function within your company and, as a result, in better managing the company overall. If we have accomplished this, then we have been successful.

Reference

Mentzer, J. T., & Schroeter, J. (1993, Fall). Multiple forecasting system at Brake Parts, Inc. *Journal of Business Forecasting, 12,* 5-9.

Index

AUTHOR'S NOTE: Page references followed by *f* or *t* indicate figures or tables, respectively. References followed by *n* indicate endnotes.

About the Authors

John T. Mentzer is the Harry J. and Vivienne R. Bruce Excellence Chair of Business Policy in the Department of Marketing, Logistics, and Transportation at the University of Tennessee. He has directed all four phases of the Sales Forecasting Benchmarking Studies, served as a consultant for numerous companies in the area of sales forecasting management, taught a sales forecasting management course every year for more than 20 years, conducted numerous sales forecasting management seminars, and published 3 books and more than 120 articles in the areas of sales forecasting, marketing, and logistics.

Carol C. Bienstock is Assistant Professor of Marketing in the Department of Marketing and Economics at Valdosta State University, where she teaches marketing research and channels of distribution and logistics. Her research, which examines channels of distribution, logistics, sales forecasting, and service quality, has been published in numerous journals.